I0825003

"If you've ever cried in the car after yelling at your kid or just felt like a complete failure because traditional parenting advice doesn't work on your 'strong-willed' child, this book will feel like someone finally gets you. Mary Van Geffen has written the parenting manual I wish I had when my kids were little. She's funny, compassionate, and real. No judgment, no perfection—just smart strategies, deep empathy, and a huge dose of relief. You'll laugh, you'll cry, and most of all, you'll finally feel like you're not screwing everything up. This book is a hug, a how-to, and a total game changer."

Mel Robbins, bestselling author of *The Let Them Theory*
and host of *The Mel Robbins Podcast*

"Raising a strong-willed child is exhausting and lonely. You don't know what you're doing, let alone how to do it right, so you just hang on tight, do it scared, and start your kid's therapy fund. *Parenting a Spicy One* is unlike any parenting book I've ever read. It helps you not to manage your child but to compassionately understand and root for them. Every page is infused with kindness and grounded in hope, not to mention all the wildly helpful tools. A must-read."

Kendra Adachi, *New York Times* bestselling author of
The Lazy Genius Way and *The PLAN*

"If you've ever lost your cool with a child who repeatedly infuriates you, you're not alone. Here to the rescue is a deeply honest account of what it's like to raise perplexing, feisty kids. This book offers personal, relatable stories, practical skills to help you in a wide variety of circumstances, and heaps of kindness to soothe your battered sense of self. This is the book you've longed for, written by the right person at the right time!"

Julie Bogart, author of *Raising Critical Thinkers*
and founder of Brave Writer

"When I first met Mary, what stood out to me most was her compassionate honesty. She tells the truth about how it feels to have a child with traits and tendencies you never expected and aren't prepared for. More importantly, she offers ideas and strategies that help because they honor spicy kids rather than faulting them. I'm so thrilled that Mary is offering the world the chance to better understand spicy kids and to better respond as adults in their lives. Full of wisdom, deeply practical, and marked by Mary's trademark humor and candor, this book will be a gift across generations of people who will feel seen and supported."

Meredith Miller, pastor and author of *Woven: Nurturing a Faith Your Kid Doesn't Have to Heal From*

"This loving, generous guide is an invitation—to connection, creativity, and forgiveness for our understandable parental shortcomings. My only complaint is I wish I had read this book when my Spicy One was younger. Can I have a do-over?"

Kelle Hampton, @etst on Instagram and author of *Bloom*

"I wept, laughed, and read most of the book aloud to my husband. Somebody gets it. Somebody gets us. Somebody gets our kid. We are not alone!"

Katy Bowman, MS, bestselling author of *Grow Wild: The Whole-Child, Whole-Family, Nature-Rich Guide to Moving More*

"*Parenting a Spicy One* is like a walk-and-talk with a wise, witty friend who gets your kid—and you. Mary Van Geffen is equal parts truth-teller and soul-encourager, offering tools you'll actually use and stories that make you feel seen. I'm so grateful this wildly practical, big-hearted book exists."

Kayla Craig, author of *To Light Their Way* and *Every Season Sacred*; creator of Liturgies for Parents

PARENTING A SPICY ONE

PARENTING A SPICY ONE

A Compassionate Guide for Raising a Deep-Feeling and Wonderfully Strong-Willed Kid

MARY VAN GEFFEN

a division of Baker Publishing Group
Grand Rapids, Michigan

Published by Revell
a division of Baker Publishing Group
Grand Rapids, Michigan
RevellBooks.com

Printed in the United States of America

Library of Congress Cataloging-in-Publication Control Number: 2025023324
ISBN 9781540905031 (cloth)
ISBN 9781493452828 (ebook)

Some names and details of the people and situations described in this book have been changed or presented in composite form in order to ensure the privacy of the individuals involved or those with whom the author has worked.

The author is not a licensed psychologist or healthcare professional. Reading this book does not replace the care or assessment of psychologists or other healthcare professionals.

Cover design by Dan Pitts.
Author photo © Rachel Walker.

The Inner Mean Girl illustrations in the appendix are by Giulia Pink Hoxie @giuliapink.design.

The author is represented by Alive Literary Agency, www.aliveliterary.com.

Baker Publishing Group publications use paper produced from sustainable forestry practices and postconsumer waste whenever possible.

26 27 28 29 30 31 32 7 6 5 4 3 2 1

DEDICATION

This book is dedicated to the red-headed Spicy One who raised me and the big-energy Spicy One who razed me.

Thank you, Mother, for being a powerful woman who modeled full-body NOs, taught me the real names for private parts, and danced like everyone was welcome to watch.

Thank you for filling my childhood with the domestic arts of propagating purple irises, passionate charades, mouthwatering home cooking, and proper table settings.

Thank you for encouraging your children to explore multiple artistic pursuits.

My exotic confidence comes in part from knowing you delight in my stories.

You have always been the discerning but eager audience I needed, long before anyone else wanted to hear what I had to say.

I hope this book makes you proud.

Thank you, Daughter, for refusing to dim your light so I could fit in. You wisely awoke a part of me that had been hiding.

Your goodness, eye for beauty, and intuition shine for all to see.

Your competence and hard-charging, decisive action inspire me.

You are a joyful doer and an expert finisher.

I can't wait to see you improve upon the ways I did things—each generation refining the art of loving.

I am so proud of you.

CONTENTS

If you are a skimmer like me, I've included some extras that are marked with one of the following symbols:

Definitions

Did You Know?

Exercises

Resources

Tips

Assignments

You could skip those and still get what you need from this book. Enjoy!

INTRODUCTION

Welcome to the Eighteen-Year Spiritual Retreat You Never Signed Up For

Raising a child who is more loyal to their own soul than to your adult agenda is not typical. Not optimal, even.

But it is your reality.

You have the overwhelming responsibility of being the parent of a Spicy One.

I should know. Finding my footing didn't come naturally. I remember one awful Thanksgiving family gathering where, once again, my child was both the outlier and the spectacle. I wrote about it in my burn book (er, I mean my journal):

> Kneeling in my sister-in-law's front yard in Bakersfield, California, I feel itchy from the grass. My skin is sticky despite the chill in the air. My teeth are clenched. I'm gripping my sweaty four-year-old daughter's body against mine while she twists her head to try and bite me. She is struggling to escape my hold. And screaming.
>
> We are thirty minutes into a five-alarm, "man your battle stations," epic hurricane of a tantrum. Trembling with my own adult rage, I fight the exhaustion that comes from realizing once again that I am not a good enough mother to prevent—or end—this embarrassing

meltdown. After four years, I still do not know what to do to make this sensory onslaught stop. It's humiliating.

Twenty feet away, my husband's extended family waits in the house to start carving the turkey. I can imagine them milling around the table, clicking their tongues. They must be wondering what is wrong with me. And with my daughter. *Why can't she get control of her own child?*

An image of covering her red face with a pillow and holding it there to muffle the sound flits across my consciousness. I have dark thoughts like this sometimes. I just need the defiance and the screaming to stop.

"Let go of me!" she wails at a volume that ricochets off the garage and back toward the audience in the window. The trees seem to shake from the noise. "You are hurting me!" she screams. *Do they think I'm being abusive? Am I being abusive?*

The sky turns from pink to purple, like my bruised arm where she is pinching me. I kind of hate this child. I certainly wouldn't choose this person to hang out with if I wasn't her mother. She's selfish, irrational, mean.

Eventually, my husband comes out of the house and taps my shoulder. He's graciously taking a turn with the beast. "What does she want?" he asks, hoping it's that simple. I no longer remember how the tantrum started. My sister-in-law gifted us matching leggings and "gobble gobble" sweatshirts. All the children were going to dress alike for a perfect family photo. *Couldn't Gigi just go along with things for once?*

No. Gigi hates the feeling of scratchy fabric on her legs. She stripped off the offensive pants immediately after the photo. She desperately wants to go see the horses even though it is dinnertime. She's away from our normal home routine and surrounded by extended family she doesn't know well.

Nothing works with this child. Everything is a power struggle. I am so sick of being the one in charge.

Do you have similar stories? No decision is made lightly when it comes to the Spicy One. They question everything. Every *no* from you brings the potential for an emotional lightning storm.

When you crack and react angrily, they either ignore you, cower, or explode dramatically. Gentle parenting doesn't work on this kid. You are forced into the role of wimp or monster swimming in a shame swamp.

You understandably feel defeated and hopeless.

Those closest to you, be they family or friends, are critical of your choices.

No one understands the mental calculus you go through to have to decide whether to hold a limit. The ramifications of your child's upset could sink the whole ship. Ruin the trip. Repel the new friends at the park staring at you with frozen smiles while your angel loses their mind.

You wake up in the morning wondering how the drama will unfold. Should you walk on eggshells, or will you get a joyful version of your child today?

You go to sleep depleted and bitter. It's lonely. You are grateful the meltdowns tend to happen in private. But it's isolating that other people don't often see the dramatic and out-of-control version of your kid. This sparkling child acts differently for teachers or even with their father.

The emotional whiplash is dizzying. When you struggle to fall asleep, you ask the existential question, "Is my child the problem or is it me?"

[*clears throat*] It's likely a little bit of both. I will explain in the following chapters.

But if you are the only one in your community leading a fiery world changer, you found the right book. Courage and positivity naturally erode when you parent through scenarios that no one else in your life can relate to, like:

- Chasing your flight-risk toddler through a parking lot, praying they don't get hit by a car
- Pulling your car to the curb while getting punched in the back by an angry preschooler out of their car seat again

- Holding your child down for the dentist so a professional can tell you if they have cavities since you constantly fight about toothbrushing
- Being told "I hate you" by the one person you work the hardest to love

Every. Single. Transition. Is. A. Conflict.

The Spicy One tests all limits. Including the ones they agreed to. Being in public with this kid can be embarrassing. And hilarious. Meanwhile, the world is looking at you to fix this kid before they become a full-time menace to society.

Come Have a "Time In" with Me

Welcome to a new season of connection and intention in the adventures of parenting your strong-willed child. You are probably worried this book won't work for your scenario. None of the other well-meaning gentle-parenting advice has applied to the chaos you are dealing with. This book will be different from what you've read in the past.

The internal postures and relational pointers you are about to read are the beginning of a powerful shift for your family. You can relax knowing I will guide you along a journey—I too have traveled—to a refreshing vantage point on your parenting. And I won't recommend spanking. Maybe you've already tried that.

I have successfully led thousands of Moms of Spicy Ones (MOSO) through the concepts laid out in this book. The MOSO approach prevails because we are recognizing this for what it is: a heroine's journey. The quest to parent someone you cannot control demands archetypal spirituality! Regardless of your faith, religion, or full-frontal atheism, know that raising this kid with your well-being intact will plunge you into a spiritual quest. You are entering a set-apart community of parents who have been called (against their will) to stay safe and tender when their child is neither. You are the reluctant hero—Moses, Buddha, or Moana (who spends the first part of her spiritual journey trying to opt out of it).

I'm defining *spirituality* as the lived capacity to be in a deep, dynamic awareness with a deeper presence or spirit of life. My approach does not require you to believe in God, but it does invite you to choose some higher power to help you make meaning from this unmarked journey. Like the recovery groups meeting in basements across the world, you need something bigger than yourself to hold on to during this roller-coaster ride.

Our brains are chemically constructed to search for evidence that we are loved, guided, and not alone.[1] And dang, you will need that when raising this child who has their own fully formed agenda. The naming of this assistance is up to you, but tapping into an energy out there that is *for you* and for your child will be your lifeline when things implode.

To look at parenting through a spiritual lens, you must try on the idea that your child is not your challenge. They are your curriculum. This book is the syllabus.

This is an outline of the shifts you will need to make in your approach, your heart, and your body to have more harmony and collaboration in your family. Your Spicy One is an invitation to grow your ability to love your child and—surprisingly—yourself unconditionally. You are not broken. Neither is your child.

Good news! The universe has gifted you with a child who will not participate in the toxic definition of love as something that must be earned. You have hit a magical speed bump to slow you down. What you are going through isn't really happening *to* you so much as *for* you. This is a big ol' opportunity to heal your own stuff through the process of parenting your spitfire. You can learn to love this prickly creature well, even though their venom will sting you from time to time. To open your heart wider to someone who disappoints you on the regular and refuses to meet expectations, you must engage in deep personal work. You must be okay when they are not.

The result of this work is that you will stop perpetuating some of the painful patterns you come from. The pain of your past releases its grip on you when you start practicing unconditional love and the holding of firm but flexible boundaries, regardless of your child's behavior. You can give what you once needed.

What to Expect from This Book

If you don't have an older woman in your life who has raised a kid like yours while staying calm, kind, and firm, I've got you. This book is here to encourage you, to carve out a safe space where you can learn positive, effective parenting techniques that help make this journey less painstaking and more (dare I say) fun. Yes, you are deserving of fun!

Here's a little secret. The ideas in this book will change *you*—not necessarily your child.

Before I can teach you tips and tricks for helping your Spicy One cooperate, or at least be more at peace, we first need to conduct a serious vibe check on what wounding and bad habits you are bringing to the party.

It's going to feel like we're starting slow, but that's on purpose. We could launch right into tactical tips, but new techniques alone won't transform your parenting results from the root. For lasting change, we need to start from the deep, dark beginning. Prepare to spend the first few chapters looking more at yourself than at your child. With your permission, I'll be gingerly pointing out areas where you might be making things worse. We all have blind spots. More on mine later.

It will be most helpful for you to read this book sequentially. These Spicy One concepts build on each other. That said, get your freak on and flip to the chapter you need if you are in pain and need immediate guidance!

Calm, Kind, and Firm

Whether you're limping into this season of life beaten down by your child, worried you are a permissive parent . . . or frightened by your capacity for cruelty and suppression of their light, you grabbed the right book. The way forward is calm, kind, and firm. I will show you how to choose those ways of being when everything in you feels chaotic, homicidal, and weak!

I am honored to help guide you to a new season of health in your parenting. My credentials are simple: I too climbed a punishing, black-diamond-level parenting mountain. In 2011, after shifting everything and finding my purpose in parenting a powerhouse, I started speaking to moms' groups and telling my story. Next I studied to become a Simplicity Parenting counselor and a Certified Professional Co-Active Coach. For years I privately coached hundreds of precious moms of strong-willed kids, discovering the universality of our journey. Every day, I showed up on Instagram, sharing a technique or tip to help others. In fall 2022, I wrote down my learnings and launched Moms of Spicy Ones®, an eight-week group program. After ushering seven cohorts and 1,700 moms through my online program, I still pore over reviews and cry seeing my prior suffering reflected in their testimonials. Their descriptions of life after MOSO are unanimously filled with relief and hope.

Three disclaimers before we get started:

1. My Spicy One is neurotypical. I'm not. I'm a full-blown ADHD, gifted, and highly sensitive person with symptoms that recently earned me a level 1 autism diagnosis. I do not have a lived experience of parenting a neurodivergent human, so I can't tell you how your child's unique brain will respond to all the techniques I share. But guess what: Your child's diagnosis is irrelevant when it comes to your necessary personal development. A third of MOSO graduates have autistic children. My approach overwhelmingly works for those parents.
2. This book is not a substitute for a medical or psychological examination of your child. If you have the access or resources, pursue a diagnosis to unlock the early intervention support your child may need to reach developmental

milestones. It'll give you more information about your child. Follow that nudge in your stomach if something feels off. Insist that your child see an occupational therapist (the unsung heroes of differently wired kids). Pursue that neurodivergent diagnosis—it comes with so much support. So many neurodivergent adults are grieving their late diagnosis. It's empowering for your kid to learn about themself and how their brain functions differently. It can shift them (and you) from seeing them as broken, lazy, or dumb to understanding that they have unique gifting and challenges to work around. But don't let what may be a long and expensive process stop you from doing the work in this book that only you can do.

3. I have an agenda. I am a bona fide Spicy One who, like your child, swings from not caring one iota what people think of me to feeling mortified that I put my foot in my mouth and let my impulsivity, odd sense of humor, and fiery emotions get the best of me again. I have immense empathy for your child. I am committed to doing everything I can to equip you so they don't grow up feeling broken, wrong, or hard to love.

This book will change your perspective, your coping skills, and your energetic capacity not just for your Spicy One but for all the challenges that life throws at you.

Pull on your stretchy pants, grab some crunchy snacks, and let's get into it!

PART I

YOUR OVERWHELMING ASSIGNMENT

Every child is a different assignment—and . . . how different the assignments can be. Within the range of developmentally normal children, some parents have a much, much harder job than others: more drudge work, less gratification, more public shaming. . . . We spend a lot of time patting ourselves on the back . . . when the easy babies and toddlers behave like themselves, and a lot of time agonizing and assigning blame when the more difficult kids run true to form.

Dr. Perri Klass, pediatrician

1

Is Your Child a Spicy One?

It is isolating to parent a spirited child who gives you fifteen *nos* to get to one *yes*.

Without support, their inner fire—which makes them an ideal future world leader but a problematic teammate—can reduce you and your family to ashes.

The world needs this fidgety child's unbridled enthusiasm, thoughtful pessimism, and refusal to conform to the status quo. Yet the genius of your gifted child is also the thing that will be most annoying to parents. Kids who debate everything will be gifted litigators. Kids who complain that nothing is fair will be social activists.

Not sure yet if you're dealing with a Spicy One?

You have a Spicy One if you believe they need more than you have to give.

No offense, but it's usually painstakingly obvious. Many bio moms of Spicy Ones are barely pregnant when they realize their feisty fetus kicks harder and longer than the rest. Fresh out the womb, Spicy Ones are fierce from the first breath, brandishing a wide-eyed thirst for life that is obvious long before their first word. However, there are a few baby lambs that ripen into dragons ready to incinerate your once peaceful life.

SPICY ONE QUIZ

Take the quiz below to be sure. This is not a diagnostic tool in the medical sense. It's an ever-growing list of the Spicy One's uniqueness that will give you some information to reflect on, no matter your score.

Choose the number that best represents how much each question describes your family situation.

0 = rarely, 1 = sometimes, 2 = often, 3 = all the time

Does your child . . .

1. Feel things intensely and express themself in big emotional outbursts (from rage to joyful screaming)?
2. Refuse to be consoled with physical touch or comforting hugs?
3. Possess a fierce drive for independence, persist at getting what they want, and fixate on doing it their own way?
4. Choose to be completely true to themself, not others?
5. Seem unafraid to take up space or disappoint others (but feel outsize shame when corrected)?
6. Vacillate between an enthusiastic zest for life and grumpy complaining that their life is awful?
7. Have energy to spare and tend to be moving all the time?
8. Powerfully negotiate with adults until they lose hope and melt down?
9. Test as gifted in some ways but seem completely inept in others?
10. Have a deep sense of justice, and are they quick to point out "that's not fair" when they want something they can't have?

11. Skip over feelings of contentedness to focus on what's missing?
12. Exude contagious emotions that make it impossible for others to have a good time if they are not?
13. Hurt folks or property unintentionally or in the midst of big feelings?
14. Default to brutal honesty with powerful words that can wound or delight?
15. Seem overly affected by others' negative feelings yet miss the social cues necessary to develop steady friendships?
16. Have moments of being incredibly sweet, caring, and loyal but refuse to say "I love you" unless they feel it?
17. Display a silly, subversive sense of humor (or dark misuse of toys)?
18. Approach games so competitively that they lose it if they don't win and/or refuse to play by the rules on the box? Often accuse others of cheating?
19. Notice every detail, from how a chair was moved to how Mom is pursing her lips, indicating a bad mood?
20. Prefer to direct the play of peers?
21. Become very upset when plans they looked forward to change unexpectedly?
22. Experience outsize reactions to slight changes in the environment, including clothing textures, smells, crowds, and sounds?

Score 0–19 Heat Index: Bell Pepper

Your child sounds like a Mild Child—an easygoing human (most of the time) who's comfortable with transitions. They allow you to lead even if you don't always know what you're doing. Your Mild Child will benefit from you reading this (or any other evidence-based parenting book) to thoughtfully determine a discipline approach free of yelling, shaming, and punishing. You are welcome to keep reading. There are lots of tips here for you too.

Score 20–35 Heat Index: Jalapeño Pepper Jam

This book is for you!

Your child is a Diet Spice. Sometimes they are a compliant little bundle of joy. Other times, they are stressful as all heck to manage. It's natural to get frustrated and thrown off your game by this mood-shifting human.

Score 36–66 Heat Index: Habanero Ghost Pepper

Yowza! Your child is a legit Spicy One! I'm honestly impressed you made it through the quiz without melting from all the nuclear heat you deal with on a daily basis! Everything is a struggle, and this can make it hard to stay connected to the absolute miracle that is your kid. Your Spicy One flashes you with genuine love and spirited sparkly clairvoyance one minute and then angry explosive meltdowns and cold defiance the next. Nothing is predictable. The amount of daily conflict is exhausting. But also, I am personally a 3 on all the above questions. I'm doing great! It gets better. You have found your road map in this book! Stay with me.

Well done for working through the quiz. You are a thoughtful parent. There's a reason your child fights upstream automatically and hugs harder than most: their natural temperament. We will explore the four most salient traits of the Spicy One's personality in the next chapter, as well as where you might be contributing to the heat.

May You Embrace the Dichotomy of the Spicy One

You've probably noticed some *inherent contradictions* in your Spicy One's nature. This duplicity, while maddening at times, to be sure, is *also* quite typical for the artists, thought leaders, and geniuses among us.

They see you as their person—the one human they can count on and be themself with . . . *but they critique everything you do with a caustic vocabulary and tone.*

They crave structure and knowing what's next . . . *but rebel and rage against plans they themself agreed to.*

They can be the tenderest, most affectionate lovebug . . . *but then look at you with disdain and contempt.*

They are annoyingly persistent when they want something . . . *but give up on anything they are not instantly great at.* It's not just your kid. Real moms share:

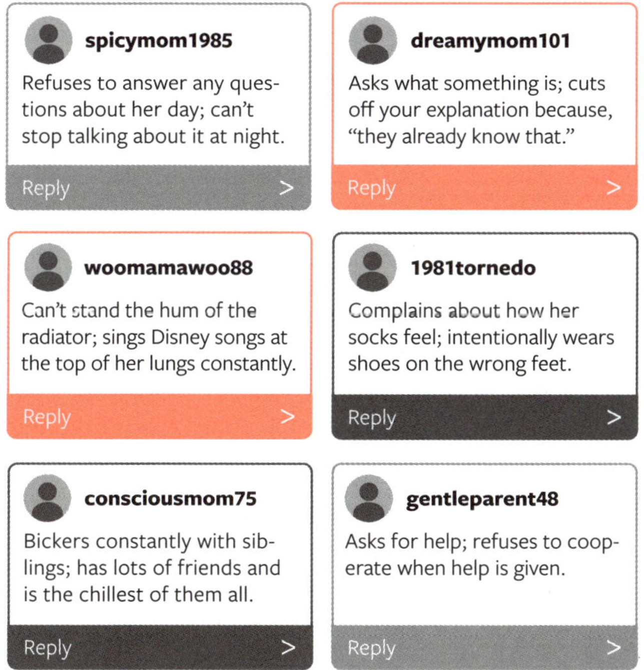

Your child's duality is an inextricable part of their white-hot intensity. These polarities are part of their gifted life. May they always be this unafraid to shine!

Holding opposites feels messy and emotionally challenging. Especially for parents who felt unseen as kids themselves. Likely, no one held the tension of your light and dark parts with care and reverence. No one waded into the nuance for you.

It's beautiful what you are doing for your child. And for yourself. I am proud of you.

IS "SPICY ONE" JUST A FUN WAY OF SAYING "DIAGNOSED"?

No. While there is some overlap between a strong-willed, big-feeling personality and the identifiable symptoms of neurodivergence, a diagnosis requires support from a certified mental health professional. This book cannot help you differentiate that.

Neurodivergence is an evolving term. Annette Estes, director of the University of Washington Autism Center, says it has to do with "how someone's brain is structured and functions, it's a part of the variability in humans and life and it makes life on earth exciting and interesting and beautiful."[1] At this writing, it encompasses autism, ADHD, sensory processing disorder, obsessive-compulsive disorder (OCD), academic giftedness, pathological demand avoidance (PDA), and other types of intellectual and learning disabilities such as dyslexia.

About half of moms who call their child a Spicy One report their kid also has a diagnosis—or presents as neurodivergent.* The other half of Spicy Ones are just unusually intense, dramatic, persistent, and deep-feeling children without the skills yet to peacefully collaborate, self-soothe, or problem-solve. *Countercultural but not diagnosable.*

Being a Spicy One is all about the personality, temperament, and sensitivity of a child (and of their primary caregiver). It doesn't tell you whether your child is neurodivergent. There's a vast variety of reasons a child can be difficult to parent. Accepting and embracing your child as a Spicy One is admirable, but it doesn't replace the professional mental health support they might need to learn to move more adeptly through the world.

* Per repeated polls in my Instagram stories, with over four hundred respondents who identify their child as a Spicy One.

CH 1: Reflection Questions

1. Do the quiz's results feel accurate for the level of heat you deal with in your home?
2. Which description from the quiz is most troublesome to you and why?
3. What aspect of your child do you most hope this book will address?

Want to share this quiz with another parent who might be navigating the Spicy One life? Visit maryvangeffen.com/quiz or scan this code:

2

Name the Hard So It Can Get Better

Let's talk about the difficulty of your unique parenting challenge. This challenge will not break you, but it does come with a serious learning curve. You are raising a baby CEO who occasionally acts like a psychopath. I know we aren't supposed to compare suffering, but yours is legitimately a more difficult parenting experience than many moms can imagine.

Putting the challenge into words will help release some of the guilt you carry about finding this little person so tough to raise. It's not all in your head. This would be demanding for anyone.

Raising a Spicy One is objectively difficult because of four challenges:

1. Their natural temperament
2. Their sensitivity to shame
3. Very little positive feedback from anyone
4. Loneliness and terrible advice

Their Natural Temperament

A diagnosis is not necessary for a child to be the kink in the garden hose of your life. Your kid might be labeled with letters like ADHD, ASD, ODD, HSP, or PDA. Or maybe they just possess personality traits that make a human unabashedly and objectively difficult to lead. Parenting is leadership, so that is highly inconvenient.

I'm not sure what's harder—everyone knowing your kid is different or them being model citizens out in the world but acting surly and aggressive at home.

Temperament traits are usually glaringly obvious "right out the womb." You didn't cause them and you can't change them. You can only hope to accept them and help your little one use their dynamic personality for good.

As one mom put it, "His personality is so large. Like I'm holding a nuclear substance from the periodic table that I have to handle just right. It could create an atomic bomb, but it could also power an entire country."

Let's examine the aspects of this child that even a seasoned childcare provider or that shiny, successful mom at the park would struggle with. This is the part of the challenge that's not up for interpretation. It just is.

There are four fiery temperament traits that make parenting your child an expert assignment:

1. High Intensity
2. Low Adaptability
3. High Perceptibility
4. High Persistence

High Intensity

Your high-intensity child experiences emotions as bone-deep, earth-shattering forces. Their unparalleled meltdowns come from access to a bottomless well of emotion that must be felt (and, unfortunately, expressed). Their feelings get expressed physically, which is why you are the only mom on your street who has to say things like "I know you're mad, but I'm not going to let you head-butt me in the stomach or start from across the room and charge me like a bull."

Their physical reactions are also powerful and in your face. When my client Lauren would take her baby girl to the library for Toddler Time, all the typical six-to-eighteen-month-olds quietly thumbed through books, one hand clutching their mother's knee for safety. Meanwhile, her kid crashed across the room like Godzilla, pacing, snatching books, and lumbering over the seated children. Lauren wanted to crawl in a hole and hide from the frightened looks the moms of Mild Childs would give her tornado offspring. She felt inadequate.

The good news is, high intensity means even their full-bodied joy is contagious and loud. Their default mode of exuberance is wonderful . . . and a lot. They emit signs of happiness at the loudest volume setting while their body bounces off the walls like Tigger from *Winnie the Pooh*. The bad news: Their disappointment is just as loud. Spicy Ones can wreck the road trip and destroy the dinner with only their attitude.

When in their feelings, the Spicy One can't be consoled physically. Oh, how the moms of Spicy Ones wish a simple hug was more of a comfort to their vexed porcupine. Their meltdowns are like riding a careening train through a dark tunnel—you can't turn them around; you've just got to move through to the other side. Their storm of big emotions will rain down on all, no matter what you try.

One mom tells a story of visiting a new city for a "fun adventure." Her six-year-old Spicy One had had enough. He refused to get out of the car. Everyone else went ahead to find a table for dinner. Mom endured full-body shrieking in an underground parking garage until her brain could take no more. She decided to take him aboveground. Sometimes a change of environment is all you need. But in this case, his shame at having a public meltdown hit hard, and he decided to run. After forty-five minutes of her son screaming and clawing away from her, Dad arrived with a cold can of Sprite. A switch flipped. Refreshed, the Spicy One went inside and calmly ate a full dinner. He posed for pictures like nothing had even happened.

Low Adaptability

A lot of kids have trouble adapting to change, but the Spicy Ones resist it on a whole 'nother level. When you most need a flexible kid, they get rigid and emotionally stuck. This child doesn't yet know how to go with the flow. They thrive on living with routine even though they constantly resist the plan. Their first reaction to any change they themself did not orchestrate is a wholehearted HELL NO. Situations they didn't see coming set them off and create stress in both your bodies. If an anticipated playdate gets canceled, it is grounds for an immediate meltdown.

Some Spicy Ones meet every day with melancholy. They see the glass half empty no matter how often you model gratitude. Like the Sadness character from Pixar's *Inside Out* or Eeyore from *Winnie the Pooh*, these kiddos often find life disappointing, and they insist on letting you know.

High Perceptibility

Your child processes the world at a deeper level than others. Every experience is a bombardment to their acute senses. They hear, smell, and notice everything. The smell of broccoli and feel of hard pants can ruin a perfectly good day.

Spicy Ones are the world's supertasters. Food is often too spicy or the texture unacceptable. The temperature of the air in the car is either two degrees too hot or too cold.

Crowds and social situations (even if they crave them) quickly turn from exciting to overstimulating. They are often aware of others' feelings before anyone speaks. Interestingly, your emotions (as the parent) are part of the stimulus they are constantly processing. More on that later, in chapter 16.

They notice the disappointment they stir up in adults, and that makes things worse. It's a paradox: They can be irrevocably agitated by what's happening around them while unattached to how their behavior and attitude affect others.

High Persistence

Spicy Ones are doggedly single-minded, especially when you desperately need them to drop their zany idea and move on. Their commitment to their own immature vision makes influencing them particularly tricky. Meanwhile these highly persistent humans give up immediately on anything new if it doesn't come easily to them. Somebody explain this, please!

One mom told me,

> My nine-year-old daughter is in a forever question phase—like the kind people talk about with three-year-olds who follow you to the bathroom. I can't breathe with all the questions. In just five minutes tonight: "What's your zodiac sign? What's mine? What's Sister's? What's Dad's? What's a zodiac sign? Do you know how much Elon Musk makes? How do you get in the Olympics? How much money do you have in your bank account? Can the president say it's against the law to send kids to school? How old is the president? If my teacher died on a school day, would you make us go to school? Who is the most popular actor you know? Do you know how old the actor who played Barbie is?"
>
> Literally all those. At the end of the day, I am so spent, and she takes me over the edge even when she's not being spicy. When she's at her most beautiful, it's still too much. I just say, "I don't know." I try to explain that my brain can't handle the questions. She gets so mad that I am not exactly what she wants me to be. And I'm heartbroken that I can't meet her. I am so scared that her memories of the years when her brain was the most malleable, beautiful, magical, stretchy little thing will be memories of an exhausted, caretaking, grieving, stressed mother whose human capacity couldn't handle it.

How many of these four temperament traits apply to your little spitfire? Circle all that describe your kid. Then underline the ones that apply to you as well.

- ☐ High Intensity
- ☐ Low Adaptability
- ☐ High Perceptibility
- ☐ High Persistence

Their Sensitivity to Shame

Your Spicy One is allergic to any perceived sensations of shame. They can't yet tolerate the sharp disappointment and sense of disconnect that traditional discipline can elicit in their inexperienced bodies. They will lash out in response to a lecture or disappointed tone of voice where another child might dutifully change course.

The Spicy One hides their self-consciousness beneath false courage, but it makes them see shame where it isn't. Like the four-year-old who screams "Stop copying me!" at the girl obliviously swinging next to her.

Once when a beloved family was visiting our home, I firmly told my friend's Spicy One that he could not put the entire loaf of frozen bread in the microwave to defrost it. I was saving it for the next day's breakfast. "Just choose one slice to put in there," I directed him. He immediately dropped the loaf on the counter, his face twisted in a scowl, and growled, "Never mind." He avoided eye contact with me for the rest of the visit. His shame monster had been released. Meanwhile, I too was feeling shame, asking myself why I made bread quality more important than connecting with my friend's child.

Spicy Ones also feel shame where it *is*, even if you think you are hiding your judgment or irritation. You might tell yourself, "I'm simply educating them," but if you use humiliation, a harsh tone, or a power-over approach, they will reflect this misstep back to you with surprising raw aggression.

I've come to think of this as a good thing. You don't want to use guilt and shame tactics on your child, and they won't let you. It's like having a kid who can't tolerate cigarette smoke, so the whole family has to stop smoking.

Very Little Positive Feedback

If you consider your child's behavior as the measure of your parenting success, it's easy to believe you are failing. The unwanted negative feedback waiting for you on every grocery trip, family gathering, or park playdate is relentless.

"Your child is a handful. Have you tried telling them NO?" says Madam Obvious at the park, clutching her pearls as your kid shows hers how to climb *up* the slide to pour sand from above.

Meanwhile, the Spicy One certainly doesn't thank you for your ministry. In fact, they hurl hexes at you, like "You are a bad mommy." They are rarely a satisfied customer of your parenting. It's excruciating to keep showing up to a workplace where people think you should be fired for incompetence. No wonder you want to hide under the covers.

Loneliness and Terrible Advice

No one loses their ever-lovin' mind like your child. Others can't wrap their minds around your experience. There aren't many helpful mentors because not many have walked this path and looked back to share the way.

Years ago, I thought I'd found the perfect therapist. This little old lady in her moth-eaten Mr. Rogers cardigan, gliding back and forth in her rocking chair, was an answer to prayer. Ready to drink up her advice like a weary desert traveler searching for water, I poured my heart out to her. I described Gigi's brazen defiance. Her four-year-old mean-girl words that wounded her innocent peers. The fierce and fiery tantrums. The disrespect.

There was a soft silence between us. The goodness was coming. I could feel it. She opened her sweet, wrinkled Yoda mouth and purred, "Have you tried spanking?"

Once again I was alone on the gentle-parenting road.

Raising a Spicy One can feel like being the only parent struggling in an empty dystopian landscape of perennial conflict with a warlord who can't even wipe their own bottom. The skills and talents that made you successful in your earlier life are often useless in leading the Spicy One. Responding to this child's lack of "get-along" is often the first taste of failure for many otherwise highly competent people. This kid would stymie anyone committed to intentional, respectful parenting.

Repeat after me. "I'm not supposed to know how to do this."

I remember gathering with my church small group to discuss the book *Shepherding a Child's Heart*—required reading for faithful Christian parents serious about raising obedient children who honor God. But the idea that parents are stand-ins for God's authority and require immediate compliance troubled me. I was hardly patient, consistent, clear, or selfless enough to adequately represent God to my child.

Meanwhile, everyone else nodded appreciatively and traded stories of their child's behaviors that could not be tolerated and required the *rod of correction*. I kept my eyes on the ground lest anyone be able to tell that despite how rowdy my child was, I wasn't comfortable using corporal punishment. Was I not Christian enough? Someone read aloud, "The heart of a child is wicked. . . . Spanking is a sacred responsibility." The words hung thick in the air.

I was having trouble squaring up these gentle, imperfect people with the idea of them as judges and executioners of their young children's sin life. I couldn't imagine my Jesus nodding approvingly as I smacked my child's behind using a paddle. *Jesus, does your Bible tell me to strike your sheep?* I asked in my quiet times. I stayed quiet for a few more years.

Have you been counseled by a faithful mentor or your own parent to use corporal punishment on your child? Have you been taught that your parenting is a battleground, with you being the instrument of good against the evil lurking within your wayward child? Let's clear one thing up. There is indeed a spiritual battle happening here. But it's not raging inside your child. It's brewing *inside you*. It's a battle to determine where your identity comes from. Is it from presenting the world with a squeaky-clean, well-behaved child so you can follow the expectations other people have for you? Or is it from honoring your own intuition, seeking the imago Dei* in your child, and building your capacity for unconditional love?

Even though this child may bring you to your knees, to a place beyond your own ability, you do not have to break their spirit. May this journey move you to prayer, personal growth, and community rather than violence. May you call on your higher power to supply the patience you can't manufacture on your own. You are made in the image of God, but you do not represent God's authority to your child. Instead, you are their favorite fallen human, failing forward and working out life with fear and trembling just like the rest of us. If you were led to believe that a disobedient child is evidence of a faithless walk with Jesus, hear me now.

That's poppycock!

No expert educated in child development endorses violence against children in any form, be that pinching, slapping, spanking, or belting. There is nothing religiously sacred about spanking. It's a relic of a brutal time and often a sign of a parent out of options and out of control. We now have enough research on attachment theory to put spanking to rest. If you tried spanking to deal with the outsize responses of your child that scare or trigger you, please forgive yourself. There is no judgment here against a parent who has done what they felt was best (and what used to be advised by past

* Imago Dei refers to humans being made in God's image and possessing qualities that mirror aspects of God's divinity and goodness.

generations of parenting experts) to build the family they long for. May this book give you numerous alternative tools and strategies for addressing problem behaviors. For a Scripture-based argument to offset the spanking indoctrination you may have absorbed, read "What about the Rod?" in *The Flourishing Family*.[1]

CH 2: Reflection Questions

1. Which temperament trait do you share with your Spicy One? Does this shared trait make your relationship easier or trickier when it shows up? Why?
2. Which of the identified challenges makes parenting especially difficult for you: temperament, sensitivity to shame, little positive feedback, or loneliness and terrible advice? Why?

3

Are You Also a Spicy One?

It's tempting to blame the explosions in your home purely on the Spicy One. Would you be willing to explore how you might be adding to the combustion?

When my passionflower was five, I went on a campaign to get her diagnosed with something. Anything. I desperately wanted a label to assure me that our power struggles were squarely her fault.

I asked the pediatrician, but he said she was progressing well. Wrong answer. I searched for a psychologist to observe her at her preschool, where she was having daily friendship flare-ups. Way too expensive. Don't wait as long as I did to ask for help. There was nothing "wrong" with her. Or me, for that matter. But I was contributing to the chaos.

You are likely playing a teensy part in the chaos happening at your home. For starters, how many of those hard-to-lead temperaments from the last chapter do you also possess? Your personality, needs, and woundings could be unintentionally adding gasoline to situations that might, on their own, slowly burn out. In fact, your Spicy

One might seem like a Mild Child to someone else with different tolerance or pain points.

May you be brave enough to make room for your part in this dance.

Let's talk about some hard truths.

Your Need for CONTROL Ignites the Resistance of the Spicy One

I once had a whole plan for how a felting art project was going to go. I wanted to bond with my energetic six-year-old niece by crafting adorable brown and purple woolen owls. We would make replicas of the exact bird shown in the instructions.

But when I brought the Spicy One to the table, she ignored my directions and began making big, garish happy faces directly on the foam felting square. Someone bring me smelling salts!

Jab, jab, jab went her needle as she mixed the brown and purple strands haphazardly. I tensed up—that's not how she was supposed to do it. I wanted to control the scenario for optimal results. I had a choice to make. I could either force my vision and kill the joy she was taking in combining colors or—*sigh*—let her lead the way we made art together.

Are you a "my way or the highway" kind of parent? Do you have a vision and need your people to get in line? The question to ask yourself is do I want to be in the right, or do I want to be in relationship with my child?

TRY THE BABYSITTER TEST

Imagine a childcare provider or your best friend is hanging with your child. The Spicy One is being their loud, directive self. Would the babysitter be as triggered as you get by their disruptive behavior, or would they giggle at this brazen creature and not take it personally?

A Spicy One will chafe and resist your insistence that your way is the correct way. On the spectrum of life, control is at the opposite end of the Spicy One's spontaneous play. Yet play is the language of children. Your opportunity to practice improvisation with this child gets lost when you are anchored to an expectation of how things *should* be. Author Steve Cuss talks a lot about how relational tension comes from focusing on how others can improve instead of changing what you have the most control of—you. He teaches that there are four spaces where anxiety resides. In life, you have some power over three of the four but one where you have almost none.[1] In the list below, circle the one you have no control over:

1. The space inside you
2. The space between you and the Spicy One
3. The space between you and God
4. The space inside the Spicy One

Did you pick out the one where you have no power? Yep, #4. The space inside the Spicy One. That dark echo chamber of insecurity, creativity, and rage is none of your business.

Managing the space inside the Spicy One is not part of your job description.

In her book *The Cost of Control*, Sharon Hodde Miller writes, "When we fixate on that fourth space, what is going on inside of others, what their motivations might be, why they act the way they do, or how we can change them—it creates anxiety because we don't actually have control over it."[2]

What does this illuminate for you? For me, it's a reminder that I can't make the Spicy One happy or content.

Where can you have an impact?

In the space between us, AKA the culture of your home and the temperature of your relationship. You can impact the space between you and within you. Don't try to control the rest. In chapter 4, we'll talk about planning how you want the space between people in your home and family to feel.

Your Need for ORDER Ignites the Anxiety of the Spicy One

We all perform better with cleared counters and clean laundry, but when you prioritize order as the goal, you trade the current imperfect beauty in this moment for a future perfection that may never come. You end up putting the status of an environment over the state of the human. Idolizing order sounds like "You cannot mix Squishmallows with Barbies" or "Children should play quietly" or "Make sure you color the sky part blue." Unfortunately, if the Spicy One interprets your meticulous insistence as a critique—or an unattainable goal—they will sabotage and detonate.

My client Melody reported having a blowup with her tween daughter every time she tried to get her into the car for her weekly specialist appointment. "I refuse to be late! It's so disrespectful!" she would shout at her dawdling child. Her throat was hoarse from yelling by the time she got her daughter's hair brushed and a nice outfit on. They would drive in stony silence all the way across town as her daughter silently cried. It felt awful. And it was becoming a habit.

I asked if maybe she could look at *lowering the stakes.*

Lowering the stakes is reminding yourself that your short-term goal does not matter much in the grand scheme of things. Lowering the stakes is demoting the perceived importance of an appointment or goal or event in order to prioritize the relationship and the supportive habitat of your home. There are concrete things you can do to make it more likely you will be on time (see chapter 11). That fine-tuning of the home rhythms is important, but it doesn't replace the need to first expand your definition of what *correct* looks like.

Lower the stakes so not everything is important. Lower the stakes so your body is not clenched nor your breath held. Your Spicy One notices the nonverbal signs of your disappointment, and it activates their fear of getting it wrong. What would happen if you arrived on time, calm and connected, but their hair wasn't properly brushed or braided? What would be the long-term harm if your child arrived late and still in their crusty pj's? This is your one wild and precious life. You get to decide what really matters.

Getting to school doesn't have to feel like *The Amazing Race*. Are the stakes higher than they need to be?

Your Need for PEACE Ignites the Chaos of the Spicy One

Desiring peace is so relatable. To want things to just feel easy is understandable. Can't your child, for once, let you put on sunscreen without a fuss or good-naturedly turn off the iPad and come to dinner?

However, you can get so wrapped up in wanting peace that you take it personally when other people in your family are struggling. As if they are upset on purpose to inconvenience you. The peace you seek isn't found in the good attitude or even neutral emotion of your child. It is within you, the only atmosphere you have some real control over.

Attempting to fix or stop other people's big emotions is called taking over responsibility. Stay in your lane.

I still remember being a sour-patch twelve-year-old moping into the kitchen on a school morning. Before a word was spoken, with her back to me as she fried bacon, my mother decreed, "Fix your face or leave my kitchen." She couldn't tolerate my adolescent funk. She needed peace at the cost of being available to listen and help me process my teenage angst. What a balm it would have been to my tortuous teen years if she could have tolerated my mood swings without it disrupting her internal climate.

Your child's not-okayness *cannot make you* not okay. Children need to feel safe with you, especially when they are chaotic and disagreeable.

Your desire for peace can show up as low tolerance for sibling squabbles. If you get flustered by any conflict between your children, you might end up creating a pressurized climate that brings more combustion to their combination. Lots of sibling drama looks like needless fight-picking, but it lays the groundwork for vital social-emotional learning. Skills like body awareness ("I guess I'm too big now to sit on my brother's head") and negotiation ("Dang! I should have asked for the front seat when she borrowed my T-shirt") are forged from irritating sibling conflict.

Emily P. Freeman asks, "How can we . . . discern the difference between true peace and discomfort avoidance?" She goes on to quote Hillary L. McBride, who says, "Being able to tell the difference between what is the relief that comes from my avoidance and what is actually peace is a whole life's work. . . . They will show up differently if you hold them side by side."[3]

When you focus on control, order, and peace, you create an environment stacked against your Spicy One. It's time to adjust some expectations, focus more on positive reinforcement, and reassess the home environment for simplicity and predictability. In the coming chapters, we'll cover lots of ways to help your wild one fit in better.

Your Sensitivity to Stimulation Is Making Things Harder

Which of these sentences best describes you?

- You are pretty unaffected by noises, visual clutter, touch, smells, and other sensory stimuli.
- You are aware of a lot of stuff going on but able to navigate through the distractions.
- You are constantly overstimulated and feel like your nerves are frayed much of the time.

The first ten years of parenting are completely overwhelming for anyone with heightened sensory perception (HSP). You may have heard it called "highly sensitive person." Unfortunately, the world treats sensitivity like premeditated dramatics, calling folks snowflakes and pick-mes if they voice their discomfort. The term *heightened sensory perception* feels more accurate.

To keep a small child alive, you must experience an onslaught of sensory and physical input. There is no way to keep up on everything you want to—the house clutter, the laundry, healthy meal prep, your friendships, and personal hygiene. Not to mention the mental labor of researching and making all the decisions. And what about all the crucial sleep you're missing?

Your body's inherent sensitivity (whether biological or trauma-induced) plays a big part in your acceptance of Spicy One counterintuitive behavior. Their frenetic movement and propensity for mischief can ignite a broiling nervousness in your body even when the play is innocent ("Esme, what are you doing to the dog?!").

To an HSP, whining is an ice pick to the forehead. Happy squealing is a visceral attack to your overactive nervous system. To a mom with ADHD, a child's joke can feel like a character assassination.*

In my first "mommy and me" parenting class, I tried to concentrate on the teacher. In the middle of our circle, babies lay on their stomachs, grasping for blocks. I heard words like *temperament* and *sensory processing* for the first time, but I was too distracted to comprehend. I could not hear above the frustrating sound of dripping water coming from a spigot somewhere down the hall. I looked around for confirmation that others were irritated by the *plunk*, *plunk*, *plunk*. But they were all locked in to the instructor's talk. Why was I the only one hearing this? And how could I get the noise to stop?

If you are in the 15–20 percent of humans who have a heightened reaction to external stimuli or experiences, noise, chatter, others' emotional expression, sound, light, or other environmental changes, you are neurodivergent.[4] Your high sensitivity is a nontypical functioning that could mean you are autistic or have a sensory processing disorder, a learning disability, ADHD, anxiety, a mood disorder, or OCD. Fun!

If this describes you, buckle up, buttercup. You will need some new tools to navigate this heightened sensory perception life.

* Google "rejection dysphoria."

PRO TIP: Avoid stimulation rather than try to recover from it. The end of the day is not the time to soothe yourself since the cumulative effects of *too much* have already crashed your capacity. Try to remove things *before* they overwhelm you, like you would allergens.

Remove the allergen of:

- ☐ Visual clutter in your home.
- ☐ Intense sensations (e.g., strong smells, tight clothing).
- ☐ Depleting environments (e.g., malls, crowds). Time in a darkened room at midday is therapeutic.
- ☐ Irritating sounds (e.g., a TV on in a faraway room). Wear earplugs. Don't have them? Wad up toilet paper and shove it in for all-day ease. You can still hear the Spicy One cry. You can still show up for them with empathy and care—but you don't have to subject yourself to *full-volume audio terrorism* all day long. That's not good for either of you. You may also need an hour a day where you bring out the big guns—noise-canceling headphones that block all sound. Confidently tell your child, "Mommy needs to give her ears a nap. I won't be able to hear you, but I will still be here, and we can use sign language if you need to tell me something. I'll start a timer so you can see when Mommy will wake her ears up again." Then smile and nod while they ask questions or complain.

May you treat your own spiciness with so much compassion.

CH 3: Reflection Questions

1. Where specifically does your desire for control, order, or peace add to the tension in your home and stop you from connecting with your Spicy One? What is one way you might lower the stakes?

2. How sensitive to environmental and emotional stimuli are you? Are there indications that you might be a heightened sensory perceptive parent?
3. What helps or could help you reduce sensory overwhelm earlier in the day?

• • • • • • • •

For a three-page PDF with tips for highly sensitive parents, visit maryvangeffen.com/bookresources or scan here:

4

What Do You Hope for Your Kid?

We can get so caught up in the day-to-day challenges of raising a little firecracker that we lose sight of the bigger picture, of what we will consider most important a long time from now.

Conflicts over potty training, a meltdown at a family barbecue, or arguments over who empties the dishwasher give us stress-induced tunnel vision. I want to lift you out of the muck of the day-to-day power struggles and tell you, "If you, as the parent, don't know where you are going, every road will get you nowhere."[1]

You've been parenting without a map. To create that map you will need to get clear on your intended final destination. You will need to define:

- ☐ Your hopes (which may entail facing your fears)
- ☐ Your long-term vision for your relationship
- ☐ Your personal values
- ☐ Your unique definition of a good parent

"But what about the kind of human I want them to be?" you may be asking. You have the most control over your part of the relationship. Even if this child grows up to be a struggling adult, you can still envision what kind of relationship you want to build by their adulthood. The more you can separate your view of yourself from your child's actions, the more you can allow yourself to enthusiastically accept them for who they are.

There is great joy in the connection you forge with a grown child who has grown up feeling seen and supported by you. My twenty-one-year-old Spicy One is both irreverent and socially adept, kind and caustically funny. I would 100 percent choose to be her friend even if she wasn't my responsibility.

If you do this parenting thing well, you get to be on the inside of their life, hearing about their adventures forever. They will invite you to have Sunday dinner together, go on vacations as adults, and be someone who weighs in on their big decisions. You will continue to have influence (but not control). This is all very possible.

But you must begin now with the end in mind.

Define Your Hope by Facing Your Fear

My worry, usually lingering just below the surface, that my daughter was mentally ill was memorialized in tempera paint.

I was sure her artwork was a symptom of a DSM* condition or defect I could not yet name. Fear was growing within me. It would be months before I worked up the courage to show a school counselor the drawings. Only then would I get the assurance that these were normal, developmentally appropriate artistic explorations.

Until then, the concern that something was very wrong was the through line of my parenting. Fear colored how I saw my daughter. Still holding the drawing, I recalled a few weeks earlier when I had

* *Diagnostic and Statistical Manual of Mental Disorders*, a book used by physicians to describe every disease and condition that impairs the mental health of humans.

asked my daughter to choose her words more carefully. She had called her two-year-old brother stupid for knocking over her blocks. "We don't want him to feel bad about himself, right? We want our words to lift him up," I pleaded, with false cheerfulness.

She cocked her tiny blonde head, grinned with gleaming eyes, and lisped, "No, we want him to hate hisself." I did not chuckle at her unmitigated gall. I felt fear. Fear I was raising someone who enjoyed being cruel.

Being afraid is a familiar feeling when your child is wired differently than the rest. But fear has a physical imprint on your body, making you reactionary and tight. It restricts you from what you really want—a deeply connected and loving relationship with your child. Fear keeps you anxious about the future instead of grateful for the gifts of the present. Fear stops your creativity and ability to see potential.

Parenting out of fear is not your best work.

Typical fears of Moms of Spicy Ones:*

- "I'm afraid the Spicy One won't be a functioning adult or that they'll be a bad person. No friends, can't hold down a job, possibly prison."
- "I'm afraid that I might squash their spirit or cause them to hold things inside, but they are ruining everyone else's moment."
- "I'm afraid that I might be the one enabling my child's brazenness because I don't know what to do with their powerful defiance."

These fears lead to heavy emotions:

- Sadness—this wasn't your dream. There's grief here.
- Tiredness, exhaustion, and hopelessness—your body is heavy.
- Frustration or anger—you can't seem to be the parent you want to be. You experience the sting of failure over and over.

* As voiced by six different cohorts of students in my Moms of Spicy Ones course.

These are legitimate emotions that can dominate your parenting when you try to repress them. When you don't yet have the vocabulary for the nuance of feelings, they can seem larger and more powerful than they need to be.

Don't treat your fear like Voldemort's name, assuming that the less you acknowledge it, the smaller the chance it will come true. Naming the fear is a crucial step for letting it move through you. Being able to parse out and acknowledge the nuance of your fears will help both of you. A fear spoken aloud loses much of its power over you.

Articulating a fear is different from ruminating on it. To let hope, not fear, drive your parenting navigation, practice focusing on the "not yet" rather than the "not ever." You aren't stuck or unchanging. Neither is your child.

A confident, hope-infused leader is easier to respect and follow than a terrified one.

One of the fears that used to clutter up my leadership was *My son's relationship with food means he's going to get sick eventually.*

He used to love sugary treats and never ate enough protein or fiber. When I operated out of that fear, mealtimes became battlegrounds. I was fixated on what went into his mouth. He began to hide his food choices from me. Thankfully, I learned to shift my focus to my hope: *I can trust my child to develop intuitive eating habits as he matures. I will keep providing healthy food options and allow him to be in charge of what goes into his own body.*

Over time, as I practiced hope and celebrated the hard-to-notice examples of nutritious choices, he morphed into a capable eater who makes conscious choices about what goes into his body. He is now a buff eighteen-year-old who refuses sugar, sodium, and processed foods. He stepped into the hope I had for him.

Notice your body's response in reading the two contrasting thoughts in the following couplets. They create a vastly different internal landscape, which impacts the energy you bring to parenting. Fear's energy gives us something to run from. Hope invites us to skip toward it.

WHEN THEIR PLAY MAKES YOU FEARFUL

"You can't play with us," the blonde Barbie screamed at the horse figurine. "We don't like you that much!" Listening to my first grader's solo play made me anxious. It wasn't nice talk her dolls slung at each other. Should I step in and enforce kinder language?

What about the tied-up dolls painted garishly? Spicy Ones are notorious for their "creative" use of toys (remember Sid from *Toy Story*?). It's a peek at the fabulously innovative adult they will become!

Messy, unstructured play is therapy for kids. Like dreams, the play is tapping into conscious and unconscious concerns and fears. They are working out their mental health right before your eyes. Do not disturb. The world your child can create from their imagination is as healing as it is entertaining.

During the school year, countless adult-led, structured activities squeeze out opportunities for real play. Hold certain parts of the day as sacred and set apart for play. Make screen entertainment off-limits during that time. Mornings might be best. Then pick up a book and seem engrossed in your own thing.

Fear: My Spicy One is destroying their relationship with their sibling and will be lonely as an adult. Too bossy, emotional, and selfish.

Hope: My Spicy One is learning to be a good friend and will develop a connection with their sibling as they mature. I hope they will learn the skills of leadership.

Fear: I'm worried this kid is going to get seriously hurt taking thoughtless physical risks.

Hope: I hope my child will learn to assess the situation and take safety precautions when testing their athletic limits.

Fear: I'm afraid my parenting reactions are making my child's outbursts worse rather than better. I don't know what to do with this surprising rage within me.

Hope: I hope to learn how to tolerate and welcome feelings I can't fix. I hope I can be compassionate with the angry parts of me.

Fear: I'm afraid I won't learn to be kind and gentle because I never saw it modeled.

Hope: I hope to heal my attachment wounds by building a secure attachment to my child. The intention I hold is holy,

NAME YOUR FEARS

In the clouds below, write out the specific fears that loom over your ability to parent your Spicy One. Take time to listen to yourself. Identify the hazy, unspoken anxiety that keeps bubbling below polite conversation. The exact issues will morph and change as your child grows. Be brave enough to pin down the current fear—to write it out and witness it.

Word to the wise: As you articulate your fear, DO NOT climb down into the fear like it's your personal anxiety hot tub. Notice it from above—with compassion but also detachment. Keep each fear to one specific sentence.

even if I mess up a lot in learning a new way of being I never got to experience myself.

WARNING: Sometimes we speak our fears out loud in a misguided attempt to activate a sluggish child. Avoid verbal hexes that curse your child to a negative future like, "You are not going to have any friends if you keep acting like that."

Instead say, "You are learning to be a good friend. Each day, I see you get more comfortable sharing."

Doom-and-gloom pronouncements work opposite of how you intend. They become the script of your child's inner self-talk. Do you want your child silently repeating to themself, "I am not going to have any friends"? Of course not. That self-talk would make the very thing we are afraid of come true.

Your Long-Term Vision: The Thanksgiving Exercise

What kind of lifelong relationship do you want to build with this child? When you know your big-picture goal clearly and tangibly, it changes how you react to the little stuff. Take time to consider your hoped-for future.

Imagine it's twenty years from now, in late November. You finished reading this book long ago and successfully shifted how you showed up for your radical thinker. Your adult child has matured and learned to cope with their big feelings. You two now have a very close relationship. They are still trying to swim upstream, but they are a functioning, successful adult surrounded by a supportive, loving community.

In this beautiful future, your child, in their late twenties, is driving home with a friend for Thanksgiving dinner. Their friend notices them crackling with joyful expectation.

"What's going on?" they ask. "Why are you so pumped to visit your mom?"

How do you hope your adult child responds? Maybe they grin and say, "You haven't met my mom yet! She's amazing. Let me tell you what it's like to be with her . . ."

Visualize your adult child describing the emotional temperature of your home. They gush about you and what it was like to be themself in your presence. They are describing the culture that you worked so hard to make happen.

What phrases do they use?

Some parents have envisioned their child saying:

- "My family was a safe place where I could be my authentic self. I felt very accepted and appreciated for just being me. Differences were embraced."
- "My mom created such a welcoming atmosphere. Something yummy was always cooking, and she allowed my friends to come over whenever. She was interested in them and me."
- "My dad cracked jokes and looked for ways for us to have fun and test our strength. He had high standards for academics but was willing to roll up his sleeves and figure out the hard stuff with me."

I honor how difficult it can be to hope for a rosy future when the present is so dingy. But making this effort to visualize your desired future is like putting the address in your car's GPS. Naming your hopes is a momentous step in getting where you want to go.

IDENTIFY THE GOOD

When you feel defeated and hopeless, stop scanning the situation for what's most upsetting about the Spicy One! I've been there—building a case to explain to an imaginary judge about what's wrong with your kid. Instead, reduce your stress by noticing all that is already good. Ask yourself this powerful question: "What's everything else I'm not noticing that's not hard?"

Make it your practice to celebrate progress rather than ruminate on what is not yet good enough. Start telling defiant stories of how far you and your child have come.

REWRITE YOUR FEARS INTO HOPES

Name three fears and write out the opposite hope that could also be true. Look under the fear for the buried deep longing and give it voice. It's easier if you channel the personality of your most positive friend.

1. I am afraid that ______________________________

   ____

   I hope that ______________________________

   ____

2. I am afraid that ______________________________

   ____

   I hope that ______________________________

   ____

3. I am afraid that ______________________________

   ____

   I hope that ______________________________

   ____

Define Your Values

When my Spicy One was two, I was part of a playgroup run by an organized mom who pureed homemade baby food, planned educational field trips, and required first-time obedience from her easygoing child. When the adults started chatting and the kids were left to fend for themselves, a child would predictably grab a toy from her son. Her response was to look at her son sternly until he said meekly, "That's okay, you can use it. We can share." She beamed with pride at his ability to stay out of drama, even if it meant giving up toys he wanted to play with.

Meanwhile, when my daughter would use her big voice (instead of her hands) to say, "Hey, I was playing with that! Give it back, please!"

I would burst with pride. She was vocalizing her needs instead of hitting!

Was one of us parenting wrong?

Nope, we just had different values. This other mom valued *keeping the peace*, while I prioritized *assertive, nonviolent communication*. Both values are virtuous. There's no moral high ground here. One person's constellation of values is not more correct than another's. One mom might want her child to be able to endure any trial, prizing independence, while another parent might want her kid to always ask for help and "know that I'm in his corner." Both sets of values are admirable.

When you ignore your personal preferences, you eventually burn out. You, oh Mother of a Spicy One, cannot afford to burn out.

Know your values and honor them. Values are your operating instructions for optimal performance. You have valid preferences around your time, space, energy, body, and food, how you like to communicate and be touched and spoken to, and how you want to parent.

Specificity in your language helps you uncover your values to bring more leadership clarity and big boundary-boss presence. If you can imagine it, and describe it, you are much more likely to obtain it. Get granular about what you long for from this wild child and from this one wild life!

Your dream for your child will hinge on your personal values: the concepts or ideas that matter most to you and that you want to embody in your life—even when it costs you something. You likely want these values for all of humanity but especially for your child.

Research shows that family culture can play as big a role in shaping a child as your actual parenting style.[2] Doesn't that blow your mind? Family culture is the distinct way a family harnesses their values to work together to solve problems, achieve goals, and relate to one another.[3] The felt sense of belonging that is inherent in shared values can greatly increase a child's well-being.

Your family culture, dictated by your conscious or unconscious values, will happen whether you actively create it or not. It's up to you (and your co-parent, if you have one) to commit yourself to naming what matters and coming back to it again to correct when folks (including you) predictably fall off course. You cannot hope for the best or passively let group dynamics take shape based on whose personality is strongest (then the Spicy One will always dictate!).

Not sure what your values are? I've got you! Check out my 500 Possible Values resource for ideas, which you can find via the QR code at the end of this chapter. Use this list as a starting place. Look for words that light you up. But you are a unique Pegasus of a creature, so your specific values might not even be on this list. Be on the lookout for phrases in books or songs that more closely describe what is uniquely important to you.

Sometimes your values are buried under the things that really tick you off. Anger is an indication that someone is stepping on the bare toes of your values. Like when your mother-in-law says she's taking your child out to lunch but then "surprises you" with your child's first haircut (and it's a crew cut—all his glorious long hair chopped off). You might feel especially murderous if your values were open communication, playfulness, respect, self-expression, and celebrating milestones.

Your values aren't set in stone. You get to change your mind. Values change because each season of life and motherhood will demand a different version of you. The purpose is to uncover what matters most to you in this current season of life.

CO-PARENTING

If you have a spouse, partner, or other healthy adult invested in your parenting and your child's well-being, talk to them about your values. Values discussions can be a compelling tool for getting on the same page. Finding the overlaps, or even just respecting the uniqueness of what matters most to each person, creates more collaboration. You might have drastically different ways of getting "there," but there is relief in articulating some of the "there." See more on co-parenting in chapter 21.

CH 4: Reflection Questions

1. What phrases do you hope your adult child will use in twenty years to describe you and the culture of your home? Fill up one page with these phrases. Imagine your child finishing these starter statements:
   - "My childhood home was a place where . . ."
   - "I love that it felt like . . ."
   - "Our family culture was . . ."
   - "My mom was the best. She would . . ."
2. Using the 500 Possible Values resource, what are your top five personal values at this time in your life? Explain why each one is important. This exercise brings your principles into focus, making it more likely you will honor your values in your daily parenting. For extra credit, write one small doable thing you could do to move closer to honoring each value in your everyday family life.

For my list of 500 Possible Values, scan here:

5

Are You a Good Enough Mom?

The quest to be a "good mom" is fraught with unconscious societal norms, delusions about the beauty of selflessness, and fantasies about family we held long before we met the Spicy One. So how will you know if you are indeed a "good mom"?

A few years ago, I was lucky enough to host five nineteen-year-old girls giggling, dancing, sleeping, and eating in my home for four days. I did my best impression of an eager Downton Abbey servant during a royal visit, canceling all my social obligations and keeping my expectations light. I made myself available to get to know my Spicy One's friends on a deeper level.

I kept up a friendly vibe by playing music in the kitchen, welcoming their song requests. We fried eggs to throbbing beats and language that would make your mother-in-law blush. I taught them how to play pickleball on my home court.

It was intoxicating to be in their fresh-faced girl gang. The next morning, before I dropped them at the airport for their giddy spring break trip to Mexico, I said a blessing out loud, asking God that they would stay together, especially at night, and that they would have patience and generosity toward each other.

Driving away smiling, I thanked God for the gift of a strong relationship with my Spicy One despite all we'd been through. That she could feel secure enough to bring these buoyant spirits into our home. That she wanted to come home. *Sigh.* We had made it through the fire and my dreams had become reality. I knew without a doubt that I was a flawed, imperfect, but good enough mom.

I want this assurance for you too!

How do we define a good enough parent?

Have you ever had a job that was not well suited to your natural skill set? I tried waitressing one college summer at Dewey Beach, Delaware. The memory of me forgetting to put orders into the kitchen, letting down table after table of hungry patrons, and trying to memorize dish ingredients and prices makes my cheeks red.

If the definition of a *good* waitress is timely order taking and food serving, I deserved to be fired. If, however, we decide a *good* waitress means someone able to flirt with grumpy grandads, make babies laugh, and loudly sing "Happy Birthday" in three-part harmony, then I should have been employee of the month.

Your job description is critical to your felt success as a parent.

Laura lived a good life before kids. She traveled around the country as a medical sales technician. A seasoned adventurer, she could decipher back-road detours, plan her route to hit exotic roadside attractions, and take advantage of the serendipity that happens in travel.

After birthing three babies in five years, the good life came to a screeching halt. While she dutifully raised them to toddlerhood, she hated cooking and sitting home marking time. Motherhood felt suffocating.

A responsible woman, she pushed through the boredom and discontent to cobble together attempts at structure and consistency. By the time she found me, she was joyless, a depressed shadow of her former self. Together we realized Laura had a toxic definition of a good mom: "Good moms make home-cooked dinners and stay home so kids can take scheduled naps and eat seated at kitchen tables."

I questioned how accurate that was. What if, for her, it's just the opposite? I invited her to write out a new job description based on her own unique values. "I value adventure and wind in my hair," she whispered, at first wistfully and then, over time, louder.

Once she freed herself from her arbitrary (and false) definition, she realized she could easily pop her kids in the car to head out into the world and even—*gasp*—grab takeout on their way home as the sun went down. Following her way of parenting brought out her inner smile, and that meant joy for everyone! When Mom is happy, everyone tends to be happy! Well, not always when you have a Spicy One, but it's a start.

The culture of Laura's home shifted when she drafted her own job definition of a good mother: "A good mother takes her children on adventures and teaches them about the world and makes sure they have food accessible to them."

Now, that's a job description she can fulfill! A good mother pays attention to what lights her up because her happiness is vital to "good" parenting.

Might you be operating out of some inaccurate beliefs about what a good mother is or does? Like these?

- Good mothers have well-behaved children.
- Good mothers make time to brush their kids' hair every morning.
- Good mothers have children who don't curse.

None of that is true. "There's no way to be a perfect mother and a million ways to be a good one."[1] It's crucial to create your own custom definition of a good mom. It will not match your mother's or your neighbor's.

You make parenting more difficult when you force your journey to look like the "acceptable journey" some other parent is on. Their ways are not your ways, young Jedi!

Can a good mom have a disobedient child?

Yes. You can have a defiant child and still be a very good mom, a mom who stays grounded and positive, who doesn't keep a record of every wrong or speak ill of her child to others. That's revolutionary work for a Mom of a Spicy One.

Can a good mom have a dysregulated child?

Yes. Your child is working through their own unique expression of being in a limited human body on this planet. Their timing to maturation may not be your timing. You are their warm, safe place, so you will witness the awkward, terrible lurching of their human development. Treat their journey with reverence. You have a window on the slow unfurling of a soul.

How you define a good mom will color your entire experience.

Make sure your definition of a good mom is not shaming you into setting an unattainable standard. "A good mom never gets angry" is neither true nor inspiring. Whoever wrote "Love means never having to say you're sorry" was a gaslighting narcissist.*

It's time to nail down what success looks like for you, even if it is an evolving definition.

WARNING: If the description of a good mom is connected to your child's behavior or to their happiness, you have set yourself up to fail at this job. You can't make someone else happy. Plus, the Spicy One's first language is disappointment. Don't make this your problem to fix.

From here on out, it's not fair to have a secret, unspoken list of things that you aren't doing well that keeps you out of the imaginary Good Mom Club.

You're finished with unvoiced rules and hazy expectations. Parenting with no set definition of success is like moving the finish line each time the runner nears the end.

Will you give yourself a break if every day you work toward that description? No one is asking for perfection. Can you allow yourself to mess up and try again tomorrow without calling yourself a bad mom? And when you do experience that elusive moment where

* It was Erich Segal in *Love Story*. Shame on him.

WRITE OUT YOUR "GOOD MOM" DEFINITION

STEP 1: What three words describe the way you want the space between people in your home and family to feel? Name the culture you want to create with specific emotional words, like *safe, fun, active, adventurous, playful, merciful*. See the 500 Possible Values resource on my website (QR code at the end of this chapter) for a list of potential words.

These three words might not match your current family atmosphere. You could long for *collaboration, togetherness*, and *laughter*, but your actual family contains *humorless* people holed up in separate rooms. That dissonance gets to be okay while you are setting a new strategy.

I am committed to creating a family culture that feels ______________, ______________, and ______________.

Well done.

STEP 2: If that's how you want the culture of your home to feel, what three words need to describe how you, the leader of that culture, must show up?

(Hint: It's usually the very same three words.)

Maybe you choose *calm, firm*, and *kind*, but you are currently a raging, inconsistent, and mean mom. That's all right. This journey requires starting with a blue-sky perspective that believes "I can get better every day."

To create the above family culture, I want to be a mom who practices being ______________, ______________, and ______________, regardless of how my child behaves.

You just wrote your first definition of a good mom!

If it's missing something important, add to it now. But not too many words. Keep it simple. Attainable.

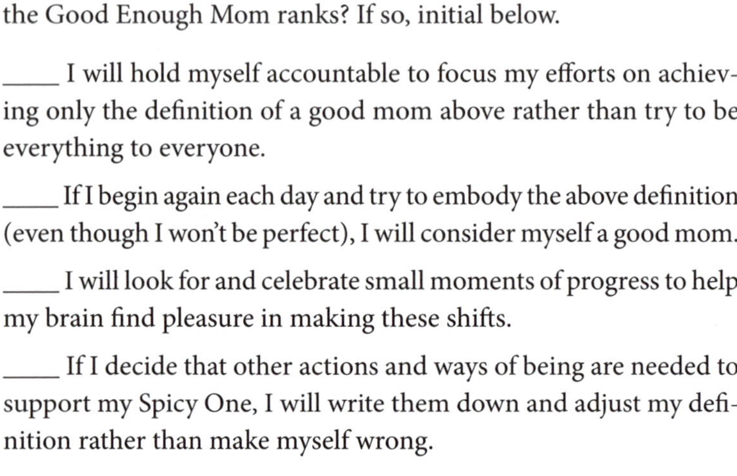

you meet your definition, will you celebrate your membership in the Good Enough Mom ranks? If so, initial below.

_____ I will hold myself accountable to focus my efforts on achieving only the definition of a good mom above rather than try to be everything to everyone.

_____ If I begin again each day and try to embody the above definition (even though I won't be perfect), I will consider myself a good mom.

_____ I will look for and celebrate small moments of progress to help my brain find pleasure in making these shifts.

_____ If I decide that other actions and ways of being are needed to support my Spicy One, I will write them down and adjust my definition rather than make myself wrong.

CH 5: Reflection Questions

1. What is your definition of a good mom?
2. What nice-to-have attributes of a good mom are you willing to let go of in this season?
3. According to your definition, how have you already met your expectations in both your actions and the way you just exist? As you write, notice and enjoy the softening in your body from experiencing a rare sensation of self-acceptance.

Download the 500 Possible Values PDF
to help figure out what matters most to you.

6

Listen to Your Inner Child

A healthy family is like a giant sequoia tree. You are the sweaty ranger planting a sapling in the forest, investing in this strong, resilient future tree that will bring joy to generations. But a hardy tree can't grow without rich, nutritive soil to nourish its roots. Toxic soil makes for stunted, diseased growth. To protect your tree, you analyze its soil, amend it, and add nutrients that might be lacking.

In this metaphor, the soil is your understanding of your own past. The roots of your parenting choices and how you cope under pressure are fed by this soil. The quality of the fruit of your parenting is dependent on the story you choose to tell yourself about your own childhood.

If you grew up listening to people you love accuse you of being too much or not enough, then you will likely see and abhor those qualities in your own child.

You cannot welcome in your child what you hate in yourself. Your backstory will either poison or nurture your parenting.

If your parents praised you for being agreeable and easygoing, you might believe it's just not worth it to disagree. Managing life under this rule will make the effort of standing up to (or for) the Spicy One insurmountable. You will resent them for something they can't yet understand. Only after you come to terms with the truth of what it was like to be little in your family will you be able to notice the parasites in the soil that keep you separated from your child.

This part of the work is a doozy. It's not easy digging up your past to hold it to the light. I promise to be gentle with you and vulnerable about my own backstory. Go slower if that feels right. Consider reaching out to a therapist to work through some of the ideas or memories this work might dredge up. What resources will help you be compassionate with yourself? Put them in place now.

When Your Past Haunts Your Parenting

When I married my husband over twenty-two years ago, I was a shiny, new evangelical Christian coming off the pain of a failed first marriage. I can now link the divorce and a few other lost friendships (I told you I was a Spicy One) to the fact that I had not yet looked beneath my own childhood. Invisible open wounds from my past infected my current relationships.

I was stuck clinging to what I learned about myself from the words my parents and teachers labeled me with: *Dramatic. Overly emotional. Too sensitive. Selfish.*

Eight years of Catholic school added more labels, like *class clown*, *sinner*, and *slutty*.

Looking back now as an adult, I admit I was a spunky little Spicy One. My mother was essentially alone in the child-rearing department. Dad was a brilliant but absent-minded nuclear medicine physician obsessed with radioactive isotopes but oblivious to kinkeeping. Parenting alongside this emotionally unavailable genius left my mother completely overwhelmed. My unceasing need for attention and limits fatigued her. Then two more children were born.

Around the fifth grade, I remember running upstairs so fast my lungs burned to make it to my third-floor bedroom before she could grab me. She was screaming, a few strides behind me. She aimed to slap me for my brazen back talk. I would catch my breath only after I had made it inside my room and slipped the lock across the door. I ignored her banging. Only a fool would open a locked door to a parent in monster mode.

Eventually, my parents began using substances as a much-needed escape from me and my neediness. Or at least that's the explanation I came to as a child and clung to well into adulthood. Let's fast-forward past my struggling teen years, where I acted out and took risks that could have killed me, and scroll all the way to me becoming a shiny new mom.

The entrenched beliefs that I was demanding, dramatic, overly emotional, too sensitive, and selfish colored the filter I looked through to make sense of my new parent-child relationship. The first two years

of parenting were a piece of cake, but that's because I gave birth to an angel baby. My chubby cherub was a show pony, way cuter than your kid. I could take her everywhere and receive praise for having such a "good baby."

But then my daughter became a devil's spawn, er, I mean a toddler. This fleshed-out, independent human being with her own intense will was like a flash flood dredging up the toxic soil of my personal narrative, poisoning our mother-child bond.

With every tantrum and willful act of defiance by her, I found myself thinking this child is so *demanding*, *dramatic*, *overly emotional*, *sensitive*, and *selfish*.

My mom and her Spicy One

Me and my Spicy One

Do you recognize those glowing descriptions? Can you see the lies I believed about myself and how they might have caused my past to bleed into my present? My perspective on my child was skewed by my parents' limited language for me. The wounding was being passed down.

A couple months after the Spicy One turned two, I gave birth to a baby boy. This meant less time for my girl and certainly less patience for her big personality. I was outnumbered.

By the time she was four, we'd established a pattern of me setting a boundary and then her melting down for twenty minutes. I would start out calm and friendly and then end up screaming right alongside her. I tried to keep firm on my boundaries, but boy was it exhausting. Her emotions spiked then plummeted with no warning. She had no "go with the flow" in her. I loved her undoubtedly. But I also kind of hated her. I was ashamed to feel that way about my own child.

I finally admitted in a whisper to my college roommate Gail (who had just finished grad school to become a psychotherapist) that

I couldn't stand my daughter. It was a flood of relief to say those dangerous words out loud to another human. And to not have her recoil in disgust at my lack of maternal instincts. She calmly suggested that I go talk with someone about what was causing those feelings. But I already knew what was causing those feelings: my daughter's awful behavior.

"No," Gail said gently. "Your relationship with your daughter is triggering unresolved feelings about what it was like for you when you were her age." I rolled my eyes as far back in my head as I could because I had already done the therapy thing in my twenties. I had checked that box. I didn't need help. My daughter did.

Gail kept talking about a new "remembering context." In motherhood, we reengage in "the intimate emotive process of caring for a baby. The ordinary acts of holding and feeding a child evoke a flow of memories about our own experience of being mothered. Spontaneously, unconsciously we draw on a repertoire of feelings and behaviors" that may not have been linked to anything else since our own experience at that age.[1]

A Pandora's box filled with emotional baggage gets unleashed when we form a new parent-child relationship. Whether your Spicy One is four or fourteen, this is the first time you've revisited your memories of being that age . . . but this time from the position of power. Part

of you is clenching your fists and insisting, "Never again will I allow myself to be treated that way." I suppose that was the part of me that rejected Gail's idea to get help and instead embarked on a quest to find a specialist who could tell me what was wrong with my kid.

I needed to diagnose my daughter with something I could fix. I wanted a handy label, a doctor's certificate with one of those tidy little three-letter conditions like ADD or ODD.* I saw my negative feelings and the way those feelings got released as her fault. I certainly wasn't like this with anyone else!

Which leads us to my low point—my rock bottom in parenting. It happened one morning when we were trying to get out the door for preschool. My four-year-old's attitude and words were so disrespectful that day. She wouldn't get dressed. She called me a "poo-poo head" with contempt on her squishy face. She pushed her baby brother down. My emotional tank was already empty by 8:30 a.m. My nerves were shot. I smoldered like a blown-out candle.

She proudly wore one of her daddy's Disneyland work IDs around her neck, marching around like she owned the place. She was the queen, which made me the handmaiden. She was shouting at me for the fifth time that morning. And then she pinched me.

The rational, thinking part of my brain powered down. [*scene fades to black*]

As she twirled away from me, I instinctively reached out and snatched the lanyard tight around her throat—yanking her back toward me. She fell to the floor, the wind knocked out of her. A thin, angry red welt emerged across the skin of her neck.

As soon as I realized what I had done, both of us were sobbing.

Thank God my husband was there. I hate that he had to live through that scene and how helpless he felt. He graciously brought her an ice pack and put his arm around me as he held her on his

* For the record, ODD (oppositional defiance disorder) is a crap diagnosis. It's handed out disproportionately to brown or impoverished children. It just describes behavior but offers no solutions or treatment. Unfortunately, sometimes our healthcare system will require this label to get you the services you need. Look up PDA instead.

lap. Then he gently pointed out that our daughter couldn't go to school that day.

"But we need a break from each other!" I pleaded.

He nodded but asked, "Do you know what happens if a child shows up to school with a bruise or welt and then tells the teacher, 'My mommy did that'?" My stomach dropped. I had crossed a line. I was a heavy sandbag of shame. I was one of those abusive moms now.

But low points are often the necessary catalyst for finally asking for help.

One week later, I was sitting outside the office of a child play therapist, praying God would use this professional to fix my broken daughter.

As my tiny dictator headed into the room behind the one-way mirror, I exhaled. Now I would finally have an answer. A reason for our pain. After a couple sessions, the therapist asked if I could get childcare and come back alone. I understood completely. This specialist had properly investigated the depths of my daughter's darkness and was ready to help me create a game plan to address her mental issues.

So I went back alone. She invited me to tell my story, her face twisting and grimacing with my words. What was that look on her face? Was this empathy? She gingerly scratched beneath my complaints, looking for something deeper. I returned the second week. Then again for the third, fourth, and fifth times. I kept going back . . . for two years. Drinking in the therapist's nurturing maternal presence I needed. My daughter never returned.

My bold little girl was not the issue. Mommy's backstory was rotted and needed mending and healing. If I hadn't sought help, I was beginning down a destructive path of autopilot, parenting from a broken narrative. Over the next two years, we unearthed my past, infused compassion into my perspective, and dressed my open childhood wounds. I am no longer bound by an old and inaccurate childlike interpretation of my current reality.

I rewrote a meaningful *new* story. Turns out, I was not demanding, dramatic, overly emotional, too sensitive, and selfish; I was

ADVERSE CHILDHOOD EXPERIENCES

Effective parenting starts with being gentle with yourself. Proceed slowly and tenderly as you walk into these self-reflections. You may have adverse childhood experiences (ACE) that require a one-on-one relationship with a therapist to safely unpack.* If this is you, visualize encapsulating this work along with your hurtful memories in an imaginary wooden box in your soul. You decide when to take out the box and look through the contents. There is no ideal pace or response you must adhere to. When your spirit feels overwhelmed by the effort, imagine putting the work and the memories back into the wooden box for a few days. You get to decide how much time you spend with it.

* ACE refers to a range of negative situations a child may face growing up that can result in trauma. These experiences include emotional, physical, or sexual abuse; emotional or physical neglect; parental separation or divorce; or living in a household in which domestic violence occurs. Other situations that can have a negative impact on health, opportunity, and well-being include living in a household with an alcoholic, a substance abuser, family members who suffer mental disorders, or an incarcerated family member; being Black or brown in an America set up for white domination; or simply trying to survive as a family in poverty.

a wonderfully strong-willed, creative, gifted, emotionally sensitive *girl* who often felt rejected and emotionally unseen *even though* my parents were doing the best they could. I grew into a strong-willed, creative, gifted, emotionally sensitive *woman* and gave birth to a strong-willed, creative, gifted, emotionally sensitive child.

This tale has a happy ending—one of connectedness; nurturing, warm, loving boundaries; and immense supernatural, God-given levels of patience. You can have that too.

My Spicy One is now twenty-one and kicking butt in a prestigious college with an impressive paid internship. May I brag a little? Back in high school, she was the first of her peers to get a job. During the COVID-19 global quarantine, she was awarded student of the month because she was one of the few to bravely keep her camera on and interact with the teacher and students. She and I have a loving, respectful relationship. She's still incredibly willful, spirited, smart, and quite capable of verbal disrespect, but she now has a healthy parent designed specifically for her.

I no longer blame her for my reactions to her behavior. I choose my words carefully, I call on God to be strong where I am weak, and I care for myself fiercely.

I have been refined in the fire of her intensity. I am different. More authentically who I am. More vulnerable—capable of more joy and deeper sadness. Like the velveteen rabbit, I was made real through this journey with a Spicy One. I stopped pinning my happiness or frustration on my kid. I started tending to my inner child, which led to creating a better relationship with my Spicy One.

Now it's your turn to look at your story.

The greatest indicator of whether dysfunctional behavior will be handed down to the next generation is whether you can give an accurate depiction of what happened to you. Can you name with compassion what it was really like for you to be little?

In his book *Parenting from the Inside Out*, Dr. Daniel J. Siegel says the best predictor of a child's secure attachment to you is not what happened to you as a child but rather how you have made sense of any difficult childhood experiences.[2] Having a traumatic relationship with your own parents doesn't have to haunt your parenting. Not if you have found a way to make sense of how those experiences affected you.

Practice New Narratives

The stories you tell about your own life help you determine who you are and what you believe about yourself. Telling yourself "I was a little terror" instead of "I was a child acting out because the adults in my life were unable to be present" can emotionally handicap your current relationships.

Your *beliefs* dictate what you *think.*

What you *think* dictates how you *feel.*

How you *feel* compels you into specific (parenting) *action.*

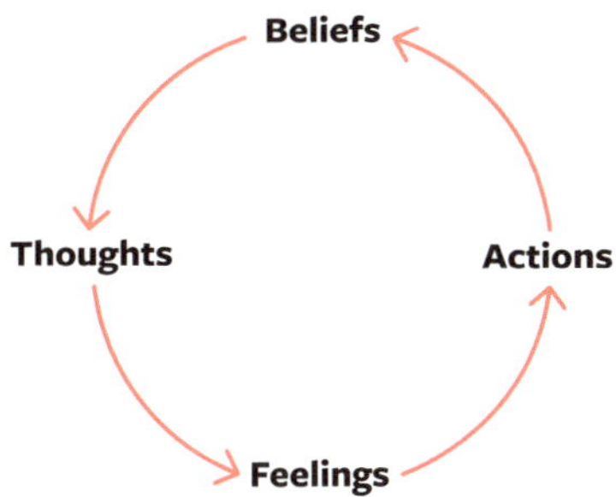

If you are walking around *believing* "I'm not enough" or "I don't matter," your mind is a hostile place. These harsh beliefs could mean you're *thinking*, "No one cares for me." This makes you *feel* vulnerable and unsupported. Now imagine you've just put your hair into pigtails. Here comes your eight-year-old, who prefers your hair down. He grimaces and says, "I don't like your hair like that." Because of your thoughts, you are primed to see his comment as vindication of what you already believe. That you are subpar.

When you feel unlovable, you act unloving.

"What a rude boy you are!" you might holler at him, your face twisting into a scowl. He will be surprised and hurt by your *action*, and a chain of negative events is set in motion.

If, instead, you actively believe "I'm more than enough," you will likely walk around thinking, "I am doing the best I can, and that is enough." You will feel at peace and playful. Now when your son makes that same rude comment, you will have a very different reaction to his snark. You might squeal, "Oh no. You don't like my pigtails? Oink, oink!" while grabbing for him. Now he's giggling, and you've made some lemonade out of his sour comment.

I'm asking you to consider what beliefs about yourself you may have developed from your childhood. It's time to pick up and examine these beliefs like litter from the beach now that you are an adult. Are they worth keeping?

Parenting is a stressful role for anyone. Under stress, we go to autopilot like faulty robots—doing to others exactly what was done to us. If you had a difficult childhood but work to develop a coherent understanding of your history, you free yourself from the unconscious pull to re-create the same negative interactions for your own children. If you did not grow up in a home that nurtured you . . . even if your parents "did the best they could," their best wasn't what you needed.

Beliefs clung to in childhood don't have to still be true. Maybe you never learned that you are a holy image bearer, reflecting the beauty of your Creator. Full of worth just for existing. Good enough AS-IS.

Your job, if you want to be a safe parent, is to excavate your calcified idea of the past to uncover fresh truth. As James Baldwin writes, "Whoever cannot tell [herself] the truth about [her] past is trapped in it, is immobilized in the prison of [her] undiscovered self."[3]

Were you called *sensitive* or *needy*? Believe this and you might see your child's needs as in direct competition with yours. You will see your complicated kid as the enemy.

Instead, see yourself as a human who struggles from time to time and longs for safe relationships where you can receive comfort and support.

Did you grow up the designated helper in charge of making sure everyone was happy in your family? The professional peacemaker believing you must earn your keep through selfless service? It will feel life-threatening to have a family member upset with you. You will avoid any conflicts that are necessary for intimacy and change.

Instead, practice the belief that everyone is responsible for their own emotions. You are working on being okay when others are not.

It's important that you notice some of the past rules you unconsciously parent beneath, like "People should know what I need."

This is a lie. People—especially your kids—cannot read your mind and need to be educated on what you need and feel.

Try believing, "I can practice asking for what I need and staying grounded even if others say no."

From a neurological perspective, there is hope. The brain is malleable. Gaining a new understanding of yourself alters your expectations, associations, and interpretations. Your brain's synaptic connections are upleveled by your active role in healing from your childhood.

By revising the stories you tell yourself to include limitless compassion for the child you were and the things that happened to you, you can develop new impulses and gut responses.

From a spiritual perspective, you've come to the edge of your own usefulness. You can't do this alone without help from something greater, outside of your limited skin. It's going to be okay, because you don't have to do this alone.

Healing takes equal parts valiant effort to change and terrifying submission to reality. Your beliefs about who you are and why or what your loved ones did or failed to do have to be upgraded. Like your favorite app that won't work properly without an update. When your beliefs change, your thoughts change, and when your thoughts change, your parenting will change.

You are doing the work to become someone who would have cherished and protected you as a child. That's powerful and slow work. Be patient.

Reparent Your Inner Child

When my kids were little, I secretly dreaded going back East to visit my parents. I tended to find myself face-to-face with the familiar feeling of being left out . . . not seen. I would experience the sting of abandonment all over again. No matter how much work I thought I had done.

One time, I was supposed to go to Park City to vacation with my parents. Mr. Van Geffen was stuck at work, so it was going to be just me and my littles.

As the trip drew closer, I started getting headaches. An adult child of parents who enjoy using alcohol to excess daily, I was filled with foreboding. I dreaded that certain time of the evening when you might expect to gather and play games or watch a movie together, because my parents would disappear. They might still be sitting in the same room, but their essence was replaced with glassy-eyed strangers.

I mentioned to my therapist the impending doom I felt about this upcoming visit. She echoed that for everyone you are on a trip with to disappear without comment sounded like abandonment. She instructed me not to abandon my inner child as well.

What was that supposed to mean? She blew my mind by saying, "Your inner child is the part of you that's been present ever since you were floating contentedly in your mother's womb. She's witnessed all the shifts you have gone through, from baby, infant, toddler, young child to gangly preteen."

As you grow into a bigger body and more logical, conscious brain, your younger self doesn't just melt away. Your inner child remembers every beautiful memory as well as your childhood fears, traumas, neglect, and significant losses. She is a part of your subconscious that has been picking up messages since way before it had the luxury of adult words to make sense of it all. She "holds emotions, memories, and beliefs from the past as well as hopes and dreams for the future."[4] When you get triggered and can't understand why, it's likely a younger part of you is screaming for your attention.*

Inner-child work is connecting to that younger part of you that is still just as scared, lonely, or unseen as she was when you were little. Turns out, my inner child was constantly wondering, "Am I too much? Why doesn't anyone want to be with me?" Those moments of disconnection with my family activated and condemned that lonely younger part of me.

* Google "burning man inner child sculpture" to see an artist's haunting representation of your inner child in relationships.

The therapist gave me life-changing advice that I now share with you: When you feel your family sinking away, check in with your inner child. Assure her, "I will take care of you," while holding your hand to your heart. With great love, ask her what she would like to do together, with you.

That was such a foreign idea to me. How do I ask myself something? Yet I often asked myself each morning, "What do I want to wear?" But that voice was usually all business, cold and removed. This exercise would require a voice of self-tenderness.

When that inevitable moment came on vacation, and I walked back into an empty room after putting the kids down for the night, I slowly exhaled. Then I asked my inner child (who was starting to spiral into thoughts like "See! No one loves me. I'm hard to love!") a question: What would she like to do?

I imagined her squealing, "I wanna scrapbook. And watch a romantic comedy! And eat that ice cream in the freezer." It was the 2000s. So I took her upstairs, and we watched *When Harry Met Sally* and glued paper frames over photos together. It was the first time in my life that I didn't sink into victim-like sadness over my parents' behavior. I didn't feel abandoned, because I stayed with myself.

I didn't leave me too.

Part of parenting self-care is reparenting the little child within you. The child who wasn't treasured or seen. She is still stuck in your neural loops. Her deep unmet needs can sabotage your efforts to stay calm and not yell. She doesn't mean to sabotage. She's trying to be seen . . . by anyone, but especially by you.

Today is the day to start a daily practice of noticing the younger parts of you still worrying about being unworthy and unsafe. Notice her and give her the loving attention you wish your parents could have. This is a step toward healing. It helps to think about you at the same age as your Spicy One. Go find a childhood photo of you. I'll wait. Looking at this photo, notice what judgments you have about you at your child's age. How would you describe her? Was she too much? Too sensitive? Did she have to earn her keep? Did she need to keep her own spiciness under wraps to get positive attention? Was she a peacemaker or an angry girl? Either way, she's pretty cute.

Inner-child work is also about acknowledging that you have access to a warm inner parent within you who can be whatever you need.* Your inner mother may have a soft, feminine feel, bringing you nurturing you crave. Or your inner father may feel more commanding and masculine, offering a protective energy. Often this warm inner parent is what you didn't have in the adults around you, so you can now locate and strengthen that way of being within yourself. You get to choose.

Reparenting is the practice of directing a loving adult energy at the young parts of you. This is a critical skill in becoming the parent you want to be. To be tender with your child, you must first give tenderness to yourself.

What does reparenting literally look like? Try this: Put your hand on your heart and your belly and say, "I'll take care of you. You are safe and loved. You are doing a good job." Imagine your younger self and say gently to her in the mirror, "I know this is hard. I'm proud of you for not giving up. You are worth it." What sensations do you notice when you bring kind attention to the younger parts of you? Noticing and sitting with those messages is reparenting. It's you taking the reins and becoming the parent you always needed.

Now try the opposite self-talk, which many of us unconsciously practice. Ask yourself, "What's wrong with you? Get over it and get going!" Notice the shift of heaviness or tightness that enters your body. Yuck!

Participate in the Loving

Have you heard the saying "You are only as happy as your least happy child"? I say, you can only be as present for your child as you are for your inner child.

---

* Learn to develop that warm inner parent in chapter 15, "Unfriend Your Inner Mean Girl."

Practice holding an internal posture of affection toward yourself. Note the stark difference between mumbling to yourself, "Get your lazy butt upstairs to wash your face," and cooing, "Let's go wash your face, sweetie. You've had a long day." How you talk to yourself is how you will talk to your child under pressure.

REPARENTING WORDS TO SAY TO YOURSELF

I asked moms on Instagram what they wish their own mothers had said to them. Out tumbled healing words full of acceptance, affection, and contrition. May you try some of these words on yourself (and your Spicy One) today.

- "Your feelings don't scare me; let's talk about them."
- "I believe you."
- "Let's spend time together. You are more important than completing some task."
- "I respect your opinion."
- "You are enough just how you are right now."
- "I like you."
- "I'm proud of the mom you are, even though it looks different than I expected."
- "What do you think? I value your opinion even if it's different from mine."
- "You mean more to me than my friends."
- "I'll take care of myself so you don't have to."
- "I love that you are a lot and have never made your 'a-lot-ness' smaller."
- "You are doing a great job. Not just 'good for now' or 'good enough' but fantastic."
- "You are worth my attention."
- "You are not too dramatic."
- "I want to spend more time with you."

Your inner child already tends to feel at fault and abandoned when things don't go well. Speak kindly to her. Then see how your parenting instincts begin to bloom!

Mother yourself while—or even before—you mother your child. Self-mothering can look like slowing down your pace, feeding yourself breakfast, getting enough sleep, finding childcare to enable some solitude, or celebrating small wins. It means creating space for systematic self-care.

"Oh, great. Thanks, Mary, but I don't have time for bubble baths and face rollers." That's not what I'm talking about, lady! This kind of self-care is deeper (and less expensive) than a spa day or girls' weekend—this is a life-defining daily investment in your well-being and your motherhood. Systematic self-care means building a life that is fulfilling regardless of how your child behaves day-to-day. It means engaging in activities that bring you joy independently of the kind of adult your child will become.

The more love you lavish on yourself by living a fulfilling life outside of your child's performance, the more generous and forgiving you become as a parent.

Showing up for yourself tenderly and fiercely is an important way to show up for your child. Pursue pleasure—it is both your maternal responsibility and your human birthright.

Don't wait for others to read your mind and meet your unspoken needs. That is the mark of a martyr.

Martyrs make terrible mothers.

Embrace parenting as a healing art. Your love for your child gets woven into the relationship you are recovering with the child you used to be. They are not separate projects. When you hug your child, you are also hugging your inner child, and she loves it!

You nurture all day long. You know how to do it for others. Join in on that goodness. This can be concrete: If you make sandwiches for the kids when packing for an outing, make yourself one too. A mouthwatering turkey, Brie, and cranberry on ciabatta bread. None of this "I'll just eat whatever they don't." Participate in the loving.

Don't save the berries for the kids. Don't just watch the splashing swimmers; slip into the water during adult swim. Barge into the photograph. Seek out moments in life that bring you a little spark of joy. Take time away from the family to just be you.

I know it's scary. That sinking guilt that you shouldn't take time for yourself. The fear that your kids will be harmed by your absence. But your family is not a zero-sum game. Meaning, if you invest in nurturing alone time or invest in a couple's weekend, your child doesn't suffer proportionately to your gain. Your child needs you to prioritize your own fulfillment and needs.

Everybody wins if Mom is refreshed and revived. Like hydrangeas soaked in a cold sink of water, you can bloom for your family once you are cared for. Conversely, no one looks back on being raised by a depleted martyr as a healthy upbringing. It is a legacy of guilt and bitterness.

There is no white knight coming to whisk you away. It's not up to your husband or friends to intuit your needs. You must verbalize what you need. Ask out loud for the support. Move forward with getting the break EVEN IF your family is nervous to be on their own without you for a bit. This is your permission to spend the money on the babysitter. To book the Airbnb.

You are worth investing in. Let *your* fun and fulfillment matter too.

CH 6: Reflection Questions

1. Find a childhood photo of yourself from around the same age as your Spicy One. Use it as a bookmark for this journey or save it to your phone's home screen so it pops into view a couple times a day. When you see her, give her some love. What are ten positive words to describe this adorable girl? Refer to the "Love List for the Spicy One" in chapter 9 if you need ideas.

2. Describe your experience of being little. Imagine you are giving directions to a movie set director to re-create your childhood environment:
   - What was the atmosphere of your home like? What were the sights, sounds, textures, and smells that shaped you?
   - Who were the characters in your home? What motivated their actions?
   - What was it like to be little in that home or with those people?
   - What did you like to do for fun?
   - Where were your safe spaces and people?
3. What's a belief you picked up from childhood that might be making parenting harder than it needs to be?
4. Participate in the loving: Introduce something you loved as a kid back into your adult life. This can be as simple as coloring in one of your child's coloring books or skipping on the sidewalk. Play in the dirt. Sing a favorite song into a spoon microphone. Read in the grass. Join a sports team. Who says you can't go climb a tree? It gets to be something just for you, without your child present. Ask your inner child, "What do you want to try or explore today?" Keep asking, even when she doesn't know the answer. Experiment with play, then write a bit about your experience.

For a guided meditation to help you access and listen to your inner child, scan here:

PART II

EMBRACE A KIND PARENTING POSTURE

It's time to get into the meat of the parenting principles that work best with Spicy Ones. We will start with "kind postures"—ways of carrying yourself and adjusting your parenting presence to de-escalate, soothe, and equip. (These techniques assume you are the calmest person in the room. If that's not you yet, skip to Part III and come back after.)

In your physical body, good posture is important to your overall health and offers benefits like increased energy, greater confidence, and less muscle tension and fatigue. The same is true for the parenting postures I will teach you. They get more comfortable and easier to hold over an extended period of practice. We are going to improve your ability to sit in chaos while exuding inner wellness.

Each of the following chapters includes concrete techniques for holding postures that build influence with a kid so headstrong that it seems you must crush their spirit or destroy your relationship to get compliance.

Holding these thoughtful postures increases the chances that your Spicy One will feel cooperative and connected to you. Kindness is critical in building trust with your caliente pepper.

Spicy Ones don't listen to people they don't trust.

Depending on the combination of you and your child, there will be some helpful tools in these lists and some that won't suit your family dynamic. Don't get overwhelmed thinking you should take on all the postures. These lessons are designed to be an assortment of ideas. Take what is helpful for you and leave the rest. Refuse to succumb to an all-or-nothing mentality.

Choose one technique at a time to practice until it becomes your own. You can always come back to read these lessons whenever you need a fresh breath of inspiration.

7

Connect Rather Than Control

When my Spicy One niece was four, I babysat her at my house for a few days. On day two, I took her to a Bible study. Frankly, I hoped for a break from her there. I wanted her to go gently into the faraway land of church childcare so I could be refreshed with one hour of conversation with stable adults.

When we walked into the unfamiliar building filled with unfamiliar kids, she declared, "I will stay with you!" This was a crossroads moment. I had the choice between control and connection with my feisty niece. Because I wanted this little girl to want to come visit me again, I reminded myself that I am an aunt who chooses to connect, not control.

After laying my desires aside, I reluctantly said, "Sure, you can come in with me, but you need to draw quietly and let the adults talk to each other."

She did not draw quietly.

Once the worship music started, this little girl felt the Spirit and began to twirl and shimmy in the center of the room of women.

Again, I had to decide what I would choose in that moment. Would I prioritize control, so I didn't have to feel like other people were judging me, or would I choose to embrace her quirky expression of joy—especially when her audacity hurt no one?

I must have been well rested, because I chose to connect with her. I smiled at her and appreciated her full-body response to the music. The other ladies were frankly blessed by my whirling dervish, even if a few might have grumbled.

You may have grown up in a home where parental control over children was the default position. Every action of the child was placed in the category of either good behavior or bad behavior. You were expected to give first-time obedience no matter what adults asked of you. If you were deemed disrespectful or disobedient, you were punished, spanked, or yelled at. Adults rattled off sayings like "Children should be seen and not heard," "Do you want me to give you something to cry about?" and "Stop being so sensitive."

If this is your story, I am sorry.

I'm sorry if you had to hide a part of you to get your needs met. I'm sorry that adults couldn't tolerate your overwhelm and rejected you for it. I'm sorry if you still can't be your authentic self with your own mother. And I'm also sorry if the echoes of your parents' harsh messages make you now doubt the gentle, respectful approach you are attempting with your own child.

You are blazing a new path now. A path where control is no longer the end destination.

When you start exploring a new direction, it's normal to be concerned that you might have inadvertently traveled into the dangerous land of permissive parenting. A place that corrodes character and spits out entitled adults.

You might not have experienced connected authoritative parenting (which you are learning here). You may not have lived through an approach that doesn't rely on kids being afraid of their caretaker. Let me assure you of a universal fact—fear cripples, while love heals.

Research shows that children who are parented with a connected, positive approach excel academically and see improvements in mental health.[1]

The benefits of connecting over controlling include:

- ☐ Increased emotional IQ and awareness of others' state of mind
- ☐ Improved ability to label and communicate emotions
- ☐ Improved self-regulation and well-being
- ☐ Improved relationships and communication[2]

It's not a hippie-dippie song lyric. Fear *cripples*, while love *heals*.

Prioritizing Connection Is Not the Same as Permissive Parenting

While permissive parenting says, "Do whatever you want," connected parenting says, "I can assess the difference between non-negotiable limits that keep you and others safe and those unspoken social norms that don't work for you and aren't important enough to disturb everyone's peace to enforce."

Your kid wants to sit in the shopping cart seat with his feet facing the basket. He's coordinated enough to pull it off. It keeps his brain challenged while you read your shopping list. Others will find it odd. That can't be central to your mental calculation of whether to allow it. And when you do identify and hold to the important limits, give your child the freedom to grieve those limits.

Choosing connection means that much of the time, things won't go the way you hoped. While your child won't be calling the shots, you won't quite be either.

As you lean into this approach, you may need to tweak your expectations and intentionally mourn any lost identity you may have held for yourself (like being a type A mom who runs a tight ship). If you are human, you may want both a warm, lifelong connection *and* first-time compliance. With a Spicy One, you cannot have both. While it's completely understandable to want both, you as a parent must choose which is most important to you: connection or control.

Your ability to get compliance from your child is not a measure of your worth as a parent.

But let me let you in on a little secret—your Spicy One behaves better when compliance is *not* the goal!

Obedience cannot be what makes you feel successful as a parent. This kid ignores unjust rules! They have such strong inner boundary lines. Breaking the will of the Spicy One comes at the cost of the relationship with that child or the relationship they have with themself. If you make a habit of forcing them to cross the lines of their own convictions, you damage their trust in you.

Connection gives you a lifetime of influence and a front-row seat to your child's beautiful adventure of a life. It is through continued connection that you maintain the position they grant you to advise them on their course. Every mother will eventually learn she does not have control over the human she raised, but as a Mom of a Spicy One, you learn that lesson fifteen years earlier than most.

What does connection look like?

- ☐ Warm eye contact
- ☐ A slight smile, a nod, and soft eyes
- ☐ Tender, slow touch
- ☐ Giving your full attention for a few moments
- ☐ A friendly tone of voice*
- ☐ Free-spirited play and laughter**

If your Spicy One is a neurodivergent kid, you may not get all of the above signs, so focus on some synched quiet, slow breathing.

---

* Imagine how you might speak to a new friend. Not a curt newscaster voice or fake, high-pitched baby voice.

** "Barbie is helping with the bedtime routine tonight!" or "Help me take the baby doll to the doctor. She's scared."

The pausing. The "being with." Notice that talking is not on my list of signs of connection. If your kid tolerates touch, give lots of long hugs. Physical touch improves performance, attachment, and feel-good hormones.[3]

Connecting Through Play

Do you struggle with playfulness? You have permission to honor your way of playing. If you don't know what that is, ask yourself, "What did I like to do when I was little?" The Spicy One and your inner child will teach you how to add silly back into your life if you listen. When in doubt, Spicy Ones love *prey games*, like being chased (consensually), playing tag, or being thrown on a soft bed.

If connecting like this feels overwhelming, aim for micro-moments of presence. Like Mel's husband, who, once a day, puts his hands on each of her shoulders to make sustained eye contact with her for six seconds.[4] Bring your full self to the presence of the Spicy One for just a moment. You both benefit.

To maintain the stamina needed to choose connection when you desperately want control, declare out loud to yourself, "I am a mom who chooses connection over control" or "I cannot control this child, but I can choose to connect with them."

You Can Stay in Charge Without Insisting on Control

Connection means you *are* in charge but not in control. Hear the difference?

To be in charge is to have self-mastery and self-management. It is choosing to be calm, firm, and kind no matter what is happening around you that you cannot influence. Being *in charge* looks like:

- The determined pace of a mother leaving Target holding a screaming, red-faced toddler and leaving behind a cart of items she won't be able to buy today.

CONNECTION GAMES FOR THE WAITING TIMES

There's nothing more stressful than sitting outside the doctor's office, realizing your child's boredom is about to make it hard for everyone. Introduce some games you played with your childhood friends. We don't need a lot of stuff to be playful!

Clapping games: "Say, Say, Oh Playmate," "Miss Mary Mack," "Eenie Meenie Miney Moe," or "Engine, Engine Number 9"

Competitive hand games: "Thumb War," "Rock Paper Scissors," or "Slap Hands"

Training Games: "Simon Says" or "The Macarena"

Back writing: With your fingertips, write something secret on your child's back that they have to guess. Maybe your favorite color or food. Be sure and erase it afterwards.

Custom handshakes: Create your own greeting sequence like in the original *Top Gun* movie.

Name that tune: Using your lap as a bongo, tap out the beat of a song they have to guess. Can't place it? Now hum the notes as you play the beat.

- The brave but quivering mouth of a mother shakily exhaling and waving as she leaves her screaming child in the arms of the teacher, trusting them to settle down once she's gone.
- The intuitive decision to let that same child stay home from school on another day because this time their school refusal seems to indicate something is legitimately off and needs tending.
- The soothing voice of a mother who says, for the second time, "No, thank you. You may not hit me. It's time to put shoes on. Can you put them on now, or shall I bring them into the car?"

You can hold the leadership position with your child without dictating the end result of their choices. In tense moments, remember that you are the emotional thermostat setting the vibe of your relationship—not a passive thermometer responding to it. You, the mother, have the power to set the mood, regardless of the intensity or upset your child reacts with.

Women are amplifiers: Give us sperm, we can grow a baby. Give us a house, we will make a home.[5] Our emotions can ripple through a family, so take responsibility for your vibe!

Allow Your Child the Agency to Make Choices and Fail Safely

The path to a deep, lasting trust between you and your child is built upon you giving them more and more say over low-stakes choices as they age. This will require both of you to self-soothe when they inevitably make a mistake and become inconsolable about the natural consequences. Acknowledge to yourself how scary it is for you when your explosive kid gets upset. Tell yourself that you are okay and this upset is necessary for them to develop resilience and coping skills for the future. It's messy to let the Spicy One fail, but it's crucial to their education.

Watch them bloom when you let them choose their outfits, even if it means a Batman costume at church or atrociously clashing patterns for a birthday party. You are learning to prioritize things that matter over things that don't. Clothes really don't matter. You've got way bigger fish to fry! It takes a lot of energy to manage the negotiations coming your way from this child who powerfully manifests their own reality. Insist they bring the coat on that icy cold day, but don't waste your energy making them wear it.

Assign less-important decisions to the Spicy One with great fanfare. "Hayden, you are now officially the one who decides what clothes you will wear on Saturday mornings. I shall write this promise to you here in bloodred ink, along with my one exception coupon

I get a week when we have somewhere to go that requires certain apparel." See what I did there?

Release Control over Clothing

Catering to your sensitive child on issues like clothing is not coddling; it's kindness. You are *not* setting them up for failure, despite what the grandparents say. Sensory processing sensitivity (not disorder) means you take in nervous system information affecting your body more thoroughly than others. You recognize, feel, and then think about the heat of your jacket or the sharpness of the clothing tag or itchiness of the sock seam continuously . . . until . . . you . . . can . . . finally . . . rip it off.

There's nothing wrong with altering our environments to suit us. Highly sensitive people have a tiny little sensory cup. It fills up quickly from sounds, scents, others' emotions, and tactile objects touching the skin. As the parent in charge, work to find ways to empty your child's sensory cup.

Believe them when they say something (like jeans!) feels yucky. If you force them to wear the offensive item, they will spend most of their body's resources defending against it all day. That doesn't make for a very pleasant student at school.

Donate all the items they hate to wear to a well-dressed Mild Child. Your opinion matters too. If you hate something, get rid of it. No more wincing when they grab that ratty T-shirt. Use the yardstick of "Is it comfortable?" and "Is it appropriate for the occasion/setting?" over the dreaded, outdated question, "Is it flattering?"* Ask your child to pick their five favorite shirts, pants, socks, and so forth. Get rid of the rest. Buy duplicates. No more fighting over hard pants if they are gone.

---

* Self-worth is independent of how one dresses. It's much more wrapped up in one's confidence and ability to set boundaries. Don't get me started on helping your daughter find "flattering" clothing. That's a code word for "slimming." Don't do that. Don't be your child's first bully. When other people make judgments about her clothing or her body, teach her to firmly say, "I don't want you making comments about my body" or "Peer pressure doesn't work on me, so please stop."

Release Control over Food

Eating is another area of a child's life that can quickly become a daily power struggle. Spicy Ones, with their selective taste buds, either ferociously crave exotic foods or refuse to thrive by insisting on only white food. Let me make it easier for you: The adult decides *what* the food is going to be, *when* mealtimes are, and *where* you eat as a family. Your child determines *whether* and *how much* they will eat.

Consider Ellyn Satter's beautiful precepts for staying free of power struggles when it comes to feeding. Allow your child to decide whether or not they will eat and how much at regular feeding times (you set).[6] This will be liberating for both of you. It provides your child with a sense of agency—a trust of their own body's signals. It also means a warm, welcoming mother comes to the table rather than an anxious warden counting bites. If this is all new, start with providing three meals and two snacks at regular, dependable times. That allows your child to know when sustenance is coming next so they can make better decisions.

Letting go of these power struggles is *hard* but so, so worth it. I know from experience that only when you let go of the rope of compliance do you get to embrace your magnificent child's true brilliance.

TO DECREASE POWER STRUGGLES, LET THE SPICY ONE CONTROL:

- *How much* they eat or *whether* they eat.
- Whether or not they eliminate (but you can choose toilet times to try).
- Whether or not they fall asleep (you choose bedtime).
- Attitude, bad moods, eye rolls, and their tone of voice.

How to Prioritize Connection over Control

Connection over control is the heartbeat of Spicy One parenting. Here are five techniques to get you firmly in the land of connection.

1. Harness a Past Golden Moment to Create New Ones

Bring to mind a time you successfully chose connection over control with your child. A moment where you were proud of your parenting and the relationship you are nurturing. A time you wished somebody would have grabbed a camera because the situation needed to be memorialized on social media as proof that you can be a good mom.

For me, it's an afternoon dog walk that I invited my fourteen-year-old son to accompany me on. He insisted on grabbing his scooter first from the garage, which meant I would be in danger the whole time of him rolling over my feet. But rather than try to control how he walked with me, I grounded myself in what mattered most: He had said yes to the walk! I was walking in the fresh autumn air next to my beloved scooter boy! Then he sped up, and the dog strained against the leash to match his pace. I had to jog to keep up. But I laughed instead of lectured. Now that boy is all grown up and far away, and I'd do anything to have him next to me casually sharing his thoughts on superheroes and Pokémon cards.

Remember your moment of past connection and jot down a few key words to give it some texture. Observe the sensations in your body when you hold this specific golden moment in your mind. Likely, it's a softer, meltier sensation. This relaxed posture makes you more creative and cooperative. This is the version of you to bring to the roughest of parenting altercations. Hold on to that vibe in your body as we talk about the opposite scenario—when we awaken the dreaded *counterwill*. [*cue ominous horror music*]

2. Beware the Counterwill

Part of what drives your child's defiant "hell no" energy is a natural phenomenon called the counterwill. It's the protective natural aversion to letting a stranger dictate your actions.* Humans are wired to take instructions only from those we have an established relationship with. That instinct keeps us safe.

The counterwill explains the Spicy One's rebellion against influence from anyone they don't feel connected to. You can almost see the bolt of energy zigzag through their denial system when asked to do something when they don't yet feel comfortable and connected.

Avoid arousing the Spicy One's counterwill. Your Spicy One's aversion to being controlled by anyone they don't feel connected to can destroy their receptivity to your guidance. The progression of compliance begins with feeling connected to *you.*[7] It is crucial that you build a strong daily bond if you want cooperation. This is a repeated effort with your child that starts over every morning. Each day is a new opportunity to build warmth and attachment.

Love doesn't keep score.

Think of it this way: I am on the constant prowl for 100 grams of protein a day to help me build strength as I age. And since protein isn't stored in the body the way carbs are, each day I must begin the hunt for eggs anew. My constant search for protein is similar to your child's daily need for a felt sense of connection. A child's attachment is fragile and thin and needs to be reestablished after every separation. Separation is a day at school, an hour in childcare, or a night of sleep in the same bed with their foot in your face.

Whether it's a phone call you took behind a closed door or a transatlantic flight you took to come home, every separation brings the potential for tension and conflict.

---

* The term *counterwill* dates back to the early 1900s and was coined by Austrian psychoanalyst Otto Rank but has gained modern popularity with Canadian psychologist Gordon Neufeld.

Your Spicy One has an overactive counterwill. To get around it, you must prioritize connection. Remember that golden moment above? Likely, that is what connection looks like in your family. To enhance compliance and avoid unnecessary tantrums, give no commands until you first build some of that warmth.

3. Connect Before You Direct

Maybe your kid is playing LEGOs, but you know everybody needs to leave for school. Come close, pause, check your breathing, and say, "Ooh, blue on red with wheels." He looks up at you. He sees that you see his creation. You are in his world for a moment. You stay there for a few beats. Now you've got his eye contact. Then you say slowly, "It's time for us to leave. Do you want to bring this with us in the car or leave it here safely?"

NOTE: Only give choices that are agreeable to you so there is no wrong answer.

Ponder the hyper-focus of childhood. It is a time of being incredibly present to whatever you're doing. They are under a spell of the world's beauty. Incapacitated by the wonder of the present moment. Deep in their own world of imagination, they cannot hear you. You need to intentionally get into their world, gather their gaze, and let them feel the warmth of you, *then* give instruction.

Connection requires your full presence, your unconditional, positive regard, and your curious attention. Your phone is put away. If you have a negative reaction to the idea of "connect before you direct" or feel like "I don't have time for that," *you need to make time for that*. You need to rearrange your life and wrestle your priorities to the ground because your unhurried presence is the marrow of conscious parenting. The lifeblood.

If your body revolts from slowing things down (hi, ADHD girls!), one way to make connecting more palatable is to treat being with your child like a meditation. A meditation that your relationship and your body desperately need. Assign your brain the job of noticing the curve of their nose and the exact hue of their eye color. Give

YOUR CHILD CANNOT HEAR YOU WHEN THEY ARE VERY UPSET

Your melting-down child is emotionally flooded; they can no longer take in the information or synthesize what you're saying. You can generally tell because their eyes are moving all around.

If that's happening, they can't hear you. Zip it. No need to hurl words at a storm. Take time to calm yourself down as a living blueprint for your child (see chapter 13 for *how* to do this). In a situation where your child has lost their ever-lovin' mind, you are no longer in discipline territory. There is nothing to teach here.

The fewer words the better. We wait now. You won't need the perfect words in this situation; you just need to calm your own body down.

your face the job of softening your eyes and arranging your mouth in a slight smile.*

Your goal is to be mindfully present with your child. Guess what this might look like to your child? PLAY! Your kid is going to interpret your full attention and positive regard as an invitation to play. After all, play is a child's language of connection. Once you have entered into a playful pattern of interaction, you will find your attempts to direct them get easier.

4. Plan for Special Time

This is not new advice. You must invest in routine one-on-one dates to build sustained connection.[8] Nothing fancy. Just them knowing ahead of time and without a doubt that they will have set aside nonnegotiable time with you regularly so that any unconscious

* Before entering the corporate world, I read a book that advised if you don't know how to arrange your face into a pleasing way for a hard conversation, go with the mouth shape that happens when you start the word *sex*. Notice the neutral face you can't help but make at the beginning of "seeeex." Maybe that's why I never got promoted past assistant marketing manager.

anxiety around your attachment and availability is soothed. This sounds like you saying, "You and I are going to start taking a walk together on Mondays. Should we plan to look for nature stuff to make a leaf rainbow, or would you prefer I hold your hand and you

SPECIAL TIME: NAME IT AND CLAIM IT

Your investment in special time will pay out even more if you brand it beforehand and afterwards. Set it apart from normal time by giving it a catchy title like "Mommy and Me Date" or "Truck Time" or "Girls Gone Wild Wednesday." Then gush about it like a fangirl, showing how much it matters to you. One mother-child duo explored ASMR (autonomous sensory meridian response) together looking for which sounds sent good shivers up their spines and which ones made them want to bite someone. Play often looks just like sensory-seeking activities.

Many Spicy Ones find anticipation incredibly pleasurable. Others may need practice waiting patiently for something and ramp up their whining during the waiting. You can endure this with a breezy attitude. Write the upcoming date visibly on your giant kitchen calendar and circle the date with a heart.* Got more than one kiddo? Use a different color for each. The kids who have to wait their turn will eventually be supportive when they realize their time is coming. "Anticipation is identity building."[9] Let your child dream into the idea of being chosen and special by you. Then talk about it later, saying, "Remember when we had a picnic by the back gate—just you and me? I like being with you."

Share golden memories of your dates. Describing positive family moments out loud can break the stalemate between you as it conjures up the feelings embedded in the memory.

---

* If you don't have a paper calendar in your kitchen, run—do not walk—to buy a desk calendar-sized version so you can make your schedule more visible and help your Spicy One feel less surprised about what's next.

try your roller skates?" or "I want you to stay up thirty minutes later on Tuesdays because I need some special time with you. Should we color in my adult coloring books or put a puzzle together?"

You have to invest in the relationship in order to get cooperation out of it.

Don't expect overt gratitude. When Mr. Van Geffen asked Gigi to go on their first daddy/daughter date, she answered, "That sounds good. But can Mommy come and you stay home?"

During special time, give no direction or correction. Let them pick how they want to spend time with you, be it geocaching or watching pups at a dog park. Ten minutes of play each day is life-changing. Explore a special interest that you can offer, like collaging, hiking, or cooking. The goal is shared laughter, touch, and warmth. But sometimes the Spicy One will use their entire time with you to complain. Be a duck impervious to water dripping off your back. Because of this time, later, when you are giving direction, it won't feel so hostile and unearned to your Spicy One.

5. Practice Big, Warm Greetings

I grew up watching *Cheers*, the TV show about a bar "where everybody knows your name, and they're always glad you came." It represented an idealized idea of home for me. The entire bar shouted "Norm!" when one regular entered. Now my family all stands up and whoops and hollers when someone comes home. We are convinced there is nothing as connecting as walking into a home that celebrates your entrance.

An important component of creating connection is the generous gift of expressive greetings. Your intentional greeting rituals pave the way for the right to direct later. Too often, we show up to pick our child up from school or a playdate with our mind still on work or, worse, actively finishing up a phone call. Still on the phone, we gesture wildly to our child with hand signals indicating "Come on, let's go." The Spicy One reads this as "You don't matter enough for me to take the time to connect with you. You will need to escalate your upset for me to notice." Or we prioritize connection with adults, speaking high above our reuniting kid's head. A lot of us are curt at reunion moments because of the stimulus of crowds and the big expectations of reconnection. So we hurl out directives—"Don't forget your art!"—and try to exit the situation quickly.

That is an abomination of a greeting.

Your sidekick has not seen you for a bit. Your prior connection has washed away. Like a boat on choppy open water, they need you to dock alongside them and throw ropes of connection aboard in the form of full-bodied, mindful togetherness.

Bring your full self to the first 180 seconds of any greeting. A warm greeting looks like full eye contact, a smile, and planted feet. The first time you see your people after a break, generate the excitement that dogs do. Wag your tail, you glorious golden retriever! Be singularly focused on your child for three minutes to set yourself up for an entire afternoon. Make hugging a natural part of your ritual. Dare each other to be the last to let go.

Sometimes establishing a connection may take a frustrating extra three minutes of hearing all your child's complaints as they unravel from a stressful day and take off the metaphorical mask they wear in public. Be sturdy enough to listen without being pulled into the negativity.

CHILD-LED PLAY

Play with your child for ten minutes in a manner where they determine all the rules and instructions. They decide and they lead. If they become critical of your playing, act as if they are a genius director and you are a simpleton learning the secrets of great imaginative play. Keep adjusting your approach to please them, like an inept underling. Fall down or make a comically helpless face so they can laugh at how clueless you are. Watch them enjoy being in the driver's seat!

COZY CARPOOL

When your tired kid climbs into the car, a warm greeting does not mean asking, "How was your day? Can you tell me about it?" That's not connecting. That's an interrogation to some kids. They don't need to perform for you to connect with them. They do need to feel like "This person likes me. I matter enough that my mother will handle her own separation anxiety to give me space to decompress." Turn on some classical music, bring iced tea and a snack for sweaty kids, and say, "I missed you. Welcome home!"

Get in the habit of collecting your child into your shared atmosphere of love before you require compliance. When the bus drops your child home, don't absentmindedly skip the "glad you are home" moment to bark a command to put their backpack in their room. That's the opposite of connection. Do not summon the counterwill by skipping this step.

Warm greetings are also necessary when a child is first waking up. Alas, yesterday's connection has already washed away. If your mornings are hectic and filled with time-starved yelling, it's time to wake up earlier and get yourself ready before you tend to anyone else. Get ready for the day so your inner martyr isn't the one who meets the family, silently complaining to herself, "I haven't even brushed my teeth and now I have to make breakfast!" Making folks wait ten minutes while you dress and care for yourself will switch the morning from a tense thriller to a rosy rom-com. Lace up your shoes before you leave the bedroom. Caveat: This advice applies only to parents who have arrived at the stage where kids are sleeping through the night. Your sleep is more important than being organized.

If you are lucky enough to have to wake up your children, make that a culture-setting event—gentle and warm. One mom brings the dog into the room and up onto the bed as she opens the blackout shades. Another sings a wake-up song while massaging her kid's twitching foot. Say a cheery "good morning," but don't initiate conversation until they come back to life.

You are a parent who is in charge. You are a parent who connects. You are a parent who practices warm greetings. You've got this.

CH 7: Reflection Questions

1. What's a golden moment of parenting for you? Describe it in colorful detail and notice the impact of remembering it on your internal weather.
2. In what parenting scenarios are you most likely to get caught up in wanting control rather than connection? How do you want to show up instead?
3. Who greets you in a way that feels good? What is it about their style that you appreciate? How can you borrow some of their approach for reconnecting with your child after you've been apart?
4. What's it like for you to let your child direct play without your leadership? How does it feel to participate without leading?

8

Find Your Inner Royalty

Have you ever witnessed the pied piper skills of a gifted early education teacher? My Spicy One's first teacher possessed ethereal grace and Mother Teresa levels of patience in the midst of absolute classroom melee.

My daughter attended a parent-participation preschool. Each morning several of us anxious adults would show up for our shift, nervous to witness our children in their natural habitat. We tried to look helpful but were essentially lookie-loos watching multiple car accidents.

One day, my child ran to the imagination corner and began spewing insults at children who also wanted to play in the dress-up chest. "I don't like the smell of your breath," she announced toward a Mild Child trying to pull a feather boa out of the play kitchen's oven. The interchange froze me. I moved toward her, ready to shriek, "That is *not* how we talk to friends!" but the teacher stepped between us and shifted the entire scene. She knelt down a few inches from my oblivious child and put a hand on both the shell-shocked Mild Child and my brazen offspring.

"I wonder what's happening over here," she said in a dreamy voice that made me curious too. "Gigi, do you see your friend's face? She's looking sad."

"Please don't say, 'That's not my friend,'" I silently pleaded.

"I just don't want her to play near me right now," my little tyrant said, shoving her pudgy arms through a ballerina dress. The teacher gently pulled Gigi closer and translated her harsh words. "It seems like you don't want to share the kitchen area with Olivia right now."

"Right! I want her to play somewhere else."

The teacher nodded, unfazed by this antisocial behavior that made me blush. "And what are you wanting, Olivia?" she asked the gentle child now crying from the tension.

"I want to play in the kitchen too." With this answer, the teacher turned to my kid and repeated the message. "Olivia wants to play here too. What should we do?" If you couldn't hear the content of the words, the whole interchange looked like a fairy godmother casting a spell on grateful children. The mood was light and instructive. Meanwhile, my inner monster seethed. My child was embarrassing me again.

Find Your Inner Royalty

This is your invitation to find a mythical royal character who resonates with you. Someone whose unshakable grace you can borrow, like the preschool teachers who inspired me long ago.* For some of us it's a stylish and demure Princess Diana. For others, it's the Mother of Dragons from *Game of Thrones*. Accessing your inner royalty is helpful in keeping your other, shall we say, less dignified inner personalities from taking over.

Some moms choose Mary Poppins, Clair Huxtable, or Mother Nature. I used to mimic Glinda the Good Witch from *The Wizard of Oz* because I needed that level of saccharine to persuade me to be kinder. Imagine me in pink and sparkles, saying, "Oh, my dear children, I'm sorry to inform you that the kitchen is closed, but we shall indeed eat again at noon."

* I'm talking about you, Miss Bailey and Miss Sandy of the now-closed Children's Garden.

Maybe you need the quiet regalness of the Downton Abbey matriarch or a joyful online queen like Tabitha Brown.

Your challenge is to find an image of a royal from history, film, or literature that will inspire you, and display her in your home. Extra credit if you post it on Instagram and tag me so I can reshare your inspiration.

Your child needs you to step into your monarchy to show them how to use their power for good.

It's a wild job you have. You are leading a leader who doesn't yet know how to lead.

May you be the seasoned queen helping your apprentice learn the essential life skills while you practice them yourself, like:

- ☐ How to soothe and calm themself
- ☐ How to connect their feelings to their needs
- ☐ How to reach out for support from their community

A good and noble queen is serene and settled in her body. She trusts herself and believes that *what she says is going to happen is indeed what will happen*. When she shows up, she makes things better. She brings neither frenetic nor loud, angry energy. She does not make the scenario worse. Imagining yourself as a queen is a great way to embody calmness, kindness, or firmness. Unfortunately, many of us show up under pressure with a vastly different character leading the charge.

What a Queen Is Not

A queen is not a beggar who feels taken advantage of or disrespected. Nor is she a teenager or a monster. Let me explain.

The Beggar

Some of us show up as the beggar in our parenting. The beggar laments rather than instructs by saying things like "Oh, please don't tell me you spilled milk on my special rug. But I asked you to wait for me to pour it!" Notice the way she whines helplessly and wrings her hands. She is permissive.

"Oh, why me?! Please just give me a moment of quiet." A beggar's posture and tone of voice are synonymous with a victim. "No one ever listens to me!" What stinks is that it's a self-fulfilling prophecy. No one does listen to a beggar.

The Teenager

Others act like surly adolescents when parenting. Imagine me, aggressive and petulant, rolling my eyes and heaving a big sigh: "Of *course* you spilled the milk yet again." Hands aggressively perched on her hips, the teenager uses eye-rolling, superiority, contempt, and lots of irritated groaning.

A teenager is not the leader anyone deserves. She sarcastically harangues her child. "Of course! Of course you are interrupting me now that I'm finally having a moment on the phone with my sister. Where were you when I asked you to come clean up your toys? I'm so over this."

Your inner teenager evokes shame and humiliation in others. We've all been "the teenager." She is not an effective leader.

The Monster

I morphed into a monster in my toughest parenting moments. Imagine me with gritted teeth: "That's it! I'm sick of you spilling milk. You are such a pain in my butt."

The authoritarian character I most embodied in my early parenting was like Gollum from *The Lord of the Rings* ("my precious") or the Demogorgon in heat from *Stranger Things*. My approach was menacing. An emotional stiffening. The opposite of soft. "Now you are going to get it. Now you deserve everything I will do to you. I won't stand for this!" The monster made hitting and slapping and yelling seem unavoidable and deserved.

I'd grit my teeth, clench my hands, and gutturally scream. My monster created fear in my child. And fear works . . . for a few years.

But scaring kids degrades long-term trust and connection. Don't sacrifice the chance of a long-term intimate relationship for terrified obedience in the short term.

Just so we are clear, that monster still lives in me. But I've learned how to notice when she's trying to run the show so I can soothe her with my inner royalty.

What about you? Who do you become when you are triggered by disrespect and noncompliance?

Is it the beggar? "Oh, I must be a terrible mom because you just won't listen!"

The teenager? "I'm so done. This meltdown is stupid."

Or do you become the monster who moves swiftly and angrily toward them, intent on stunning them into obedience?

Each time I teach Moms of Spicy Ones, women share creative descriptions of unhelpful archetypes they notice within themselves. They freeze and panic like a cold robot. They turn into a "Mama Werewolf."* It's normal to have a shadow side that comes out under stress. Whatever you call it, this character works against you because she evokes shutdown and defiance in the Spicy One. They end up acting out in compulsive and illogical ways to get out from under the shame that's coating the room like a smog cloud.

The Demeanor of a Good Queen

Let us conjure up a royal leader with the best interest of her kingdom in mind. Kim John Payne calls it your inner "benevolent governor."[1] Decide *who* you want to be when setting limits.

Good royals do not deign to follow the edicts of tantruming princes and inexperienced princesses. Royals are wise. Unflappable. Steady. This is how you will hold yourself.

Go ahead and stand up. Take this sacred moment you have set aside to improve your parenting to find your unique inner queen. Go ahead. No one is watching. Embody your most royal stance. You

* A song by Brandi Carlile.

may notice that it feels good to have your feet hip-width apart rather than close together. We don't want a teetering queen. Find your most confident and solid standing posture. Notice that you can afford to soften your belly because everybody in the royal court believes in your sovereignty. No one wants to overthrow you here. Choose a strong back and a soft belly.

Maybe your nose is regally lifted. Look out over an imaginary cliff and survey your kingdom, swaying your arms out on either side of your body. What do you notice about this regal posture? How are your shoulders? What about your jaw? Hands open or closed?

While you hold this stance, know that there are *more* packets of information traveling up the vagus nerve *to* your brain right now than heading in the other direction—*from* the brain into your body. Your body tells your brain what to do as often as, if not more than, your brain calls the shots. That's where the idea of power poses comes from. Stepping into the body position of royalty tells your brain, "I believe in my authority to lead this countercultural kid."

Conversely, what might the body be telling the brain when you are inhabiting one of your shadow characters? Yikes! Not good.

Remember this royal body posture so you can find it again when it's time to discipline.

Well done. You may sit down. Thank you for being brave and giving your body the chance to get involved in your parenting. By the way, notice that I said, "You may sit down." Did that feel rude or harsh? Nope. Just leaderly. It's okay to use directive commands. "You may clean up your Magna-Tiles now so that we can leave for school." Or "In this family, we are allowed to make mistakes, and we join in to make things better. Go get the paper towels and let's clean up this milk together."

(And then button up those luscious lips. You don't need as many words as you think you do.)

How Do Royals MOVE?

Slowly. Queens don't run around, shouting, "We've got to go!" unless they're about to be overthrown. Royals slow down and will not be rushed. They move purposefully. Queens glide with a soft but strong core, their shoulders relaxed, their jaw soft.

Some royals have their arms high, like a modern dancer. Others have palms open and facing up. Your body is unique to you. What will signal "I can be calm, kind, and firm" is different for each of us.

What Do Royals THINK?

Since they are not heading up a democracy, they think, "I am in charge for a reason." This approach makes the most sense with Spicy Ones eight years old and under. But many an intense and persistent older kid has appreciated a strong-backboned leader. Royals think thoughts like "There is no emergency. I have all the time I need." To think like a queen is to be self-assured that you were hand-selected by God for this kingdom. It means believing you were awarded this challenging child for a purpose. That you have what it takes (or are developing what it takes) to show this tiny despot what it's like to stay calm, firm, and kind.

Royals also think, "I am enough. I was made for such a time as this."

Or "I was created to be this child's parent." You are the leader. You are the one you've been waiting for.

What Do Royals SAY?

There are three phrases that help a lot in the elementary school years. During this season, use phrases like *you may* and *in our family, we*, and when faced with unacceptable behavior, *no, thank you*. Royals say, "You may clear your plate" and "In this house, we touch the kitten with two fingers."

Let's look at some examples.

Royals *don't* ask, "What do you want for breakfast?" That has a shadow of the beggar. The part of you that wants to please and placate. The freezer and the fawner.

Instead, your inner queen states with assurance, "We have oatmeal on Mondays. I know you love Tuesdays when we have egg burritos."

You are not a beggar, so you don't whine, "Why can't I have a cup of coffee and journal in the morning before you ask me for something?!"

Instead, you make proclamations: "I start my day with writing in my journal and taking some quiet time. I know that might make you sad. You are always welcome to sit quietly next to me and color."

You are not a teenager, so you don't criticize: "I'm not dealing with your drama today." A royal says firmly, "It is okay to have big feelings, but you may not hit me."

You no longer give in to your inner monster (who seems to be most potent at bedtime) by growling, "Everybody shut up! I can't stand it anymore. I am done!"

As a royal, you say, "In this family, we turn lights off at eight p.m. You have ten minutes left before we head to your room. Anything you need to finish up first?"

Practice saying these next phrases out loud. Listen to the tone of your voice articulating each of these convictions (now, while alone) so it's easier later, in the presence of your fire-breathing Spicy One.

"You may go wash your hands."

"In this family, we ask for help with a kind voice."

"Oh, no, thank you. You may touch the baby gently."

Can you imagine growing up in a home where the adults stay calm, kind, and firm rather than shouting, "Not you harassing the baby again. Cut it out!" Which home would you rather live in?

Here you are becoming more aware of how you show up even in the toughest moments! It's healing to notice the posture you have been resorting to versus the message you want sent to your child and yourself. Only then can you make an informed choice of who you will be.

CH 8: Reflection Questions

1. When you think about the unconscious character you embody when you are stressed or pressed, who does she remind you of? What do you notice about the physical posture she

causes you to take on? How does your body move? What happens inside your body? Be brave and imagine it now.

2. Whose big queen energy will you borrow from? Choose the vibe of Michelle Obama, Maria from *The Sound of Music*, Marmee from *Little Women*, or someone else who uniquely speaks to you. Peruse pictures of some of my favorite queens at maryvangeffen.com/bookresources.
3. Where specifically do you need to bring more benevolent queen presence to parenting?
4. How can you find the royalty in your body and claim it and practice it? What would that look like? How would you move and think, and what would you say? Fill this out to help you:

9

Aim for Curiosity and Delight

May I confide in you about my marriage?

A few years ago, I realized my attitude toward my husband needed a tune-up.

Crumbs on the kitchen counter meant he didn't consider me. Never mind that they came from the BLT he'd made me. Anytime he forgot something I had told him—like who I was meeting for lunch—I saw it as an intentional rejection of what mattered to me.

After a lonely winter of becoming exasperated by the man I chose to marry, I decided to stop repeating the same behavior while expecting different results. I made my mind up to do something about my spirit of discontent.

For my New Year's resolution, I chose to actively nurture the belief that my husband is *always working for my good*. Regardless of whether I could see evidence to support it. I resolved to perceive every choice he made and word he said as an act of wholehearted love. Proof that he is committed to securing the best life possible for me.

- If he chooses In-N-Out burgers for dinner, even though I don't care for them, he must want me to have more iron to keep me strong.
- If he's interrupting my reading to show me a YouTube clip of dogs befriending goats, it's because he wants to make me laugh.

I chose to believe that his soul desired goodness for me even when his flesh might not.

When I made this mind-flip and began to *assume positive intent*, the unspoken current between us shifted dramatically. I became more tolerant and able to stay curious rather than jumping to irritation. This helped me take a conscious pause in scenarios where I used to react with swift defensiveness (see chapter 13 for more on this).

Since then, each year has been the best year of our marriage to date! I am inviting you to make a similar perspective shift with your child.

Choose Curiosity over Judgment

Parenting with judgment is dangerous territory with a Spicy One. When you are looking with hard eyes at your child, thinking, "Why can't they let me be the boss for once?" they feel that energy. Their subconscious steps in to defend them, asking, "Why can't Mommy let me be the boss of myself?" or "What does she know about me that's bad?"

I remember my five-year-old planning her birthday party. So much imagination and savoring of her fantasy for the future! The only problem was she didn't want to invite her good friend who was also our neighbor. My first instinct was to squint my eyes and say, "That's ridiculous. That's being a bad friend." Judgment. Instead, I paused, softened my eyes, and got curious. "Tell me more about that." Her answer was illuminating.

"I don't want her to meet my school friends," she admitted. I glimpsed her insecure heart and desire to be loved. I wondered aloud, "Sounds like you are worried they might ignore you to hang out with her because she is so fun. That makes sense. What do you think it will feel like for her to look out her window and see you playing birthday games with your other friends?"

Staying in curiosity rather than judgment is a game changer. It softens us and our children. Curiosity keeps communication lines open. True hospitality is welcoming the parts of your child you can't understand—the parts that seem foreign.

How can you stay curious?

Assume Positive Intent

Choose to believe that your child is *not* being difficult on purpose or to get attention. Believe that they are wired to be part of the team and want to please you but don't always have the mental capacity to know how yet. Their anxiety, hopelessness, and aggression are not personal.*

Look at Behavior as a Form of Communication

Your child is not randomly losing it. There is always a catalyst for big feelings. I don't believe in "they melted down for no reason." If you react to their poor behavior, you miss the deeper problem they need help solving. Focusing on behavior alone is like medicating the symptoms of sickness while letting the disease continue to ravage the body. Same with emotions. Anger is a signal—information you need to understand your child's experience.

The Spicy One's "non-compliance is [often] self advocacy."[1]

Ask yourself what the human *need* is behind this wildly inappropriate behavior.

* When their obstinance is most intractable, ask them if you can interview them. Write out their point of view like you're a journalist talking with the smartest person on the planet. See how they respond to your intense focus on their point of view.

In the case of my daughter's birthday planning, her need was to feel secure in her friendships and able to predict and prepare for the social stress of being the hostess. With curiosity, I could embrace her needs as neutral and understandable; I could be on her team to solve the problem rather than treating her behavior *as* the problem. (We invited the friend and scheduled party games that gave structure to the event.)

Common reasons for misbehavior:

- ☐ Lack of skill needed to handle a situation*
- ☐ Desire for power, influence, and belonging
- ☐ A basic unmet need (i.e., HALT: Is your child Hungry, Angry, Lonely, or Tired?)
- ☐ Their body budget** is approaching empty

Practice Being a Delighted Anthropologist[2]

Imagine an anthropologist with her canvas vest, her pockets filled with treasures, as she has the honor of witnessing an Indigenous group's rites of passage. She listens, learns, studies, and recognizes she does not fully grasp the what, why, and how. She does not have all the answers. In the midst of conflict, a delighted anthropologist keeps a neutral tone. She draws close and asks questions that respect the sovereignty of all involved.

This technique is helpful when you don't actually feel that curious. When you think of a delighted anthropologist, it gives you a way to *pretend* to be curious. To act as if you are until curiosity can grow within you and become real for you. This is your permission slip to fake it until you make it.

As you think about how to choose curiosity with your child, notice where it's easy for you to stay open and nonjudgmental and

---

* For example, a child dragging another child across the schoolyard because he doesn't yet know how to ask someone to play with him.

** This helpful concept is from the book *Brain-Body Parenting* by Mona Delahooke. See explanation in chapter 16.

where it takes all you've got not to find fault. Practice taking your child's perspective. When they say something explosive like "I hate my sister," it's not helpful to try to persuade them otherwise with "That's not true; you love your sister." Inquire about what's underneath the big feelings. "Something must have happened today that didn't feel good. Would you like to talk about it?" Be a delighted anthropologist who doesn't take their subject's culture personally.

Delight over Duty

Writer Toni Morrison once described how, when her children entered the room, she would show them care by fussing over their appearance. She wanted to "see if they had buckled their trousers or if their hair was combed or if their socks were up." But later in life, she realized that was not what they had needed. "You think your affection and your deep love is on display. Because you are caring for them. It's not. When they see you [anxious about their behavior], they see the critical face. What's wrong now?" Toni offered a different way to think about mothering. "When a kid walks in a room—your child or anybody else's child—does your face light up? . . . Let your face speak what's in your heart."[3]

PRACTICE BEING CURIOUS

Try being a delighted anthropologist with your child. Spend a few minutes observing how they approach a task or moment of their day. Do not interrupt or even try to join in. Do not correct or direct them. Notice what matters to your child. Take in everything about their facial features and gestures and the way their body moves with an appreciative mindset. Let there be no need for them to act a certain way because every choice they make is a discovery to you.

The Spicy One is looking to see if they brighten your spirit or depress you by being themself near you. They desperately want to delight you. You want that too.

Who else is going to delight in your child? You, your co-parent, and perhaps their grandparents are the only people in the world assigned to delight in this child.

Cultivating unconditional high positive regard for your kid is your sacred duty. No one has the positional power in your child's life to impact their sense of identity like you do. No one else can make them feel as significant at this tender age of self-becoming. You are the only one in their life tasked with truly, deeply delighting in them. You have the influence to offset the onslaught of negative reinforcement they will receive in this life. Show your Spicy One just how amazing they are and how much you love to be with them, beyond the fact that you "have to" take care of them.

I am saying your primary responsibility is *not* the duty of skill-building. Skills are nice, but your Spicy One can learn those elsewhere. YouTube University will teach them how to clean a toilet or the basics of algebra. The hardest, most soul-shaping work of parenting is learning to love and be loved unconditionally so eventually you can teach it.* The most delicious kind of love is laced with delight.

Growing up savored by an adult who actively likes you is heaven.

Meanwhile, a mom who can't see the goodness of her child is living in a kind of hell. A hell that gets worse the closer your child comes to leaving. So much time was wasted being oblivious to the miracle of their brief existence in your home. Time does eventually run out. I'm imploring you to delete their past infractions and start over today noticing the dazzling virtue of your chaotic child. Love them as-is, even as you long for them to be an improved version of themself.

A client struggling with her strong-willed ten-year-old daughter once asked me, "What am I supposed to do to connect with this kid?

* Did I just quote *Moulin Rouge*?

I hate drawing, and she corrects everything I do if I try to play with her. I don't know what it looks like to delight in her."

I gave her the assignment to enter her daughter's room and lie down on the floor. No phone and certainly no agenda. Her only purpose: Find something positive to meditate on about whatever her tween was up to. No deep talk needed. She bravely gave it a try. At first there was resistance. "What are you doing in here?" her daughter demanded. This question was understandable, given the tension in their relationship. Usually her mother would come in hot, angry about the state of her room or another poor grade.

"I just like being with you," her mother said. Mom took a gamble and said what she *wanted* to be true because, frankly, it wasn't much fun to be with her daughter. Like a dried sponge under tap water, her child began to swell from the attention. Her posture softened, and she began to chatter about the doodles she was making at her desk. "That looks fun," Mom observed. Eventually there was laughter. A golden moment of connection born from a mom slowing herself down to enjoy her daughter rather than improve her.

Go beyond the drudgery and duty of motherhood into the Wild West of delight. It may feel like your child's vast wilderness of need is unending, an insatiable hole you can never fill. Like your best isn't good enough. That's not true. Read your child with the prejudice of love.[4] Seek to enjoy rather than tolerate. Ask yourself, "Is my response *from* love or *for* love?" Let it be *from* love. No correct response needed from your child to make your offering complete. Love does not keep score.

But, Mary, how do you delight in your child when they act so un-delightful?

1. Be a Proactive Bucket Filler

I tell you this from experience: The leaky bucket of your child's heart is not unfillable. Their need for attention and affection can feel never-ending and exhausting. Not so, if you shift the dynamics a little. You will have to make your care more visible with words of affirmation (see chapter 10) and obvious pursuit of them.

They likely feel shame for continuously being the initiator of connection. That stops today. No longer are you going to allow yourself to be the one being chased, feeling touched out and taken from. Pivot to become the pursuer. Initiate affection before they can. Be a mother who is sturdy enough not to crumble when her loving bids for connection are refused. Give your child the generous gift of rejecting you to find themself. Your child needs this gift, even though they don't have any idea how to ask for it or the awareness to thank you for it.

Filling their bucket can look like you turning away from dinner prep to yell, "Where's my baby?!" dramatically. Burst through the house desperately searching for them, crying out the whole time in mock terror, "Where is my baby?" Only once you find them and hug them does your search end. If they roll their eyes, mission accomplished.

This can also look like verbally blessing them as you go about your day. Whispering in their ear as you walk by them, "You are my child in whom I am greatly pleased."

If you're overwhelmed by the "Watch this, Mom!" and "Look!" requests, I get it!

My child's need to have me witness everything often felt like an irritating obstacle to the "real work" of getting us out the door, cleaning the house, or preparing meals.

But the real work of parenting is delighting in your child. Look up from your to-do list.

Set productivity aside, wipe your hands on the towel, and go see what your child has to show you.

Get down on the floor and marvel at their invention. Insist they practice three times before they invite you to their show, but then watch every minute. And please know, dear lady, that the "Watch me" requests fade away and get replaced with "Leave me alone" and "Why are you asking so many questions?" Now is when you show them that they matter. Now is the time to invest in the relationship and teach them that what they think and do is a wonder to you.

2. Focus on Your "Why I Love This Kid" List

Sometimes you get stuck in a mental loop, noticing again and again how hard this child makes your life. It takes active mindset work to shift this and become softhearted toward them again. Can you name ten things you love about your child? Begin to actively search for the facets of their personality that already please you. Write out words or phrases about your child that encapsulate what you respect or admire. Come up with as many positive traits as you can, even if your child isn't consistently the poster child for that trait. Some of the time is better than never. Add to it throughout the week. The resulting list allows you to meditate on what you love about the Spicy One. To ruminate on the good by finding positive descriptions for their big personality.

Celebrate who your child is instead of who you hoped they would be.

So much of what we see as negative about a child turns out to be an instrumental talent in an impactful adult. There are so many flattering ways to spin your view of a challenging personality so they can shine.

Visualize this: Imagine it's thirty years from now. You are now the grandmother of your Spicy One's child! This new little rascal wants to know what you loved about their parent when they were little. How would you answer?

After freewriting for five minutes, one Mom of a Spicy One read her list out loud to the group: "His perseverance and ability to be

LIGHT UP!

Practice delighting in your child by lighting up with excitement when they enter a room or request something from you today. Go a little over the top in your expressiveness and affection with them to see how it feels to both of you.

scared and do what frightens him anyway. His belly laugh. His openness to new adventures with me. When he says thank you or apologizes after a time has passed, he really means it." At this point, a lump in her throat cut off the words. Tears were in her eyes. She hadn't thought about his sparkle in a while.

Once she regained her composure, she added, "How affectionate he still is—hugs, kisses, cuddles."

What is the feeling in your body as you read glowing words about a Spicy One? Try to allow that feeling to inform your parenting. You must actively gather the good and seek out the "flecks of gold"[5] in your child (and in yourself).

Coming up dry? Borrow a word from the list of possible Spicy One attributes on the next page.

3. Ask Generous Questions

One Friday afternoon, my son threw a bouncy ball at the living room wall. The ricochet knocked over my carefully crafted fall tablescape. I instinctively muttered, "What is wrong with you?!" He paused the cleanup to repeat back to me in a neutral tone, "What is wrong with me?" Darn these steady Mild Childs. Hearing the question echoed back helped me realize how destructive it was. Asking that question, even when I didn't say it out loud, had become a habit. I made him a promise on the spot that I would not say it again. To motivate myself, I committed to paying him $5 every time I messed up. I was so sure I would never say it again. By the end of the weekend, I owed him $15.

Be aware of the inner questions you ask about the Spicy One.

The inquiry you allow to rattle about in your head becomes a spotlight pointing straight at possible ideas to bring closure to your open question. When we ask, "What is wrong with my child?" we initiate our brain's endless ability to brainstorm negative answers. Your imagination begins creating a case *against* rather than *for* your child.

Try asking yourself, "What is miraculous about my child?" or "What do I already love about this kid?" and see how your brain jumps in to help you with warm stories and tiny glimpses of goodness.

LOVE LIST FOR THE SPICY ONE

affectionate
animal-loving
artistic
assertive
bold
bright
capable
caring friend
charming
compassionate
confident
considerate
creative
curious
decisive
dedicated
determined
diligent
energetic
exuberant
fashionable
fierce
freethinking
friendly
fun
funny
go-getter
goofy
hardworking (e.g., at school)
honest
hyper-focused
impervious to crowd thinking
inclusive
independent
inquisitive
insightful
intelligent
inventive
knowledge-seeking
knows what they want
lovable
loving
loyal
mature
motivated
natural leader
no-nonsense
old soul
openhearted
original: limited-edition
otherworldly
passionate
persistent
playful
powerful
questions everything
quick-witted
remorseful
self-advocating
self-assured
self-honoring
sensitive
silly
snuggly
social
spunky
strong
studious
thoughtful
unafraid to shine
unafraid to speak up
unapologetic
unapologetically themselves
unashamed
upstanding
welcoming
wholly themselves
willing to repair
witty
zealous

To send this Love List to someone who needs to remember the goodness of your child, scan here:

4. Delight in Thyself

There is a relationship between your willingness to delight in yourself and the capacity you have to delight in your kid. The most reactionary moms I know are usually harder on themselves than they are on their kids. They are the women on the pickleball court muttering aloud, "That was awful," when they miss a shot. When they invite a friend over, they apologize profusely about the state of their house because inside their brain they are lambasting themselves for not cleaning well enough. They are mean to themselves. Their inner mean girl is rampant (more about her in chapter 14).

It is difficult to like your child when they remind you of all you do not like in yourself.

Often, the parents who protest loudest about their children being spicy wonder if they themselves might have been a stifled Spicy One! Your child's stubbornness and fierce independence may be a hereditary gift. Perhaps this child—who has never been good at being anybody other than themself—was sent here to invite you to step more wholly into self-acceptance. Do you like who you are? Unfortunately, it is not possible to skip self-compassion and still give compassion to your kid. Loving yourself is a critical step in being the parent you want to be. Be kind to yourself so you have the patience needed for this endurance race.

CH 9: Reflection Questions

1. Who is or was curious about you in your life? When have you been on the receiving end of warm curiosity? Name a time someone allowed you to flail a bit and even fail in their presence without judging you or trying to fix you.
2. Where is it easiest for you to be curious about your child's behavior rather than judging or insisting on your way? Where

is it difficult for you to access curiosity? In that scenario, how might it make sense that this child is behaving this way?

3. Take the jacket off the cover of this book. Which positive words on the cover underneath can you show to your child as you smile broadly, letting them know you love that about them?
4. What would it look like to be able to stay curious rather than enter into judgment? How do you know when you are curious? Explore some of the ways you want to hold yourself, think, and communicate by writing out and adding ideas to each column on the chart below.

Do	Think	Say
Keep my eyes soft	my child has good intentions	Hmmn. Tell me more I'm here to help

10

Speak Words of Warmth, Not War

There's a moment in the 2011 family movie *We Bought a Zoo* where a father and his troubled teenager are spiraling into a communication breakdown. Yelling and hurt. Not hearing each other. Finally, at the end of their fierce shouting match, they both slump down, their backs against a wall, neither looking at the other.

The son says something like "Sometimes I wish I knew what the hell you want me to say to make you happy."

The dad replies, "That's easy. 'Dad, you are right. I know you care about me and are trying to help me be better.'" Silence falls for a moment.

Then the dad, feeling generous, asks, "What do you wish I would say?"

The son stares ahead and says, "I like you, son. I like you just as you are. You don't have to be better."[1]

Your words matter in parenting. Use the power of your language for good with your Spicy One. Words shape the culture of your home and the self-concept of your child.

Your words build kingdoms within your child. Speak to a king and a king will appear. When you speak blessings over your child and say things like "Every day, you become kinder" or "You always seem to figure things out" or "Your persistence is your magic" or "Your deep feelings are going to be the key to helping others," you help make these things come true. Your words plant seeds in your child's heart. They believe what you say about them.

There's a saying, "If you tell a child nine times who they are, they'll tell you themselves on the tenth time." Your words matter so much. It's okay if you have been speaking curses in the past. Now you are aware of it and working on it. You were operating out of old programming. You get to start over. Speak positive words over your child each day like those in the list in chapter 9. Not to improve them or get them to do something but to follow the mission of your life, which is to build up this human and make them aware of their irrefutable goodness.

Before I share techniques for harnessing the power of words to increase cooperation and decrease meltdowns in the Spicy One, let me request that you reduce the sheer number of words you speak in your home. The more you fill the space with talking and the more questions you bombard them with, the less value your words will carry. WAIT. Ask yourself, "Why am I talking?" Often an easy silence will do more to calm your child than anxious chatting. Your quiet now gives more importance to what you say later.

Identify What You Want

You need to tell your child what you want. This sounds easy enough, but it's hard to do. So many parents can easily explain in detail how much they detest certain behaviors of their inflexible child. But when I ask what they want to happen instead, they are stumped. "Just not that," they say. When I give them space to express what they are longing for, the answer doesn't tumble out easily. It takes a second.

Your thoughts don't naturally go to the positive goal you want. It's easier to perseverate on the unwanted situation—to wallow in what's not working. It can be confusing to fully grasp (and explain) what you specifically want instead.

It's your job as the leader to create a word picture of exactly what you do want.

Imagine your child has been outside playing. They dug a mud puddle and are pumped to tell you about it. They are standing at your open front door with hands covered in red dirt. Three feet away from your dirty child is your gleaming white couch.

Most parents yell, "Don't you dare touch that couch!" When you tell a child that, into their brain comes an immediate, clear visual of touching that couch. The "don't" part falls by the wayside. To a young child with limited impulse control, it's like you just suggested they go touch thc couch.

What could you say instead? With your hands straight up to give them a visual, say, "Keep those muddy hands all the way up above your head. Good. Come with me over here to this sink. We're going to wishy-wash together. Yes!"

What Is the *Yes*?

Before directing your child, ask yourself, "What is the *yes*?" When you name what you want, you are an inspiring movie director guiding an actor who wants to please you. This is real manifestation. Words create meaning. Meaning creates culture. Naming your yes communicates way more cooperation and warmth than harping on what isn't working.

When you seek to name what you do want, you will feel awkward at first. You are going to stumble to come up with the most effective words. It's a new language of positivity to name the yes. You aren't going to know how to phrase it in the beginning. That's okay; you haven't asked yourself this before. Can you be patient with yourself?

When you communicate negatively (e.g., "Oh, don't do that"), you miss the opportunity to teach a skill. Children need a replacement behavior to consider. If I tell an addicted teen, "Don't vape," I need to supply a substitute habit. Like "chew gum." You must replace a negative habit with a neutral one.

Create a word picture in your child's mind that helps compel them to do the thing you need them to do. Let's look at some real-world examples of finding the yes.

You are at the pool, where the wet concrete is slippery. Instead of "Don't run," try "Walk slowly like a turtle. Oh yes, look at that turtle moving so carefully!"

Instead of "Don't throw sand. We don't do that. That's not nice!" try "Hey, keep the sand low." Show them the sand trickling down safely.

Whole-body learning includes touch. Extra points if you are physically modeling the action you want to see. Adding physicality to a young child's limit helps little people comprehend better. They need multiple modes of communication.

How about this one? "Don't stand on the couch!"

What does that compel them to do? Get up on that soft mountain and start climbing.

Instead say, "Keep your feet on the floor, please" or "In this house, we keep our bottoms on seats. Come on down. Thank you."

Avoid blurting disrespectful threats like "We're not going until you clean up." That is like a boss who says, "You aren't getting paid until you clean up." You don't have to replicate the demotivating cultures you have been a part of.

Instead say, "After we clean up, we are going to the park." After this required thing happens, then we get this fun thing. Connect the request to the yes. "After we brush your teeth, then we read books." Children want to succeed for us, but they are fighting a hundred inappropriate thoughts a minute with no prefrontal cortex to tamp down the impulses. Be more concrete with your yes language so your idea is more obvious and real than theirs.

WHAT'S YOUR CHAOS CATCHPHRASE?

When one Spicy One was being especially difficult, instead of saying, "Noah, you're driving me crazy," his mom would squeal, "I'm crazy about you, Noah!" She'd say it with the same intense energy because she was at the end of her rope, but the words stayed generous. Find a phrase that lets you expel some frustration but is still respectful to your child. One mom says, "It's my job to teach you to get along in the world, and I'm happy to do it." They will hear this correction often, so let it be thoughtful.

Front-Loading

Review your expectations ahead of time to increase cooperation and helpful behavior. Identifying the yes is most potent when we communicate what we want *before* entering a tricky situation. Especially in not-so-child-friendly environments. "We are going into Target. When you sit in the shopping cart, you will get to play with a toy, but it stays at Target. It does not come home." Notice I don't ask, "Is that okay?" You can't ask that and be surprised when they reply, "No. I don't want that." Do not ask. Tell. You can tell and still be gentle.

"We are going to leave the toy at Target, and you might be sad when that happens because you like bringing all the toys home. But even if you are sad, we're going to leave toys we play with at Target. What do you hear me saying?" Let them try in their own words. Gush over their attempts.

You could add, "What would you like Mama to do if you cry and are sad?"

The goal is to co-create a prearranged ritual with some buy-in from them. You are talking about it before things heat up.

Before you leave for your mother-in-law's house, say, "Remember how Grandma has the no-no area—her fancy figurines that we are not allowed to play with? What do we get to play with instead?" Ask questions to engage active participation from their brain.

"Yes! You get to open up her drawer of vintage toys. That's what you get to play with. I'm reminding you that you must stay in the family room and leave the figurines alone. At the end of our visit, I can take you to touch the figurines with two fingers, like I taught you."

Next Time!

A phrase that will help your communication stay constructive is "next time."[2] I used to say it on repeat in the early days. My husband found it hilarious. He became a game show contestant, waiting to catch me saying it. If I said, "Hey, next time will you . . . ," he'd scream, "NEXT TIME!"

It's okay. I'll take the teasing because "next time" is so powerful in casting a picture of the future you want rather than focusing on what you don't want. Imagine you walk back into the kitchen you cleaned an hour ago, and now there are leftover sandwich fixings all over the counter. What I used to say was (and listen here for my monster) "Are you kidding me? Who comes in and makes a total mess and leaves it for someone else to clean up? Do you think we have a daily maid service here?!" That's divisive, violent communication.

Instead, pause and think about what you wish would have happened. Now speak it into existence, creating a word picture. Look at the scenario and decide what you wish they would have done. Find the words and then go to that family member and say, "Next time you make a sandwich, please use the cutting board and put the condiments back in the fridge." (Pause for comprehension.) "What am I asking you to do next time?"

This can also sound like,

> "Next time, please put wax paper down to protect the table before you take out the glue gun."

"Next time, put dirty clothes right into this hamper." (It helps to be doing it together to demonstrate the behavior you want.)

Instead of saying, "You weren't very polite to Grandma," say, "Next time Grandma comes over, you have to acknowledge that she is a guest. You can say, 'Hello, Grandma,' with your loud words, or you can give a high five or even a hug if you want to." Nobody has to feel wrong to change behavior. Good leadership is casting a very clear vision of what is expected in an empowering way. Without shame.

Words of Affirmation

I attended a fabulous party the other night and woke up feeling depressed. I wondered aloud, "Why don't I have the skills to make that kind of soirée happen?" There was a table of gourmet fixings like chimichurri sauce with mini salted potatoes, charcuterie plates, roasted ham, and three different signature drinks. A blues band and glorious twinkling lights completed the evening.

Before I could wallow in my entertaining incompetence, my husband said, "Some people aren't supposed to host the party. They are meant to be invited to the party because they make every party better." And with that, my funk was gone. Isn't it wonderful when someone sees us? Isn't it gratifying when someone generously names our strengths just when we get stuck staring at our limits? Be that for your child.

The Gottman Institute determined that the number one indicator of whether a marriage will survive is a consistent ratio of five positive experiences to one negative experience. Five different instances of connection, kindness, and respect for each single instance of disrespect, anger, or hurt.

While this may be a marriage statistic, it absolutely applies to parenting. There's a strong chance your positive-to-negative ratio with your Spicy One is broken. Their intensity and fierce independence means you often have to correct them, discipline them, and verbally disagree with their actions. Even when we stay unflappable and centered, their behavior can be so off-track that your simple acknowledgment of reality may still register as a negative event to their tender spirit.

Words of affirmation help get the relationship ratio back to a healthy state. When you affirm the Spicy One with positive, specific language about their innate goodness, they are much more likely to feel connected and motivated to please you. Some phrases to casually speak over them:

- "Every day, you become kinder."
- "You always seem to figure things out."
- "Your persistence is your magic."
- "Your deep feelings are going to be the key to helping others."
- "You have such a powerful heart."
- "You are a brave and loyal human."
- "Your passion is contagious."
- "You have a tender heart and lively mind."*

Be ready to follow up with a detailed example. Spicy Ones are suspicious of generic praise, but regardless of their response, it warms their heart.

The most effective parenting tool in your box is positive reinforcement.**

You can help shift behavior when you focus more on noticing, articulating, and praising what your child is doing right rather than correcting what they are doing wrong. Praise can be as simple as naming and affirming the character trait they displayed: "I saw you share with your sister. You are a generous big sister."

* Said to me by my pastor Brenna Rubio of City Church Long Beach.

** At least twenty-six different parenting research studies show that one of the most effective parenting tools is positive reinforcement: https://www.sciencedirect.com/science/article/abs/pii/S0890856718319804. The other two are particular praise and natural/logical consequences.

PRACTICE WORDS OF AFFIRMATION

Challenge yourself once a day to speak life into your child using your Love List for the Spicy One from chapter 9.

It can sound like

- "You are a boy who brings ice to people who are hurting." (Even though they caused the welt on their brother's cheek.)
- "This family is blessed by your imagination. We appreciate how you share exciting adventures from your day." (Even though it takes mindful patience to live through these long stories.)
- "It's so much more lively and fun when you are home." (Even though your body craves peace and alone time.)

Each February, I run a challenge on Instagram to motivate parents to write out words of affirmation on hearts they tape to their child's door. Many a Spicy One, in a fit of rage, has ripped their Valentine's hearts down. A week later one mom found them all taped back together, carefully added to the wall, hidden behind his dresser. Your words of affirmation are not falling flat, but you may not always get the pleasure of seeing the joy and confidence your words bestow on your child.

Ugly words live louder in our memory than kind ones. Positive words need reapplying to stay stuck in our minds. I still can't shake the words my mother said offhandedly once when we were bickering: "You and I are like oil and water." That comment haunts me in its hopelessness. And it's not true. We are both vinegar.

As the parent, you can change the course of history with specific and well-timed affirmations that might begin with:

- "I love watching you . . ."
- "I appreciate how you . . ."
- "You are a person who loves to . . ."
- "I really respect how you . . ."

Comments that start with these phrases invest deposits in the relational savings account of your child's soul.

Celebrate the Behavior You Want to See More Of

I'm still haunted by the stranger whose Spicy One was climbing the handrailing outside a restaurant bathroom. "Get down!" she spat. "Stop being so bad!" she seethed. When he finally got down, I couldn't help but rejoice and say, "What a good listener!" I wanted to help ease the deadlock he and his mother were in. A continual loop of negative feedback and negative behavior. But she immediately corrected me.

"No, he's not. He's a terrible listener." The curse was cast. What a lost opportunity to point out the good and watch it expand.

So often, we fixate on the disruptive, annoying behaviors because they are so glaringly prevalent. But if you want to change behavior, take out your magnifying glass and catch your kid doing it right!

Your boy's always whining? Celebrate when he asks for something in a respectful voice. "I appreciate how you asked politely for juice. It's a pleasure to serve you when you use that mature tone!" Your girl's hitting her brother? Praise her when she peacefully walks by him. "You are a kind big sister. Thanks for giving your brother's body space to move safely."

Set Limits with "Yes, And . . ."

When my instructor for Intro to Improvisational Comedy called to deliver the distressing news that I had failed my first Groundlings class, I got off the phone excited rather than defeated. How could that be? He used the old "yes, and . . ." improv technique on me! He assured me, "*Yes*, you have great comedy instincts, *and* you would benefit from another six weeks of training to be the best partner on stage." I felt proud despite being fired!

Your Spicy One has caviar dreams with a can-of-tuna budget. They are in a constant cycle of ideating and insisting on big ideas that

TRY THE OVERHEARD BRAG

One way to celebrate and effect positive change is to initiate the *overheard brag*. This is you saying loudly to your partner, for example, "Honey, do you know what your daughter did today?" Watch the Spicy One's ears perk up, expecting to catch you bashing them. "She took it upon herself to wipe down every counter in the kitchen. It is sparkling in there because of her generosity and elbow grease!" The Spicy One believes you more when they think they have eavesdropped on your conversation.

can't work, given today's technology. They need your thoughtfulness to avoid feeling defeated. To save face. Here's the "yes, and . . ." formula: You say, "What I like about that idea is [*here you name the positive aspect of your child's plan*], *and* I need [*add your own wiser parental idea here*]." "Yes, and . . ." is a Moms of Spicy Ones pro move.

Leaving the park with a screaming child would sound like "You love it so much here. I know it's hard to leave. And guess what? We will come back tomorrow!" "Yes, and . . ." reminds you to lengthen the time you spend in your child's perspective. So many of us jump across it, straight to what we need from them, like "You don't want to wear closed-toe shoes but you have to."

For more cooperative results, we need to pause and give a few more beats to the child's perspective. Rest on the empathy note for a bit longer than you used to. "You don't want to wear closed-toe shoes to school." Pause here and then add, "I'm wondering how we can give your feet a break once you come home."

Imagine your preschooler begging for dessert at a restaurant before dinner has even been ordered. Find the *yes*, such as "Yes, you can have dessert, *and* we eat it *after* dinner." Naming what is acceptable without the cold, hard slap of *no* is a diamond in the coal of your child's struggles.

Practice Reflective Listening*

I was in awe the first time I watched a mom use the power of reflective listening with her overheating child. She said something basic, like "You do not like waiting when your cousin is using the microphone. You like bringing it all around the house, and it belongs to

* Also called empathic listening, active listening, or mirroring, this communication technique is a true gift for the Spicy One. It's what seasoned therapists and professional coaches do to bring clarity to their clients' emotional confusion and distorted thinking.

IMPERATIVE VS. DECLARATIVE LANGUAGE

Notice the difference in these two sentence structures when you say them out loud (best done with a transatlantic accent):

- Imagine a proper gentleman with a top hat pointing with his cane and saying, "It's imperative that you do as I say. Pick up my glove!" That's an *imperative* statement. It's phrased as a demand.
- Now picture a demure debutante batting her eyelids who announces, "I do declare my glove has fallen." This is a *declarative* statement that's phrased more passively.

As a parent, you get to choose which approach to use with your Spicy One—and here's what makes this choice crucial: Research shows that strong-willed children have what scientists call *heightened sensitivity to perceived control attempts.*[3] Their brains are literally wired to resist anything that smells like someone trying to boss them around. But the same kid who will dig in their heels over "Close the door!" will often cooperate when you say, "The door is still open." Declarative language states the problem without demanding someone do something about it.

Neither form is morally superior. Which communication you use depends on your child and your culture. Spicy Ones with a pervasive drive for autonomy (AKA Pathological Demand Avoidance) can get aggravated by imperative commands because a direct command triggers their internal rebellion alarm.[4]

you." Her vibe was business as usual but her "all-caps" tone matched that of her upset child. The transfer of energy that happened in front of me was palpable. The child's body softened. Their anger had been named, understood, and shared. The upset child did not magically get their hands on that microphone, but they did feel seen and heard, so a meltdown was less necessary.

Reflective listening centers your child's experience to open up communication. There is no evaluation or criticism of their feelings.

(continued)

Imperative: "Go grab the forks and napkins so we can sit down to eat."

Declarative: "We are going to need forks and napkins to eat dinner."

The declarative form invites a child's brain to engage as a collaborator rather than a subordinate. When we honor their need for autonomy while still communicating our expectations, we're speaking their emotional language. Sophia is constantly leaving the front door open. Each time, her mom could say imperatively, "Close the door!" Sophia may close it quickly, but she's doing so on autopilot. If you use a declarative statement like "Sophia, the door is still open," Sophia's got to think. "Okay, the door is open. Why is Mom saying the door is open? Oh, because it should be closed. Oh, I should close it." The theory is that declarative statements stimulate a child's inner voice for problem-solving and planning, leading them in a more advanced and critical thought process than an imperative command might.

Some particularly spicy situations need an imperative voice with eye contact and physical proximity.

Imperative: "Try that again, please. You may ask me with a respectful tone."

Other parent/child combinations might warrant a more passive style.

Declarative: "My body shuts down when you yell, and my brain doesn't understand the meaning of shouted words."

Communicating well with your Spicy One is an art that no one can dictate to you. Who would've thought we'd have to be so dang conscious about our words?!

Demonstrate that you have connected to the cause of their feelings, as in, "You are mad because you hate peanut butter crackers." Console yourself knowing that validating their feelings doesn't mean agreeing with them. This practice requires you to be observant and nondefensive and to pause for their response. You must savor the need they are expressing without necessarily meeting the need.

Phrases like "That isn't what you wanted to happen," "You weren't expecting that," or "You are disappointed" can help short-circuit some tantrums. In taking the time to understand and reflect your child's point of view, you create more buy-in than hitting them with the hundredth *no* they've heard today.

Label the feelings you hear. Grab the Feelings Emojis sheet from my website (QR code at the end of this chapter) if you are working on expanding your emotional fluency. Try any one of these phrases to help:

- "You are ______." Take a shot at describing their experience for them. Name and validate their emotions. For example, if you're late to pick them up and can see their gritted teeth as they come toward you, try saying, "You are angry that I'm late."
- "It sounds/seems like ______." Seek to pinpoint and clarify their emotion. "It seems like you are frustrated that I made you wait out front for so long."
- "What I'm hearing is ______." Verbalize your interpretation of their experience with a statement. "What I'm hearing is that when Mommy is late, it feels like I don't care about you." Allow them to clarify and disagree. That means you are getting closer. One family repeats the phrase "true or false" when their child is dysregulated since he can still confirm or deny in his altered state.

Once you say one of these phrases, be quiet and listen to their response. Give them space to bubble over with the emotion you noticed. This will only be a gimmick if you don't have the sincere intent of listening and understanding. As your child shares their experience, respond minimally with encouraging sounds, like "mmmm" or "uh-huh." Feel free to translate their unfiltered expressions:

Spicy One: "I hate my brother. He won't let me play with him."

You: "I can see you are very frustrated that your brother won't include you."

If this is a new skill for you, practice it with a partner. But be ready; some zesty demand-avoidant kids dislike being perceived this way. They might interpret your sincere observations as critical, mocking, or a micromanaging test to see if they feel the correct way.

I used to say to my three-year-old in her times of great obstinance, "You have so many *nos* in you!" It interrupted her habitual (and age-appropriate) negativity and opened a tiny window into how she was feeling. Some of those *nos* were the result of stuck frustration. She felt relief because I wasn't fighting against the *nos*. Another parent picked her son upside down to "shake out the *nos*," causing much giggling. My daughter would *not* have liked that. Every kid is different.

Reverse Psychology Could Work . . . or Backfire

How might you use the Spicy One's contrarianism to the family's advantage? One mom gets her kid giggling by asking, "Do you like saying no?" He sputters and laughs, unsure how to answer. Another mom says playfully, "Whatever you do, don't you dare put your shoes on!" and also "For this next picture, no smiling allowed!" For a season, the Spicy One will gleefully do the opposite.

Two Spicy One twins refused to get into the shower until their dad shouted, "First one in is the first one out." Suddenly the argument switched to who got to get in first.

A grandma once said, "You would probably think this tastes bad. You would never want to eat this edamame." The Spicy One insisted on proving her wrong.

Some Spicy Ones love these games; others get quickly agitated and suspicious, yelling, "Hey! Don't do that! I know what you're trying to make me do!" Then move on.

The idea is not to set up a habit of deliberate disobedience, so keep a twinkle in your eye that makes it clear this is a game. Like when a

WHEN THE SPICY ONE'S WORDS HURT YOU

It's hard to stay centered or kind when your child experiments with wounding power words like "You don't love me" or "I wish you were dead." Don't take it personally. This is a phase of grasping at anything that will help them express the depth and pain of their fiery upset. Here are some things you can do:

- Search for the need or pain under the offensive words. For instance, "This screaming child is desperate for my attention" or "This child is terrified of being embarrassed."
- Translate their venom into a socially acceptable version, as in, "You don't want to leave this playdate. I hear that!"
- Visualize the nasty statement flying past you as you dodge it and move toward them emotionally to reach for their heart.
- Remember that their rejecting words are a projection of self-contempt onto you. "I hate you" is actually "I hate how this feels." A desperate effort to avoid feeling the pain of a disappointing limit.
- Imagine they are a puppy barking wildly at you. See the cuteness of their childlike sputtering before you. No sense in taking their irrational and obviously not true words to heart.
- Recite W. H. Auden's poem "The More Loving One."

Spicy One freaked out because his little sister dropped a car down his Hot Wheels track. His mom pretended to agree with him but too voraciously. "Ugh! Totally! Since this is a single-use toy, now we'll have to put it in the trash. What a nightmare! Pack up the track and let's throw it away." The silliness shook him out of his train of thought. He laughed and said, "It's not that big a deal, Mom." Meltdown averted.

You can try delicious dares that are more gamification than reverse psychology: "There's no way you are fast enough to fill this entire chest with blocks in under sixty seconds." Or keep it general, like "Kids your age are afraid to try spicy things." Use exaggeration to challenge them, as in, "I bet you don't know how to make your bed on your own." Or "You would never shake the teacher's hand. It would be too scary." The line between motivating and manipulating can be blurry, but I approve of silly dares like "You better not trick me into brushing my teeth because I see you brushing yours." This won't work for long. But Opposite Day might. Tell them it's Opposite Day and you hope they will have a terrible day at school. Watch the smile spread across their face.

Reverse psychology is hit or miss. The Spicy One will quickly see through any manipulation. One nine-year-old decided he didn't want to go to Disney World two weeks before the big trip. Mom knew it was more about autonomy and less about Disney, as evidenced by his "Do I *have* to go, or is it my choice?" questions. She surrendered internally and accepted that he might choose not to go. She and her husband privately figured out who would stay home if he chose to stay. Then they gave him the choice. An authentic choice with no strings attached. He triple-checked that it was indeed up to him, and then he decided wholeheartedly YES. This is radical acceptance—not reverse psychology. If they hadn't really meant it, his genius spicy brain would have ferreted out the dissonance, and he would have doubled down on his *no*.

Words can be weapons or tools of great healing and hope.

You are using the power of your language for good, and your Spicy One is better off for it.

CH 10: Reflection Questions

1. What is one misbehavior that's stealing your peace these days? Name the *yes* of what you want instead. Describe exactly what you want your child to do and say, like you are writing a corporate handbook for a very junior associate. Spell it out.
2. What words of affirmation or curses of denigration still live rent-free in your head? What does that memory make you want to say or not say to your child?
3. What are ten attributes or behaviors that specifically delight you about your child. For help with possible words, see the "Love List for the Spicy One" in chapter 9.

To help you name all the feelings in your house,
scan the following code to download my Feelings Emojis PDF.
You can also access a growing version of the Love List there.

11

Sprinkle In Rhythm

Humans are created for rhythm.*

In our mother's womb, we are lulled to sleep by the sound of her heartbeat. The act of breathing in and out is the metronome to our lives. Our bodies find comfort in the predictable daily arc of the sun and the rise of the moon. We orient our traditions around the anticipated seasons of the year and the holidays that sparkle throughout.

We also find comfort in the simple, rhythmic elements of everyday living, like stretching upon waking, making the coffee, and walking the dog.

Children thrive on knowing what comes next in their day. Though we haven't met yet, I can guess that it's the transitions without rhythm where you see the most explosive behavior from your Spicy One.

What Are Rhythms?

Let's define *rhythms* as predictable moments of connection, play, or experience that sweeten the sting of transitions. It's the dependable

* I was introduced to the idea of rhythm in the book *Simplicity Parenting* by Kim John Payne with Lisa M. Ross. I earned my certification as a Simplicity Parenting Counselor in 2011.

notes of being awoken by the scent of pancakes and the singing of your mother. It's playing on the hanging bars for fifteen minutes after school rather than being rushed to the car. It's eating oatmeal with brown sugar on Tuesday mornings or watching a family movie every Friday after backpacks are cleaned out. It's lighting a candle, turning down the lights, and gathering everyone to the dinner table. Or a dance break after dinner, before the bedtime routine begins. Or singing a goofy song when it's time to brush teeth. The specifics will be personal to your family.

Moving a child from one thing to another is where a lack of rhythm—and therefore explosions—typically happen. Transitions are where we see the power struggles inherent in "stop doing this" and "start doing that."

Transitions can be:

- Preparing for the school day
- Coming home from school
- Leaving the house to go anywhere
- Getting off screen time
- Stopping a play activity
- Sitting down for a meal
- Getting ready for bed

It takes so much personal vivacity from you to move your born-to-challenge-the-system child through the basic progression of daily life. Adding rhythm can bring warmth and musicality so parenting doesn't require so much forcing.

Children can't make sense of adult frenzy over looming deadlines—too conceptual for their immature brains. Their confusion often leads to meltdowns, lack of cooperation, and emotional irregularity. Bring visibility and warmth to moments of transition to help your child feel like they have more control over what's coming next.

Three Guidelines to Help You Add Rhythm

1. Make the Choreography Visible to All

Write out your daily transitions to make them robust and real to you. If you, the adult, don't know the time needed for each step to get out the door in the morning, your child certainly doesn't.

Try reverse engineering a sticky transition. If you must be at school by 8:00 a.m., what time does that mean leaving the house? With that in mind, what time does everyone need to get dressed/ finish eating? If your kid is not hungry when they first wake, what time do they need to get up? If you want them to have ten to twelve hours of sleep, what time does that mean lights out the night before? If lights are out at 8:30, what time is story time? The smoothest mornings begin the night before. That might include packing lunches and picking out the next day's outfit. Like the *Give a Mouse a Cookie* book, it just keeps going. The more you work it out and write it down ahead of time, the more likely you will leave the land of magical thinking to create a well-planned process.

Post the steps where the whole family can see them so everyone feels included in and connected to the plan. Get yourself a giant desk calendar, and post it on the kitchen wall with each child's responsibilities highlighted in a different color. Make your thinking visible and the schedule obvious so you aren't holding the weight of that information in your pretty little head.

Determining the extra time needed for a long process like bedtime helps you set more realistic expectations. If you realize it takes two hours rather than the twenty minutes you wish for, then you won't resent the Spicy One for getting in the way. You will realize they *are* the way.

Same thing with heading out the door. If you figure out it can take ten minutes to exit with shoes on and five minutes to get car seats buckled, then you can allot fifteen more minutes in your existing process. This planfulness can lower your anxious "we are running late" energy that makes a meandering child dig in their heels.

RHYTHM IDEAS AROUND TRANSITIONS

Daily

- Friendly greetings and goodbyes.
- A wake-up song as the curtains are opened (be ready to dodge a thrown pillow).
- Quiet time at midday.
- Kitchen dance party.
- Breathing together.
- Neighborhood walks after dinner.
- Time with a pet.
- Floor time with the family.
- A game of tag.
- Politeness (I say please; you say thank you).
- A cleanup or toothbrushing song.
- Car DJ time: Everyone gets to pick a song.
- Putting away lunch boxes on a designated low shelf.
- An obstacle course to get to the bathroom for toothbrushing.
- Reading a book together.
- Telling stories about when you were your kid's age.
- Chores: Talk about future responsibilities earned by age. "In this family, when you are six, you feed the cat. When you are seven,

Observe when things feel pinched—where you might need to slow down to the pace of childhood. Children are easily overwhelmed by the adult-paced speed of life. The gift of slowing down is a generous one for them as well as for you. It gives you the opportunity to bring more presence and acceptance to the beauty of this fleeting season.

For maximum buy-in, enlist your child to help create the schedule. Let them pick out the colors for the list of responsibilities or fun graphics from the internet for their assigned chores.* A schedule

* Google "visual schedules" for some great ideas.

(continued)

you help take out the trash. By the time you are twelve, you get to take it out on your own."

- Family cheer when someone accomplishes something small: "Smith family, Smith family—what did you do? Smith family, Smith family—we are proud of you!"
- Sharing your day around the dinner table ("sweet, sour, and service" or "rose and thorn").
- Wrestle time.
- Bedtime rituals of reading and snuggling with parents' full attention.
- Laying out clothes for the day ahead or sleeping in fresh ones if it helps the morning.
- A romantic preview of the day ahead: "In the morning, I will wake you up with tickles, and we will have breakfast together."
- A blessing said over kids at bedtime.
- Parent preparing for next day by cleaning kitchen and packing lunch.

Weekly

- "You are special today" plate at breakfast.
- Weekly foods like Taco Tuesday, Friday night movie and pizza, and pancakes on Saturday mornings.
- Park visits.
- Game nights.

can be a regulating tool, signaling the nervous system into a state of hopeful expectation, anchoring the brain to a positive future.

Practice cooperation by asking your child, "What are you going to say when I say it's time to go?" Limit the expected steps your child must complete to three tasks. Together, repeat those first few steps over a few weeks. Then add another step. Ask the Spicy One to teach the finished schedule to the rest of the family. They love to be the leader.

Part of a successful rhythm is giving obvious cues to alert everyone that a transition is approaching. My husband equips me (and also irritates me) by shouting into the ether, "Ten minutes!

Tennnnn minutes!" like a demented train conductor. He's doing his best to get us to leave on time. Then, what feels like thirty seconds later, he yells, "Five minutes! Fiiiiiiive minutes!" As I feel the countdown coming to a close, my ADHD body kicks into gear. It works. Try it.

If that's not your speed, set a more acceptable time cue together. Ask, "How would you like me to let you know when you have five minutes left before cleanup? Should I ring this bell . . . or come give you tickles?" Add play to the transitions by singing, doing a family cheer, or high-fiving. Try sprinkling in a call-and-response game or affirmation throughout the routine.

Use actual times on the clock for transitions rather than when the adult feels ready. Your feelings are too arbitrary when it comes to leading the Spicy One. Leave when a song finishes or when the clock hits noon rather than when you happen to remember. This not only lessens your mental load, it helps your child feel like they have some control over their destiny. Set alarms on your phone with specific sounds and labels chosen by the Spicy One. Technology can help move things forward and give the Spicy One more ownership of their day.

As you write out your emerging schedule, decide how many days of patience and persistence you are willing to give it before trying something else. I find that three weeks makes for a solid attempt at a new rhythm.

2. Repeat the Chorus of Connection

As Ursula K. Le Guin writes, "Love doesn't just sit there, like a stone, it has to be made, like bread; remade all the time, made new."[1]

The repeated chorus of your relationship is dependable moments of time together. See chapter 7 for more details on that special time. Your sassafras needs intentional, predictable time with you interspersed with moments of breathtaking independence. Your prickly Sasquatch craves your full, undivided attention. Make repeated

NO SCREENS IN THE MORNING

While a fantastic babysitter when you need a break, screen use can block cooperative behavior. Technology can *disconnect* your kids from helpful natural morning rhythms. Especially when kids get to self-serve their screen use. Scientists have examined the relationship between screen exposure and attention abilities and recorded altered brain waves from screen use.[2] Screen exposure is correlated with attention-related issues. Reducing screen time is always painful for the first seven days, but if you stay firm, the Spicy One will relax into the habit of finding their own independent healing play, setting their brain up for a more successful day.

efforts to draw them close, show interest, read a book, or share a snack.

These connecting pauses don't need to last long. The purpose is to come together to fill up your child's emotional bucket with connection *before* they act out to get it. Release them into their own self-directed world with a full tank of connection. The most potent moments for connection (and culture-setting) in a child's day are the fifteen minutes when:

- They wake up
- They are eating
- They come home from school
- They are going to bed

To set an easier tone for your days, fill these sacred times with touch and vocalizing back and forth. You will be most successful if you schedule this time earlier in the day (like the joy of a surprise party scheduled *before* the birthday rather than *after*). Expect resistance, anticipate meltdowns, and allow your children (and you) to have moments of frustration and failure. Bathe your attempts at rhythm in grace for both of you.

TRY THE ASTRONAUT MASSAGE AT BEDTIME

Ears: *Gently cup and massage earlobes with light squeezes up and down.*

"Mission Control to Astronaut Taylor. Initiating presleep protocol. Activating communication systems. Zero-gravity helmet seal confirmed."

Forehead and Scalp: *Spread hands across forehead and stroke back through hair.*

"Helmet visor engaged. Oxygen circulation optimal. Brain-wave monitors now calibrating for sleep mode."

Shoulders: *Gently squeeze and make circles on shoulders.*

"Suit connection points secure. Pressure stabilizing in upper quadrants. Releasing muscle tension from mission activities."

Arms: *Make long strokes down arms from shoulder to fingertips.*

"Decompressing control arm circuits. Releasing today's command sequences. Suit flexibility restored to optimal levels."

Chest: *Make light circular motions on upper chest.*

"Heart-rate monitors engaged. Breathing systems calibrated. Reducing respiration to sleep-cycle levels."

Legs: *Make long, firm downward strokes from thigh to ankle.*

"Mission Control confirming gravity anchors. Releasing tension from walking circuits. Preparing for weightless sleep state."

Feet: *Gently knead soles, focusing on arch and heel.*

"Landing gear now in rest position. Pressure points releasing. Energy systems powering down. All body stations reporting ready for sleep mission. Countdown to dreamland commencing. 5 . . . 4 . . . 3 . . . 2 . . . 1 . . . Sweet dreams, Astronaut Taylor."

Give yourself mercy when entering non-child-centered environments, like Grandma's house, with all her breakables. Rhythm is a pipe dream when you have houseguests or during special events, holidays, or travel. Lower your expectations. Expect inflammation and meltdowns in these situations. No need to judge yourself or the Spicy One harshly.

Another daily rhythm worth repeating is unstructured play in nature. This could look like running around outside, collecting leaves together, or you lying in the grass and looking at the clouds while they figure out how to keep themself busy. Either way, nature time deserves to be on the schedule, as does time where they must figure out their own destiny without the interruption of an adult or screens.

During elementary school, every Tuesday afternoon I took my kids straight from school to the park with nothing but carrots, hummus, Capri Suns, and a blanket. We spent two hours decompressing from the school day. Half the time my child would collapse on me and loudly find something to be disappointed with. (I counted it as a blessing to work through that in the fresh air and wide-open sky of the park rather than my dark, cramped kitchen where the sounds bounce off the walls and into my aching ears.) I had to plan well. If I tried to stop at home in between school and the park to gather our provisions, it would have been Meltdown City.

Get outside where wild children are meant to be. This is more than a suggestion. Your kids need it, and *you* need it regularly to off-gas the pent-up emotions of cohabiting with a honey badger. Plus, outside allows for lots of new modes of physical touch, made-up games, and affection, like wrestling and yoga acrobatics.

3. Leave on a High Note

Don't wait until your child is fussy or overstimulated to exit a situation. Prolonging the goodbye sets your child up to be at their worst during a difficult transition.

If your child usually struggles at the ninety-minute mark of a playdate, let everyone know you are down for a short and sweet visit. Leave on the hour. Set an alarm on your phone so you are constructing a successful end time rather than waiting for the Spicy One's anguish to signal your goodbye. Start bedtime before your Spicy One is exhausted. Serve meals before they are starving.

Talk about the exit plan ahead of time to help your unyielding child end well. Try discussing the hard things early rather than hoping for the best. Cast a vision of how you would like it to go so the Spicy One has more time to acclimate. Like "So, Clara, you will get to play with your cousins until dinner, and then right after dinner, we will head home to sleep. It may make you sad that your cousins get to stay up later to watch a movie. That's understandable. And our family cannot stay late. What will help you feel better about leaving before everyone else does?"

Get your child's input on how to make the transition feel better for them. Allow them agency by partnering in the problem-solving. For instance, you might say, "When we sit down for dinner at our friends' house, you will need to stay at the table for fifteen minutes before you can get up to play. Your body might want to wiggle and move. What will help you to stay seated—sitting next to me or with the other kids?" (Listen here.) "How do you want me to help you if you forget our agreement and try to get up before it's been fifteen minutes?"

"Persuasion is not about how bright or smooth or forceful you are. It's about the other party convincing themselves that the solution you want is their own idea."[3] Let them win more while they are doing what you want.

The more you weave predictable connecting moments into your rhythm, the more security and peace you and your Spicy One will enjoy.

CH 11: Reflection Questions

1. In which part of your daily or weekly schedule is there the most conflict?
2. What changes could you make to reduce that conflict?
3. What planned moments of rhythmic warmth can you bring to the triggering transition you identified in this chapter?

12

Teaching Life Skills to a Hellion

An overdose of confidence and magical thinking combined with a drive for independence and high sensitivity to any criticism makes the Spicy One a difficult pupil.

One of my husband's favorite stories about me is the time I stood outside a music store on one of our first dates, pausing in the glow of a shiny blue drum kit. I was adept at playing the air drums, especially the tricky solo from the song "In the Air Tonight" by Phil Collins. I assumed the transition to actual drums would be seamless.

At this point in telling the story, Mr. Van Geffen will look at the couple across the table and say, "She would throw the imaginary sticks up into the air, letting them twirl above her head before she'd catch them and land the finale—without missing a beat." It's true. I am talented at air drums.

Standing there at the window, at the age of thirty, I thought, "Oh yes, finally a chance to actually *play* drums rather than *pretend* to play drums." I walked into the store toward my destiny, sat down behind the kit, grabbed the sticks, and . . . felt immediate confusion. Disappointment. Shock.

I could not reproduce the beats ticking away in my head. I was not a Foo Fighter.

Why Are Spicy Ones So Difficult to Teach?

The Spicy One feels powerless when they let someone instruct them. Like they are taking the subservient role in a doomed partnership. Letting someone else be in charge of their brain ignites a perceived loss of autonomy. They refuse to lose face or the ability to captain their own ship! This applies to learning to tie shoelaces, play an instrument, or keep a friend.

Your Spicy One is not aware of the *hidden curriculum*—all those subtle social customs people should know but are never directly taught.[1] Neurotypical people learn them automatically, without formal instruction. Meanwhile the Spicy One struggles with the reciprocity of friendship. It doesn't occur to them to modulate the volume of their voice to fit in. They will struggle to behave like others in structured spaces with rigid expectations, like at school. They have trouble with courtesy under pressure. Alas, you cannot protect them from making countercultural decisions.

If this were a typical gentle-parenting book, I would walk you through the three steps to teach your child anything. It would be simple! However, you have a child who insists on learning by doing. Whatever the lesson, they legitimately believe they already know how.

The Spicy One is the absolute worst student of anything they are not begging you to teach them. Even then, it will be a tug-of-war of who is teaching whom.

There is nothing more laborious than trying to teach the Spicy One something before they are ready to learn it.

newfrogparent commented: My 4 year old daughter, who was trying to convince me to research how to find frog eggs and take care of tadpoles, looked me straight in the eyes, "I'd rather struggle with the real thing than play with a toy!" when I offered to buy her toy tadpoles and frogs to play with instead 😅 I'm slowly learning my spicy one doesn't want an easy, no conflict, smooth sailing life. She wants the struggle and finds it far more interesting and fulfilling... I need to jump on board!

But this human needs to learn how to:

- Be flexible and adapt to unexpected changes
- Make and keep a friend
- Do household chores
- Conduct themselves appropriately online
- Project a pleasing tone of voice
- Connect nutrition to how their body feels
- Talk to service workers (e.g., order a pizza)
- Share resources, the limelight, and leadership
- Notice and react to bodily needs
- Be patient with others who think differently or need more time/space to be heard
- Apologize and repair ruptures
- Keep up with hygiene
- Identify and navigate different families' rules
- Tolerate frustration
- Maintain a positive mindset during a challenge
- Tend to their anxiety
- Be kind to siblings
- Wait their turn to talk
- Cook eggs
- Use coping skills and calm-down exercises
- Etc., etc., etc.

I asked my young adult Spicy One how she came to learn patience. I hoped it was some illuminating lecture I'd initiated or some long-suffering act on my part that she'd witnessed and wanted to emulate. Nope.

She said, "I learned patience when friends gave me feedback that I was too much for them." My heart thudded into my stomach imagining my girl being her Kodachrome self and getting rejected. Made to feel excessive. That happened to me too. [*Imagine the scene glimmering out of focus as I take you back to my college days.*]

My freshman year of college offered a harsh lesson. Leading up to sorority rush, I bragged to anyone I met about being one of the best lacrosse players in my town. I didn't take in much about the people I was meeting, but you better believe they got an earful about me. At the end of sorority rush week, not a single house I picked offered me a bid. I was devastated. I wanted to set fire to the whole school and go home.

My mother must have recognized her own Spicy One journey in my pain. The letter she wrote me (this was before cell phones) in looping cursive read, *You have a strong personality. And you are a woman. Most people will not be lukewarm about you. They will either love you or they will hate you because of your power. Learn the lessons you can and then go find the people who love you.* There was no "I told you so" needed. The natural consequences were in full effect. I was learning the hard way, the only way the Spicy One knows how.

Your Child Is an Experiential Learner

An experiential learner needs to initiate or at least understand *why* the lesson is necessary, try out different solutions for themself, make decisions, and be accountable for the results. They require support to reflect upon and synthesize their understanding.[2]

Experiential learners need firsthand experience trying multiple self-directed options and viscerally feeling the painful differences in the results. They need to fall down holes of avoidable failure first.

Only then might they be willing to chat about it. Success for the Spicy One comes *after* failure.

Your child may burn through many a friendship to eventually become a good friend. They have to bake a chewy cake with baking powder clumps before they want to see your recipe. Giving them the space they need will feel like practicing benign neglect, but they want to learn it the hard way.

You Are the Flashlight Holder

Follow-up conversations (about failed experiments) help them learn. Your role is to ensure reflection happens. Looking back (even though they want to avoid it) helps them integrate and assimilate the information. The trick is that you must remain neutral. "I told you so" will get you locked out of the shotgun seat in their life. Set an alarm for three days later to ask them what they're thinking now about the concept you brought up earlier. As in, "Remember when we talked about making space for your quieter friends to share their thoughts? Have you noticed anyone doing that or not doing that in your friend group?"

Bad experiences give birth to beautiful conversations.

Think of your role in these chats as the holder of the flashlight, not the keeper of the map. You are facilitating the learning environment, bringing the curriculum into focus rather than playing the teacher. Let them run the show and fail. Let them taste their mistakes.

When you do share instruction or host reflection chats, treat them like you would an annual pass to your favorite theme park rather than a onetime visit that needs to last all day.* Annual pass holders don't have to cram all the rides into one day. They can enjoy one ride and then leave. That's you keeping it short and painless. You can always come back a few days later to add more context and check for comprehension.

---

* Shout-out to Lisa Dunn for sharing this metaphor.

You are the sounding board as they collect experiences and core memories you could never orchestrate. You will have conversations that won't stick. Then they will learn firsthand, and you will talk more about it. A rich learning environment allows for lots of risk-taking, adventure, and failure. Ask yourself:

- Can I be a parent who allows for answers I have not considered?
- How can I learn as much from the Spicy One as they are learning from me?

The outcomes of their risky learning cannot be predicted. (My condolences to Enneagram 1, 5, and 6 parents.) Experiential learners must experience natural consequences. They learn as much from failure as success. One dad used to announce, "We either win or we learn!" before any grand experiment.

Tell Parables to the Spicy One

Social stories,* first developed to assist autistic folks but helpful to us all, make abstract social information more concrete. Imagine those airplane emergency cards detailing how to exit the plane in the event of a crash. Steal this idea for sharing clear visuals and specific steps required to problem-solve, attend to social dynamics, and interpret what is expected of the Spicy One in unfamiliar scenarios.

Use the science of storytelling to help your child work through a fear or repeated negative habit. Parables are stories with indirect guidance that help teach a lesson without the pesky aroma of a lecture, which the Spicy One can smell from miles away. They will exit the room as soon as you talk about how they treat their sibling, but they crave your imaginary tale about a mouse named Bruno who used to hit his brother with the top of a giant mushroom.

* For more detail on writing a Social Story, visit CarolGraySocialStories.com.

IDEAS FOR TEACHING AN EXPERIENTIAL LEARNER

Break down the lesson into discrete parts. (AI can help with this!) They need tasks chopped up into smaller pieces than other kids need. Clearly identify what success looks like. Let them evaluate themselves on a score sheet you make together.

Ask them how others did—they love judging others!

Make thinking visible with a picture checklist. Allow them to check off each small step.

Body doubling: This is you staying nearby, doing another task while your Spicy One completes their task. Initially, do the task together—if they'll let you—several times while narrating each step out loud.

Modeling: Point out where you are practicing flexibility or tolerating something uncomfortable. This includes modeling failure. Have they seen you screw up and not have some magical solution to remove the sting?

Practice guesstimations: Build executive functioning by daring your child to estimate how many minutes they think something, like walking a dog, will take.

Know when to outsource: Thank the Lord for neighborhood retirees, grandparents, and coaches. Call in others who can teach, like older kids, cousins, or aunts. Invest in professionals. Who can you bring into their world to teach a concept? Get a tutor. For the first half of her fourth grade year, I tried to help my Spicy One with math. I knew geometry—I could teach it! But our combustion brought the tears and character assassinations that made things worse. I fought against it, thinking, "I'm supposed to be the one who teaches," until I finally hired the sweetest guy to come over and show her how. Drama-free. If money is tight, check with your child's school or the Big Brothers Big Sisters organization in your area.

(continued)

Follow their interests: Share the big picture or list of concepts you want to teach, but then let them choose where to get started. It goes better when it's their choice. Notice what lights them up.

Pretend: Practice friendship talk by role-playing what sounds friendly versus insulting. Act out exact conversations with playfulness. Provide scripts for repeat situations, like how to ask the librarian politely for a book. Provide low-stakes situations where they can practice and fail on their own.

Involve them in the domestic arts: Assign them important roles that if done poorly will be valuable learning and not catastrophic. Like inputting the family grocery pickup order, planning a family outing (including checking prices and business hours and purchasing tickets), and using the phone to make their own doctor appointments. Most of these things you will have to do together *way* more times than you think should be humanly necessary while making it as fun as possible (music helps).

Repeat, repeat, repeat your values so your voice saying "We treat people's bodies gently" becomes their internal mantra.

Gamification: Introduce some kind of competition to get the dopamine pumping.

Celebrate! Notice tiny milestones of progress out loud. Watch that skill literally grow in front of you, like "I noticed you looking at your calendar on Sunday night. You are managing your time well." After mentioning it and being specific, see the Spicy One dig further into that practice.

Cues: Establish agreed-upon shorthand reminders, like American Sign Language for "thank you," to gesture a reminder rather than use your words again.*

---

* Sidenote: Please don't force "please" and "thank you" on difficult days. You consistently saying it on their behalf, when the cat's got their tongue, is building the skill.

Include specific sensory details to engage their brain. What was the hero wearing against their skin? What was the setting (a forest? a cottage?), and what colors or textures could they see/feel? End the story with the hero figuring it out—maybe with a little help from their favorite adult. Resist the temptation to moralize by ending with "the point of the story" or a "therefore you should" statement. No need to directly relate the story back to your child's life. Let *them* extrapolate.

During a tough season, tell tales about you at their age. You once had a hard time. Normalize mess-ups and adventures in learning. Give them options to reflect on by taking the hero character through different scenarios.

Stories help loosen a Spicy One's intractable stance. When my daughter refused to start kindergarten, making bold pronouncements that she was going to stay another year at preschool, I told her stories to help her. She happened to be obsessed with Scooby-Doo, so I began with a whisper: "Do you know what happened when Scooby-Doo was old enough to go to kindergarten but was worried?" Her eyes widened. I could almost see the neurons connecting as she realized even Scooby-Doo had to go to kindergarten. "Tell me," she demanded.

"Well, before Scooby-Doo went to school, he and his mom would go and stand outside the kindergarten playground to watch the kids play. He figured out through the fence where the jungle gym and swings were. Even the bathroom. But he didn't know any of the kids, so he was worried. What if nobody knew his name? But he was brave, so he went to school the first day of kindergarten, and do you know what happened? Every kid had a chair with their name written right there on it. It turned out that the other kids didn't know anybody's name either! Scooby-Doo felt so much better and ended up making lots of friends. Then he came home and told his mommy all about his first day of school, and they had ice cream to celebrate!"

After several retellings of the story, with modifications (sometimes Scooby was figuring out how to ask to go to the bathroom; sometimes he was learning about circle time), my daughter's fear decreased. She warmed to the idea of school.

OFFER FORBIDDEN LESSONS

You can interest the Spicy One in learning calm-down techniques (see chapter 13) by letting them stumble upon you working on one. Imagine them "catching" you pushing a wall or blowing out pretend candles on each of your fingers after a frustrating phone call. Their curiosity will have them begging you to teach them. You might even want to play hard to get and say they aren't quite old enough to learn.

Don't worry about telling a perfect story. Plot is not important. Your child will enjoy a meandering tale that echoes their experience and includes characters and interests they love.

Parables are perfect for when you are concerned about a trend or phase your child is going through and you want to enlarge their understanding and perspective. It takes repetition for these stories to sink in. This strategy is not for immediate fixes.

Parenting a Spicy One is a massive exercise in learning to let go of outcomes. As one mom said,

> I teach, she pretends she doesn't hear and rejects, does it her own way, fails, rejects feedback, tries again another way and gets too frustrated, doesn't ask for help but listens to half of some guidance before anticipating the rest of it and trying again and succeeds and thanks nobody but her smarty-pants self.

Alas, your sassy-pants will not give you the satisfaction of nodding their head and saying, "I understand, dear Mother," let alone repeating back their comprehension for clarification.

In fact, they may even hit you with *malicious compliance*, the act of exposing the absurdity of a rule but following it ridiculously to the letter. You ask them to speak respectfully to adults. They take on an exaggeratedly formal, Victorian-era style of speech: "Good evening, Mother Dearest. I do hope you are feeling quite well this fine evening. Might I humbly request permission to partake in the consumption of a frozen dairy treat?" The tone is technically respectful but so over-the-top that it's clearly mocking.

But your messages are seeping in! I'll leave you with a share from one giggling mom:

> I have no idea how, but I do believe every once in a while that things are going in and sticking. When my SO was five he wanted a certain game really badly, so I told him Dad and I would research and discuss whether or not it aligned with our family values. He asked, "What are family values?" I said, "Things that are really important to us as a family." He suddenly started spouting them off from the back seat even though I had never written them down or even sat down and said, "These are our family values." He goes, "Oh, like giving and being kind, you don't have to do everything perfect, saying 'okay' when someone says no?" I was shocked and heart-warmed! I hang on to that story for dear life because we still have some very tough days. But maybe we'll all be okay after all.

CH 12: Reflection Questions

1. How can you create an environment that invites your Spicy One to learn from their mistakes without shame? What have you said in the past that might need to be reversed to create a safer space for them to experiment and fail without fear of your judgment?
2. What would it look like to balance giving your child independence and necessary guidance? What could you do to become more of a flashlight holder than the keeper of the map?
3. What struggle is your child going through that might be soothed with a story featuring your child's favorite character (or a family member as a child)? How could a story either normalize their struggle or give them an example of a new path forward?

PART III

BE THE CALM ONE IN THE ROOM

Obviously, you want your distracted and distracting child to learn to calm themself down and to notice (and care) when their behavior upsets others.

Unfortunately, your potential to teach this skill is dependent on your own ability to settle down.

Can we take a moment of silence for the times you have headed into an emotionally charged situation and your agitated presence made things worse? Your zero-chill approach can blow up emotions that were initially just a small fire. It happens when you are raising a zesty human.

The goal is to become the safest and most grounded person in every room.

Your child's human brain learns best when it can let go of the energy-depleting job of keeping itself out of danger. If you want your child to learn from whatever issue has you seeing red, then you must calm down first. When the teacher shows signs of being open and at ease, the student can relax enough to learn the lessons.

Let's work together to help you notice and adjust when you are moving outside your *window of tolerance*, a concept coined by Daniel J. Siegel in his 1999 book, *The Developing Mind.* Siegel proposes that everyone has a range of intensity in which they can comfortably experience, process, and integrate emotions. When you feel triggered by the Spicy One, you move outside your window—into hyper-arousal (fight/flight) or hypo-arousal (shutdown/numbness). Your ability to think clearly, respond thoughtfully, and connect with your child becomes compromised. But you can expand that range with practice!

Learning to find your calm comes *before* helping your child get calm. We will start by practicing techniques that help you experience a felt sense of safety in your own body.

13

Stop Yelling

Co-Regulation and the Conscious Pause

Tunnel vision. Breath caught in your collarbone. Heat flooding your face. The pulsating volume of blood in your ears blocking any cohesive thoughts. Loneliness.

Screaming in the dark car, my four-year-old refused to put her seat belt on to go home from a friend's house. She was distraught that we were leaving before she was ready. She was tired, and so was I. Our beds were just a fifteen-minute drive away, but she was not getting in her car seat. The power struggle was drawing us into its vortex. We got physical. And per usual, I added to the drama.

Likely, you too have felt this way at some point in your parenting. Feeling physiologically overwhelmed by your "whiskey-bent and hell-bound" Spicy One is understandable. Perhaps, like me, you have found yourself shouting menacingly or gripping a tiny arm tighter than necessary.

We've all parented in ways we told ourselves we wouldn't. Despite the abandonment I experienced as a child exiled to my room,

I locked my own screaming banshee in her bedroom while she charged the other side of the door. Like my mother before me, I hoped a time-out would settle her.

It didn't.

When you are activated by the Spicy One on top of all the stimulation and responsibility of your life, you exceed your brain's capacity to take on stress. Your body thinks you are in danger. Everything feels like a threat, be it a child pulling on your shirt or shrill whining in your ears. When your brain is beyond its capacity, it's natural to want to scream and hit. Or disassociate. When you come back into your right mind, cloudy and confused by your actions, humiliation weighs on your heart. Once again, you became a monster. You can't help but look around, hoping someone else will step in and make it all better. Someone to comfort you as you wish you'd been comforted back when you were little.

If no adult from your past was able to model the rise and fall of anger in a healthy way, then self-regulation and self-compassion will be foreign concepts. Even a compassionate face can seem mocking when you've had no practice receiving comfort. You will need a plan to self-soothe in the tense moments.

Staying calm means figuring out the safety sequence your unique body needs to know there is no emergent threat to your life and limb.

No snarling predator in your midst.

(It's just a small, tyrannical human who really wants french fries.)

Let's hone your parenting power of staying calm no matter what. If you made it this far, I'm guessing you are open to learning how to accept and tolerate your big feelings . . . all while *not* lashing out at your child (who, BTW, is also learning to accept and tolerate *their* big feelings). What a dizzying tightrope you both are walking!

There are a lot of intense emotions happening at your house and likely in your body. You are using up precious patience bouncing back and forth between resentment and guilt. And then you keep hearing about this concept of co-regulation.

CO-REGULATION (NOUN)

co·reg·u·la·tion

The art of quieting yourself internally and maintaining your composure under stressful situations while simultaneously supporting a child's ability to do the same. Your embodied calm and grounded demeaner help your child to self-soothe and build their coping skills to eventually handle life's triggers without you.

From repeated warm, safe, and responsive co-regulation episodes with a trusted adult, kids are learning more adaptive strategies for modulating their reactions to challenging situations. Wouldn't it have been nice to have an adult co-regulating with you when you were growing up? *Sigh.* Alas, you are starting from scratch, and I respect it! Co-regulation is about learning how to show up both for the child and for yourself. It's learning to evaluate what your child needs as well as what *you* need to help calm you both. It's strengthening your distress tolerance for your child's emotions. Being okay when they are not.

Eventually this will be an intuitive dance between you, but it requires building some self-fluency. Self-fluency is knowing yourself well and listening (and responding) to your own body and soul's needs. The tricky part is recognizing how you feel and experiencing your own emotions before you can focus much on helping your kid.

For most of us, co-regulation is not a process we saw modeled. It is also not effortless. Instead, it is a learned skill. Before you can help your child regulate, you will have to dive in and expand your own understanding and awareness of your emotional experiences. Put another way, it's time to grow your emotional IQ (i.e., the ability to regulate your emotions). Emotional maturity means feeling the full spectrum of your emotions but not responding in permanent ways to such fleeting feelings. Buying yourself some time.

Your emotions are as contagious as the Spicy One's. Since the universe decided you are the one in charge, it's you who will have to lead by sharing your calm rather than taking on your kid's upset.

Calm doesn't come naturally for everyone. It didn't for me. I'm a redhead, for goodness' sake! I needed a plan for staying calm. I needed skills I hadn't seen modeled. I needed specific step-by-step instructions to learn how to take it down a notch. Now that I figured this out, I'm teaching *you* those principles! If you were raised by an angry parent whose bursts of emotions were unpredictable and didn't make you feel safe to explore your own feelings, I've got you. Or if your caregiver was naturally calm, but you never learned the coping skills needed to lead an emotionally distraught passionflower who wilts daily, I've got you. Here are some calming principles to play with.

Technique 1: Define Your Version of Calm

Let's get personal. Your unique version of calm matters. Allow yourself to contemplate these five questions:

1. What Does Your Calm Look Like?

To get clear on your personal version of calm, imagine a brilliant director is filming a movie version of your child doing the thing that most upsets you. Maybe the Spicy One is anxiously stalling outside the expensive martial arts class that started fifteen minutes ago. What would the director tell the gorgeous actress playing you (staying calm in this scenario) to do? What might the audience notice about the way your calm body moves, the way you breathe, the expression on your face, and your posture? What words, if any, would the actress say, and what would her calm tone sound like?

Take a moment and write out this vision. For me, I'd have soft eyes, melted shoulders. Calm me also wouldn't be talking. Just breathing and thinking about the warm air tickling the sides of my nostrils. What does calm look like for you? Parents have used words like *still*, *smiling*, *swaying*, *relaxed*, and *openhanded*.

2. *Why Is Getting Calm Important to You?*

Connect to what makes this work matter. What could getting to calm make possible for you? Your individual reason will motivate you to consider de-escalation when your body is screaming at you to ramp it up. Maybe calm is important so your child will feel safe to be their full self with you and more willing to tell the truth. Or is it because you want your child to like themself, and that might not be possible when they can sense they infuriate you?

3. *When Is It Hardest to Stay Calm?*

Think about the *most irritating* situation for you. That behavior that brings up visceral disgust or rage or hopelessness in you. The last time you lost your cool with your child. What led up to it? Where were you? What was your child doing?

Choose one scenario where it's most difficult to stay calm and describe it. The more specific you are about an unacceptable moment and the way you poorly handle it, the easier it will be to recognize the danger zone and shift how you show up in the future. This is a version of you that might react in a way you feel sad or ashamed about. Be curious rather than judge yourself.

4. *How Does Your Body Signal That You Are Heading out of the Calm Zone and into the Raging-Bull Zone?*

How do annoyance, rage, disappointment, and overwhelm show up in your body? Picture that moment you just wrote down. Where do you feel the upset in your body? For many, rage has a memorable sensation. Moms have described it as:

"Feeling trapped."
"My whole sensory system is throbbing."
"Fiery hot flames engulfing my body."
"Tightness in my chest and belly."
"Crackling electricity in my bones."

"Heart racing."

"A flood of heat."

"Feeling frozen and foggy."

Intense emotions are a normal part of parenting. You are doing holy work to allow those emotions to come, be felt, and then eventually recede so you can come back to calm.

5. What Negative Thoughts Happen?

You know those science fiction movies where the space station is minutes from self-destruction and the automated voice keeps repeating, "Mayday, Mayday. Detonation in two minutes and thirty-four seconds . . . Mayday, Mayday. Detonation in two minutes and thirty-three seconds"?

That petrifying announcement does not help the hero determine what to do. It causes more stress. You've got the same thing happening in your brain. Pause to imagine your mind's inner landscape during your worst parenting moments. The thought that plagues you during stressful moments is likely the fear you uncovered from chapter 4. Or maybe it's a snide declaration, like:

"Once again, this child is trying to manipulate me."

"Can nothing ever be easy with this kid?"

"I'm the wrong parent for this brat."

We'll discuss changing your thoughts more in chapters 14 and 15 but for now, notice your negative ones. This is important reflection work. You are gathering hidden intelligence about what is happening in the present so the future can be different.

Technique 2: Understand Your Brain's Role in Calming Down

Let's step back and review a teensy bit of brain physiology—specifically the two processing centers of your brain.

Dr. Daniel Siegel, author of *The Whole-Brain Child*, uses a hand model to illustrate the prefrontal cortex and amygdala and the role they each play in your behavior under pressure.[1]

Make a fist with your thumb inside, like this:

A calm brain

The thoughtful, relationship-nurturing part of your brain is the prefrontal cortex (symbolized here as the knuckles of your fingers). It controls impulses, emotional regulation, intuition, and empathy. The prefrontal cortex makes attuned communication possible. It's where your brain lights up when you're calm. It's also the part that is very underdeveloped in children. The prefrontal cortex is supposed to monitor the amygdala . . . unless you've "flipped your lid," as Dr. Siegel describes it.

Open your fist but keep the thumb bent against your palm.

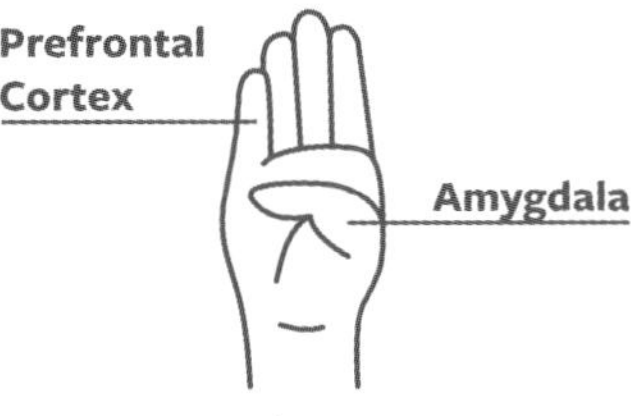

Know when you've flipped your lid!

The thumb is your amygdala. The amygdala is the oldest part of your brain and the first portion to develop in infants. The least evolved. It's prehistoric. The amygdala engages with the body in sensations, not conscious thoughts. It has one priority—survival. If it could speak, it would do so in caveman verbs with exclamation points. *"Run! Hit! Scream!"* It's an unsophisticated threat-detection system.

You don't nurture relationships when your amygdala is in charge. When you feel overwhelmed or flooded, you've temporarily lost connection with your rational-thinking brain. Unfortunately, your high alert, reactionary primal brain (amygdala) is doing the (poor) thinking.

This is optimal when a bobcat attacks you on a hike. You don't need the prefrontal cortex slowing you down to identify the kind of cat or whether it's young or old. You just need to make your body as large as possible and back away slowly and deliberately.* It's your amygdala's job to get your body to move. Not to reflect or assess.

You can recalibrate your brain's sensitive threat-detection system (*"You dumped out the entire box of cereal! What were you thinking?!"*) through the process of getting out of your thoughts and into the sensations of your body (*"My chest feels tight and hot"*). Being witnessed with compassion helps the body feel safe again.

Getting triggered by your kid is your mammalian body skillfully flipping into survival mode. Your system automatically senses and prepares to deal with danger without any conscious thought on your part. You can't think yourself out of feeling triggered because no thinking is possible. Remember, you've flipped your lid!

In a conflict, you will need to soothe and stall the amygdala with time and movement (imagine me closing my hand slowly back into that calm fist) so the thinking part of your brain has time to come back online. You can do that by slowing everything down to tune in to your body's signals. This gives you the power to choose your response instead of reacting automatically.

Technique 3: The Sensory Check-In

Reading the thermostat of a boiling hot tub stops you from jumping in and scalding yourself. The sensory check-in helps you gather vital

* Never run from a bobcat.

information about your current state before you act unconsciously. It gives you the space to slow down and shift your energy. It aids in self-fluency. Part of learning to come back to calm is about raising your attunement to yourself. To notice, like a caring friend, when something is off.

Observe two spectacular universes within you: your body and your mind. The weather in your body and your mind are a gauge for where you are on the spectrum of calm to raging. This self-reading indicates what you have available to contribute to your child's emotional state.

Check in with your mind and body. Where are you on each sensory line? Give yourself a number.

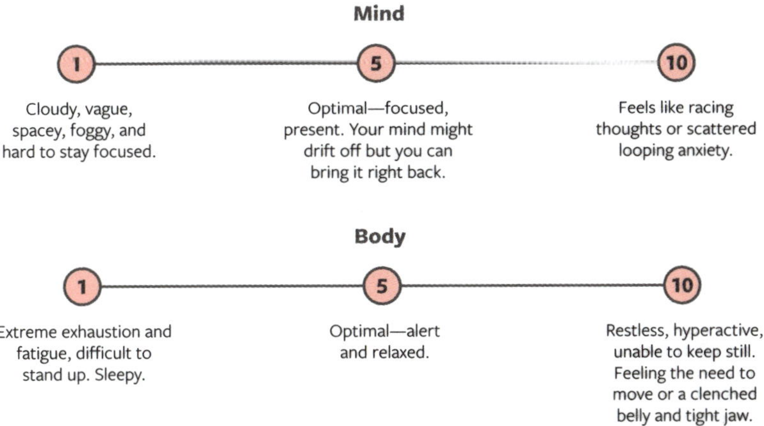

Whatever your numbers are, it's okay. You are simply gathering data, checking in with the soft animal of your body (and maybe letting your inner child be seen). In this book, you will learn exercises for moving to the middle of that range.

A sensory check-in interrupts all the automatic sequences in your brain. It alerts you to your subconscious spamming spyware running in the background, corroding your peace. It gives you an opportunity to choose a new path of thought. During a sensory check-in, ask yourself:

- How are things going in my body?
- Is my breathing quick or slow? Shallow or deep?
- Where do I feel aches and pains? Or a relaxed ease?
- What's the weather in my stomach like?
- What thoughts have I been thinking?

Technique 4: Expand the Conscious Pause

Thirty years ago, Stephen Covey wrote about the elusive space that exists between an irritating stimulus and our response.[2] That space is the moment *after* your child spills paint on the carpet (even though you clearly said to keep the art supplies outside) but *before* your reaction—be it screaming or a deep, cathartic exhale. It's the nanosecond *after* the involuntary thought pops into your head, like "This kid is trying to destroy my house," but *before* the new belief you are practicing that "we have years to develop roommate skills. Right now we are working on keeping paint outside."

This space is the conscious pause. Your conscious pause gives you the power of choice. The goal is to expand the stretch of time between a triggering event and your response to it. A conscious pause can be as short as thirty *seconds*, or maybe you need thirty *minutes* before your fangs retract. Take enough time to give your sentient, wise, compassionate-thinking brain what it needs to come back online and be the one thinking.

When you expand your conscious pause and wait before you act or speak, you are less likely to react out of habit or history. You won't yell or hit back just because that's what was done to you.

I used the conscious pause on a phone call with my college-aged Spicy One last week. She FaceTimed me while walking across campus and squealed into the phone, "I've finished my classes for the week. Now I'm gonna jumpygym!"

I replied, "What's that, honey, jumpygym?" (I was excitedly putting my earbuds in. My baby was calling!)

CONSCIOUS PAUSE EXERCISE: THE 60-SECOND HAND MEDITATION[3]

(To listen to me read this meditation to you in my sexiest mom voice, scan this QR code.)

Set down anything you are holding. With empty hands, begin to rub the fingers of one hand across the palms and fingers of the other hand, more slowly than you may want to.

As you drag one hand across the other, bring your full attention to the sensations in your finger pads and the sides of the fingers and the palms of your hand.

Notice each ridge and wrinkle. Other thoughts will come in; just let them glide by like leaves on a stream and come back to your job of paying attention to the sensation of your hands.

Your mind will wander; you just re-command it to come back to noticing the feel of your skin gliding across your skin.

Just the tingle and sensation of skin dragging across skin.

Something might distract you. There's no judgment needed. You just come back to the sensation of fingers running across your palm, maybe a slight smile on your lips, as you see and feel your hands like you haven't ever seen them before, not like they are in this moment. Each time your mind wanders, recommit yourself to the task of being with your hands.

As you near the end of the meditation, you can bring your hands up to one of your ears and listen to the whisper of your fingers gliding across each other. Now you are using three senses—sight, touch, and hearing—to invite yourself even deeper into this moment.

In the time it took to read that, you just did the hand meditation for sixty seconds!

Her temper flared, and she spat, “Ugh, I can’t deal with you right now.” She finds my trouble hearing irritating when she’s on the move. And she’s often on the move.

Because of the work you and I are doing right now, I was able to take a conscious pause. Rather than snarl back, “Can you be patient for once?! I never get to talk to you, and when I do, you are rude!” I exhaled while counting down from five. Then I replied warmly, “Oh, okay. Well, call me back at a better time. I love you.” Eruption averted. Limit set with connection still intact.

The conscious pause gives you a liminal space where you can observe your feelings. Maybe even allow yourself to feel them rather than stuff them down only to vomit them out later on your loved ones. During the conscious pause, note that your only job is to cultivate your *energy*—not to deliver some award-winning *response* to your struggling child.

What would shift for the better in your family if the only thing that changed was you expanding your conscious pause?

Word to the wise: This skill develops over repeated episodes of *failing* to hold a conscious pause. Fun!

Like an emotional muscle, self-regulation must be built over time. Start with religiously taking a three-second pause in the neutral moments. Literally counting down “three Mississippi, two Mississippi, one Mississippi” before responding to a request for juice. Then expand that time and add some of the other ideas below.

Practicing makes it easier to access this skill in the hard times.

Your conscious pause is not gritting your teeth or holding your breath passively. If you need something to focus on, one way to expand your conscious pause is to do a body check-in like the following hand meditation or the fingertip exercise in the next chapter.

How was that for you? Some find the 60-Second Hand Meditation peaceful. Others notice a million thoughts—their brain doing everything but focusing on their hands. Maybe your mind was screaming out thoughts ("Ooh, this is cool" or "Ooh, am I doing it wrong?"). Or maybe you felt an immediate relaxation. It takes effort to stay focused for a full minute.

Still other adult Spicy Ones find the dragging of fingers across skin irritating.* A moving meditation, like any intentional stillness of the mind, is not easy. Part of creating a new habit is noticing where you're falling off or giving up and coming back to it without criticizing yourself. No big deal. Try again. Give yourself little micro chances to stay focused on your hands or body.

Good news for failures! Each time you guide your wayward stallion of a brain back to the task at hand, even as it tries to wander, you are training your brain to flit back to this state of presence more easily. Growth in calming yourself comes from observing your brain going off the path and recommitting yourself to the exercise. Failing at any of these one-minute sensory exercises I share is the right way of doing it. You are training a meandering beast. Repetition (and recommitting when you fail) builds your ability to more quickly shift your thinking from a negative thought to a positive one.

Resetting your brain with a conscious pause helps to bring peace. It's like closing all the open tabs of your computer and rebooting. You become aware of the unhelpful ideas you were unconsciously meditating on (that often lead to yelling) and get to move forward with a deliberate calming thought.** It helps you get *out* of the autopilot of habitual behaviors and ingrained responses. It leads to

---

* If that's you, there are a million other ways to conduct a one-minute body check-in. Try modifying the meditation and squeezing your left arm with your right hand, starting at your left wrist. Inch by inch, squeeze your way up the arm, tightening and releasing your grip on your arm. Squeezing and releasing. Invite all your attention to focus on the sensation of skin and bone being pressed together and then the resulting release of letting go. Repeat on the other arm with the opposite hand.

** You are increasing your mindsight. Mindsight is the human capacity to perceive your own mind and that of others. Mindsight is the focused attention you are doing with your body check-in that helps you notice the internal workings of your own brain.

observing the emotions you are experiencing rather than being overwhelmed by them.

Technique 5: Marinate in a Calming Metaphor

When co-regulating, it's helpful to choose a calming metaphor to live within no matter the external conflict. An idea that gives life. An image that resources rather than depletes you. So many people unknowingly find themselves rehearsing violent metaphors, like "This kid and I are at war" or "I'm sick of being locked in battle with this kid." One mom working with me said, "I'm in the gladiator ring every day." That violent metaphor turned her into a warrior bent on subduing her child at all costs. War metaphors, steeped in a domination framework, will bring a sense of aggression and anxiety

PLAN YOUR CONSCIOUS PAUSE

Practice a one-minute conscious pause twice a day. This could be a sensory check-in, the 60-Second Hand Meditation, or another mindful moving exercise.* The easiest way to build this new habit is to link your pause to actions you already do during a typical day. Do you sit in the carpool lane every day? Do it before you drive away from school. Do you eat lunch every day? Do it before you open the fridge to assemble lunch. Decide now to stack your one-minute conscious pause onto an existing habit or set time on the clock.

I will practice my first conscious pause when

____.

I will practice my second conscious pause when

____.

* Google "mindful moving exercise" for lots of examples that might work better for you.

to your collaboration with your child. This leads to unneeded hostility in your spirit and theirs.

Your inner language matters. It frames your understanding of your world and your family. Words affect your ability to get back to calm. So rather than war metaphors, try on one of these images:

Shared Scuba Tank

To get certified, scuba divers must demonstrate that they can share one source of oxygen with another potentially panicked diver at the bottom of a dingy pool. (That's a hard pass from me. I failed lifeguarding class in college. They wanted me to swim ten feet down and grab a brick. Nah. I'm good.) This prepares you for if your partner's tank malfunctions and you must split your meager resources underwater. You must share your ability to breathe and stay calm with another diver.

In this metaphor, the oxygen tank is your self-regulation, filled with patience and self-kindness. You will draw from the tank before gently passing it on. Two people with only one tank. One mouthpiece.

Two scuba divers with only one tank aren't exactly in a great position. Having only one oxygen source is stressful, but a measured approach will get you through. To make it to safety, you need to breathe in deeply through the mouthpiece, then pass the oxygen, letting your partner breathe in while you slowly breathe out. It takes trust, eye contact, and attunement to pass your oxygen to someone else. Then, once again, you bring the mouthpiece back to your mouth before handing it back to your partner.

Wrestling for control of the oxygen would lead to harm. Starting the rescue by calming your own breathing allows you to pass the fresh air of regulation to your child. Your child is reading your signals to figure out whether this is a meditative scenario or catastrophic one.

Your nervous system staying calm helps them stay calm.

The Seedling

For a seed to sprout, it must first go through so much. Tomato seeds have to ferment into a moldy mess. Artichoke seeds need to freeze first to break down their tough outer shell. Some seeds require immense darkness. This not-yet period of a seed's development is uncomfortable (even stinky) but absolutely necessary to get to the miraculous growth phase. Your child, and your connected relationship with them, is a seedling thriving just below the surface.

Every time your child melts down but you stay calm and connected, their brain is being positively rewired. Their lived experience of you regulated and in control of your own body is perceived by their mirror neurons, helping them learn to eventually do the same over many repetitions. You may not see the growth for a while, but long before you witness their sprout pop through the soil, there are beautiful roots growing beneath the ground. Trust yourself. It's happening, day by day.

Sloth Mom

Remember the DMV scene from the *Zootopia* movie? The fidgety rabbit detective is in a hurry. She's trying to save a life. "We need this information immediately," she says rapidly and intensely to the sloth worker.

"Of . . . course," says the sloth worker slowly. "Let . . . me . . . just . . . get . . . a . . . pen."

I want you to respond that slowly to the Spicy One's most triggering and obnoxious demands. You are stalling while you wait for your prefrontal cortex to come back online. We can't rely on your amygdala driving the bus. A sloth mom is cuddly and available and measured, but her ability to get stuff done is lacking. Her jungle house is messy but cozy. She's not batch-cooking dinners or dressing the kids in ironed outfits. But she's smiling and calm. It's enough.

It's okay to take longer to respond to a disrespectful question. To move more slowly than a red-faced child wants you to. You must be okay letting customer service levels fall dramatically. You have a bigger responsibility than immediately tending to your disgruntled child's desires. Your sacred calling is to build a safe, trusting long-term relationship with this human.

This may mean refusing to negotiate or explain why for the hundredth time. You don't have to justify yourself for pulling over when your car is overheating. You are the car! Give yourself permission to pull over.

It's more important to cultivate your calm energy than to craft the perfect response to your child.

Save the teaching and discipline for later, once all parties are calm. All your heated communication does is send your child further into fight or flight, thereby flipping their lid. This is the moment to expand the time between incident and response. To practice your new conscious pause. Your child will have to wait while you take on this new skill.

The Spicy One won't like it, but they'll be better off for it.

CH 13: Reflection Questions

1. Define your version of calm:
   - What does your calm look like?
   - Why is getting back to calm important to you?
   - When is it hardest to choose calm? Describe the scenario.
   - How does your body signal that you are heading out of the calm zone?
   - What negative thoughts happen?
2. What was it like for you to practice the 60-Second Hand Meditation or the sensory check-in? What did you notice?

3. Which metaphor will you choose to marinate in for your calm-down journey? Circle the one that you want to hold on to and explain why:

14

Identify Your Inner Mean Girl

Sarah signed up for parent coaching because she was tired of feeling belittled and judged by others in her moms' group. Her kid was the only one who wouldn't eat at the snack table. Even when the scariest mom commanded the Spicy One, "You will eat at the table," her child "forgot" and cruised around the host's white sofa, smearing jam on a pillow. Sarah was mortified and sure they thought she was a bad mom. She wanted me to teach her to be a good mom. As she shared her story, she said things like:

- "I'm an inadequate parent."
- "I feel guilty about getting angry with my kid."
- "I'm acting like my mother, and my mother was not a good mother."

Notice who is judging this woman, dear reader?

There is a horror movie where the main character calls 911 to trace a repeated phone call from a heavy breather. After a pause, the operator replies, "Ma'am, the call is coming from inside the house!"

Often, when we feel judged by others for how we parent or for our child's behavior, "the call is coming from inside the house." We are judging ourselves. So much of the pain and stress of raising a neurodivergent or an intensely disobedient kid is an internal battle of self-sabotage.

The concept of bringing awareness to the automatic thoughts passively broadcast in your head—to actively choose to think helpful thoughts—is a cornerstone in parenting, personal development, mental wellness, and all-around life flourishing. My work teaching moms to recondition their thought life and quiet the influence of the vicious inner mean girl is based in part on the work of Shirzad Chamine, author of *Positive Intelligence*.* But once you learn this principle, you'll see it everywhere.

The inner mean girl is that exhausting, critical inner voice of yours that observes and analyzes everything you (and others) say or do. She categorizes everyone and everything in your life as either good or bad. Acceptable or unacceptable. Humiliating or worthy of great praise. She is a black-and-white thinker, constantly berating you: "Why can't you get this parenting thing right?" or "What is wrong with your child?" She throws your past mistakes and current struggles in your face as proof that you are not enough.

Your inner mean girl causes more exhaustion and hopelessness than the Spicy One ever could.

News flash! You are not the egoic voice in your head narrating and judging absolutely everything. You are the one listening to her. Your inner mean girl is your biggest source of resistance on this parenting journey. She appears to want to keep you safe and comfortable. But

---

* Positive intelligence is not the same as toxic positivity, that knee-jerk pull toward looking for and talking about the bright side no matter how painful or tragic the present is. Growing up with a parent who has toxic positivity is brutal. They leave no room for exploring the shadows of life that bring self-knowledge and make the sunny times even brighter.

she chains you to your old habits, outdated coping skills, and harsh ways of assessing yourself and your child.

The inner mean girl is a coping mechanism from childhood that you don't need anymore. Old programming that needs updating. This habitual pull to the negative gets in the way of connecting with your child. Your inner mean girl is often well disguised. You might not even realize you are judging your child through her eyes. But you'll know she's here by the stench of her emotional farts: stinky stress, anxiety, and guilt. She's the part of you that keeps marinating in negative emotions long after your child erupts at you and is ready for snuggles.

When you are under her influence, your body feels heavier, and your hands are clenched along with your jaw, neck, and belly. Try checking in with your body the next time you notice your thoughts sounding critical or unkind. Observe the tightness of your rib cage or the cramp in your stomach. Where exactly you carry her caustic weight will be unique to you. Be a student of your body's cues. Your internal listening is the first alert system to resetting your thoughts and mindfully choosing the way forward with compassion.

When you turn down the inner mean girl's critical chatter, everything improves. The words and tone you use with the Spicy One become more encouraging and useful. As your internal landscape grows less hostile, your outer reality shifts with it. That's because your inner voice determines how you talk to your child.

And how you talk to your child becomes how they talk to themself.

Let me repeat.

The words you speak quietly to yourself influence how you speak loudly to your child.

And how you speak to your child becomes their inner voice. The way you look at your child changes your child. Your private perspective on your child is potent. Let it be steeped in optimism and resourcefulness so you positively impact your child's lifelong self-concept!

You can no longer afford to be your own worst enemy. It's time to stop your inner mean girl's criticism and negativity from harming your child . . . or yourself.

But how?

Step 1: Identify Your Inner Mean Girl (IMG)

Deflate the IMG's power over your parenting by becoming aware of her go-to script.

How does your IMG routinely judge you or the Spicy One? Do you hear yourself say things like the following?

- "My child is a bad friend."
- "I'm not capable of helping this kid learn how to calm themself down."
- "I didn't do that right. Other mothers wouldn't lose their cool like that."

The ways we humans get in our own way are rarely that innovative. There are universal critical inner personalities that work against us. For example:

- The Perfectionist says, "You aren't parenting well enough."
- The Anxious Auntie says, "Your kid is too much."
- The Star Performer says, "You are messing it up."
- The Puppet Mistress says, "Nothing will be okay if you aren't in charge."

Let's pinpoint how you routinely sabotage your own happiness and negate your worth as a parent.*

* In his book *Positive Intelligence*, Chamine writes about nine inner critics that sabotage your happiness. His saboteurs dovetail nicely with the nine deep-seated fears of each type in the Enneagram, a personality test that divides folks into nine categories based on their core wounding and deepest desires. My favorite source for an explanation of the nine types of the Enneagram is Ian Morgan Cron and

KNOW THINE ENEMY

Pause now to read through each of the nine IMG descriptions in the appendix. Check the statements that match the harsh thoughts ricocheting in your head. Based on those results, choose the top three meanies who most often steal your peace:

- Perfectionist
- People Pleaser
- Star Performer
- Martyr
- Logical Learner
- Anxious Auntie
- Impatient Princess
- Puppet Mistress
- Escape Artist

Your IMG will take your greatest strengths and convert them into weaknesses. Are you naturally organized? The IMG will make you obsess more about the state of your child's room than their positive sense of self. Do you care about others' feelings? The IMG will have you taking responsibility for others' emotions rather than choosing your own state of being. The IMG abuses your unique powers by either overusing them or inserting them at inappropriate times. Her negative interpretations are not objectively true.

Step 2: Notice Your Toxic Friend's Influence

Have you ever stayed in a hurtful friendship way longer than made sense?

I made a friend in my Spicy One's weekly toddler playgroup. Christine was stylish and sophisticated. I wanted to be like her. The

---

Suzanne Stabile, *The Road Back to You: An Enneagram Journey to Self-Discovery* (IVP, 2016). I've renamed the nine archetypes to capture how they make parenting extremely difficult.

only downside was her habit of lobbing barely perceptible passive-aggressive comments, like "Look at you wearing jean on jean. Is that back in style?" and "Wow. You let your kids eat saltines. I'm too health-conscious to resort to that." When I declined to buy expensive cosmetics from her multilevel marketing company, she called me selfish for not supporting a friend's business. In the flurry of chasing preschoolers around, I ignored the name-calling. The relationship felt familiar to me. My mother had also called me selfish.

Then one evening when we were co-planning a preschool fund-raiser, Christine yelled at me in front of other people . . . in my home. Seeing the other ladies' surprised faces shifted something inside me. Their discomfort with her disrespect toward me helped me see it too.

Once you see it, don't allow your inner mean girl to disrespect you any longer. Her reign of nasty is coming to an end. You can break up with her by simply noticing her. You notice her by practicing your conscious pause a few times a day. This quieting of yourself to check in and observe your thinking (and your body's needs) changes everything!

WHAT'S MORE IMPORTANT FOR YOUR PARENTING PEACE—LESS NEGATIVE THINKING OR MORE POSITIVE THINKING?

Question: If you have a choice between thinking more positive thoughts about the Spicy One or reducing your negative ones, which effort would most improve your parenting?

Answer: The bigger bang for your buck is to reduce your negative thinking.[1] Negative and positive thinking happen in two entirely different regions of the brain. Negative thoughts originate in the same parts of your brain that focus on physical or emotional survival. That's not a good location to parent from. Less survival-brain activity means a greater sense of well-being for mom. Take negative thoughts captive.

CONSCIOUS PAUSE EXERCISE: THE FINGERTIP EXERCISE

With one hand, tap your thumb to each finger in a soothing rhythm while thinking a different prayer for each finger combination. Pause to notice the sensation of the pressure of your fingertips against each other and the effect of each phrase on your body. Say these blessings to yourself or just focus on the sensations.

- Thumb to pointer finger: "God bless you."
- Thumb to middle finger: "Peace be with you."
- Thumb to ring finger: "I love you."
- Thumb to pinkie finger: "Have mercy on me."
- Repeat!

Under the spell of exasperation with the Spicy One, let this ritual help you find your way back to affection.

You are building the habit of noticing negative thinking and then switching to resourceful thoughts. Practice observing your mind at low-stakes moments—on the toilet, during bathtime, while filling water bottles, or standing in the line at the grocery store. This creates the muscle memory needed to make the flip in more tumultuous times when you desperately need compassionate thoughts.

You'll be surprised how often you consciously pause only to notice that your thinking was being commandeered by the inner mean girl. You thought you were just chopping carrots, but your People Pleaser was telling you, "If I make this meal perfect, my family will behave at the table" or some other hogwash.

The brain is a calorie-saving organ. It sets up macros: "When I see this, I think this. Then I feel this, so I do this." Becoming aware of your IMG requires interrupting this old pattern to build new neural pathways. Your brain doesn't necessarily like this. It may send out some stress hormones to warn you, "You don't know how to do this so it's best not to try." Good old resistance. It's a positive sign that you are onto something big!

CH 14: Reflection Questions

1. How did you identify your top three inner mean girls? What part of the description in the appendix resonated with you? Why might that trait be unhelpful to your parenting?
2. Notice your inner mean girl's influence: What's one example of your IMG sabotaging your parenting?
   - Describe the challenging situation.
   - What did your inner mean girl say to you at that moment?
   - How did her critical voice make things worse?
   - What sensations did you feel in your body when she was talking to you?
   - How did you respond to the situation because of what she said?

15

Unfriend Your Inner Mean Girl

I hat my mom."

The carefully written but misspelled note lay forgotten on my six-year-old's bedside table. Setting her clean laundry down, I read it like a gut punch.

Scanning the childlike letters might not have upset a more optimistic mother. "Look at her practicing writing!" or "Wow, so young and already using journaling to work through her emotions." But my Star Performer inner mean girl ripped into me, saying, "People would lose respect for your parenting if they knew your daughter thought that."

Reading the words hardened a part of me. The phrase did not feel innocent or out of the mouths of babes. It was another sign of my failure to parent this child well.

I was angry but also convicted. Was she just mirroring my dark energy back to me? Days before, I had whispered to a friend at the park, "I love her, but I don't have to like her," as my daughter gleefully scrambled over monkey bars. My friend nodded wide-eyed, her concern evident. I carried on, the words hissing out like air from a flat tire. "I would never let anyone else treat me the way she treats me."

Meanwhile, my daughter laughed as she beckoned a new friend to try the monkey bars. "She's not a nice person," I muttered almost to myself as my kid hung upside down, shouting, "Mom, look what I can do but my friend can't!"

Later that night, I stared at the ceiling, thinking, "You are not a good mom. You shouldn't talk about your child like that. You don't know what you are doing. This shouldn't be such a struggle."

Imagine how life with my daughter might have improved sooner if, instead of rehearsing corrosive thoughts, I spoke to myself with a compassionate inner voice. How my suffering would have subsided if I had been able to think, "You are going through a tough season, but there is nothing wrong with you or your child. You are lovable and so is she, regardless of your behavior."

I needed to grow my capacity for positive response (CPR).

CPR is your ability to remain calm, clear-headed, stress-free, and optimistic even in the midst of handling huge disappointments, triggers, and all the other challenges of being in charge of a Spicy One. Strong CPR muscles mean your brain works for you, not against you, in high-pressure parenting moments.

Consider two different moms raising relentlessly complaining Eeyore-like children. These two lucky ladies will respond differently according to their CPR. One with hopelessness and disappointment: "Why must I have the one child who hates the beach?!" The other with lighthearted humor and a twinkle in her eye: "Bless this little curmudgeon I'm raising. Only my little spoilsport would be enraged by sand at the beach!"

The difference is their capacity for positive response.

Most of us don't naturally skip to the brightest, most merciful interpretation of life events. That's fine. You can build this skill. Listen, you must lift weights and walk routinely to reach *physical* fitness, so why shouldn't there be daily work to build positive *mental* fitness?* To grow your CPR muscles is simple but not easy.

Your path to true transformation is not just to change the circumstances (which aren't always within your grasp) but to change your thinking (which is solely up to you). I'm going to show you how to reinforce neural pathways associated with discernment and compassion.

There are four steps for increasing your capacity for positive response—and you already completed two of them in the previous chapter! Look at you.

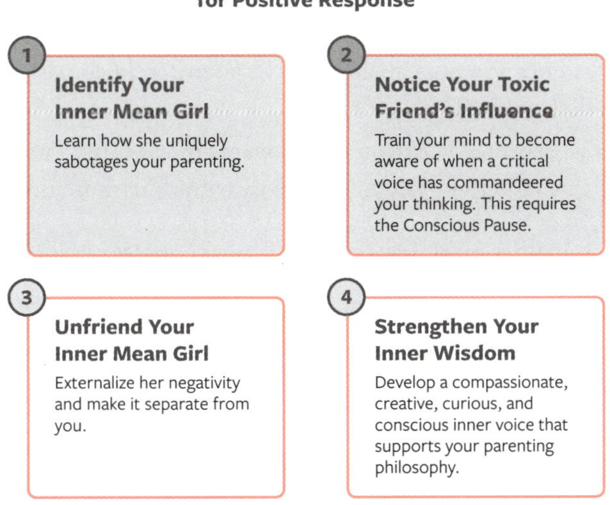

Step 3: Unfriend Your Inner Mean Girl

"How does one unfriend their inner mean girl?" you may be asking. You are already doing it! You are now aware of her. That is half the

* The overall conclusion of an analysis of over two hundred different scientific studies was that the more adept someone is at shifting their thoughts from critical ones to resourceful ones, the greater their success in work, marriage, health, friendships, and social and creative domains (Chamine, *Positive Intelligence*, 8). So why not parenting—one of the most complex relationships you will ever find yourself in?

work. You have identified her and started studying her predictable playbook in the appendix. Noticing her anxious chatter unlocks the power to change it. Now comes the effort of training your mind to separate your identity from her nasty thinking.

After practicing *noticing* your inner mean girl, it's time to start externalizing her thoughts!* Externalizing means making her voice separate from you. It turns out you aren't anxious. You have an anxious part of you.

You get to stop identifying as the one thinking negative thoughts and realize that it's just one part of you, separate from your wisest, most grounded parts.

Here's an example of how to externalize:

> Instead of: "I'm not capable of helping my child coexist with other humans."
>
> Think: "My Star Performer IMG wants me to think I'm not capable of helping my child coexist with other humans."

Notice the difference? Try saying this next couplet out loud.

* Chamine refers to this as weakening your saboteur in *Positive Intelligence* (51–52).

Instead of: "I'm a failure when it comes to disciplining my child."

Try: "My Anxious Auntie IMG thinks I'm a failure when I try to discipline my child."

What do you notice about the impact of this grammar shift? As the philosopher Janet Jackson says, "Who's that thinking those nasty thoughts?"[1] The inner mean girl is—not you!*

Instead of: "I'm not 'doing parenting right.'"

Say out loud: "My inner mean girl is telling me that there is a right way to parent in this situation, and she thinks I'm not 'doing it right.'"

Your job is to move the thought from first person "I" to third person "she."

Instead of: "I'm messing up this kid."

Think: "My inner critic is telling me I'm messing up this kid."

Instead of: "This child will resent me just like I do my own parents."

Say: "My Anxious Auntie wants me to worry that my child will resent me."

When you externalize, it gets easier to separate yourself from the constant judgmental teleprompter in your head.

Make your IMG the active subject of every single sentence you tell yourself about your fears. Otherwise, after a couple sentences, you will find yourself drifting right back to taking credit for the negative thinking, like this:

* This technique gels well with internal family systems (IFS), which sees each person as a system of protective and wounded parts led by a core self. It teaches that the mind is naturally multiple—like a family of parts (e.g., bratty teenager, big sister)—each with helpful or unhelpful roles shaped by past survival needs.

"My inner mean girl thinks I'm a bad mom for not spending the day with my family. I feel bad for choosing my happiness over a shared experience."

That second sentence should be externalized like this: "*My inner mean girl wants me to* feel bad for choosing my happiness."

One client imagines her IMG as a gnarled old grandmother in black, rocking in a chair in the corner, shaking her fist, and shrieking, "They are all going to laugh at you!" Another client imagines her IMG as a one-inch version of her overcritical father. The little guy in her head is wearing army fatigues even though her dad was never in the service. He stands inside a trash can, yelling, "You can do better than that!"

You don't need to hate your IMG *or* debate her. No need to gather up some voracious anger to scare her away. Like any other part of you, she deserves compassion and a place to be heard. And yet . . . she is not fit to lead you anywhere but toward heartache. Try saying, "No, thank you, IMG. I've got this," to her fears and complaints.

Step 4: Strengthen Your Inner Wisdom by Calling In Your Highest Self

It's time to lean into the part of you that brings more compassion, curiosity, and creativity to your parenting. This means cultivating your intuition or inner knowing. But how?

Call In Your Highest Self

Your highest self is the version of you that can rise with the tides and resist getting carried away by the emotional flood of a meltdown. The part of you that is at peace regardless of how messy the house is or how late your partner is getting home. Imagine the oldest, wisest, most compassionate part of you. This is the part infused with the Holy Spirit. She's always believed that you are enough. She is immune to the lies of the IMG.

Your highest self is you when you find the most generous explanation for tough moments. She is constantly curious, intrepidly creative, and conscious about her choices. She wants more for you but sees the beauty in what already is. She sees you as better than how you sometimes show up. It's that part of you that has a deeper knowing. That says, "I can." That says, "I deserve goodness." That says, "I long for something, and I am worthy of pursuing it."

The more you can tune in to the intuitive voice of your highest self, the more you can be guided to parent by the merciful parts of you that cheer you on rather than judge. Think about the last time a beloved friend was down on themself and that glorious pep talk that spilled out of you to shore her up. Or the version of you that stands at the doorway of your sleeping child and clearly sees their innocence and beauty. That's your highest self.

Your highest-self perspective on parenting challenges is that they are either a gift or an opportunity to develop a gift. Your highest self knows that your Spicy One is the greatest thing that's ever happened to you. That this rascal is happening *for* you, not *to* you. That this larger-than-life child presents a death-defying opportunity for intense personal growth.

When you are thinking from your highest self, you have access to four powers of an effective parent, and you can tap into those powers at any moment to meet any challenge. The four superpowers[2] are

1. Curiosity—wondering what's underneath this moment instead of demanding it change or be fixed.
2. Compassion—giving oodles of grace to everyone, including yourself.
3. Creativity—conjuring up new perspectives and outside-the-box solutions.
4. Consciousness—operating out of your values rather than doing what fear dictates. Focusing on the big picture rather than the present skirmish.

Ten years ago, I gathered my daughter and three other thirteen-year-old girls with their moms for a coming-of-age getaway in Lake Arrowhead.

My Puppet Mistress inner mean girl immediately flared up like those inflatable tube goons on the side of the road, beckoning drivers into used-car lots. She wanted me to know, "You need to maximize this weekend! For it to be a valuable experience, there is a right way to do it, and it is all up to me."

I was already years into growing my CPR, so I decided to pause and ground into my highest self.

I imagine my highest self as Octavia Spencer in the movie *The Shack*, playing the role of God. She's affectionate, caring, and so alive to the moment. She's up for whatever. Channeling her, I loosened my grip on how the weekend *had* to go and became curious about how it *could* go. When I asked the other women what they wanted from the weekend, they had so many great ideas, like inviting each of the girls to share three songs they love to make a group playlist we could karaoke to.

I leaned into compassion, remembering what it was like to turn thirteen. My creativity came online when there was no longer one right or best way. (What if we pasted posters up on the wall for each girl where everyone could write affirmations we would read aloud on the last day? What if we assigned breakfast-cooking to the girls with a fun recipe they could follow and then serve the moms?) And I was conscious that *community* and *celebration* were my most important values here—not *performance*.

It feels different when you let the highest self lead your thinking during a parenting conflict. Notice your internal weather when you're accessing your wisdom. There's a relaxed spaciousness in the body. You might notice open hands, soft eyes, melted jaws, or a calm belly. Remember that feeling in your body. This expansive state of being is where your best parenting decisions come from. Chase that sensation rather than making do with the lethargic and cramped experience of listening to your inner mean girl.

Speak Kindly to Yourself

Do you have a Scripture or positive thought you cling to when things get hard? This could be a metaphor from chapter 13 like "I am a sloth mom." Or a pronouncement like "This too shall pass." Or maybe you remind yourself to *breathe*. As you lower the volume of the incessant inner mean girl's negativity, you will need to replace her vitriol with kinder words. See examples in the appendix for each IMG.

- Rather than saying, "My kid is so disrespectful," you can say, "This child is trying to communicate something to me."

CONSCIOUS PAUSE EXERCISE: COMFORTING THOUGHTS

Look through the blessings below, noticing what it feels like in your body to read your favorite one slowly out loud. Take it one step further and gaze with full sincerity into your eyes in the mirror, tenderly saying one of these phrases to yourself. If the idea of that makes you shudder or tear up, this one is for you! Write it on your mirror with a dry-erase marker.

- "I am giving myself permission to take the time I need to reset myself."
- "Parenting feels hard because it is hard, not because I'm doing something wrong."
- "Behold the One beholding me and smiling. I am not alone."[3]
- "I was made for such a time as this."
- "I care about your suffering."
- "All behavior is communication. Well done for listening."
- "If I can teach bad habits, I can teach good ones."
- "My child's struggle is not my fault. They're trying so hard, just like me."

- Instead of "My child is trying to make my life miserable," you can plan to think, "My child needs me. This is not personal."
- Instead of "I can't tolerate her upset," you can remind yourself, "I can let her feel this without fixing it."

Do you feel the difference in the curses versus blessings of these thoughts? Don't make me get out those famous photos from Dr. Emoto's water experiment, where the water changes its molecular structure depending on the emotional energy of the *words* people speak over it. Water exposed to positive words formed beautiful, symmetrical crystalline structures when frozen, while water exposed to negative words formed disorganized, asymmetrical patterns. You are made of water! So instead of "If I was a good mother, they would be happy," decide to think, "It's normal for kids to whine when they are overwhelmed. We are doing just fine."

When all else fails, cling to any scraps of humor you can muster about the situation. How can you not laugh at the irony of your leaning so hard into healing your junk only to likely create more opposite-style issues for your child to take to their own therapist one day? You can't win! So, can we laugh at how wonky and hard parenting is?

Negative thinking leads to poor decision-making in parenting.* It's easier to let distressing judgments go when you aren't claiming them as your own. Raising a Spicy One gets so much easier when your capacity for positive reaction gets strong enough to hold a compassionate mindset.

* According to PVD Psychological Associates, "When your brain is flooded with emotionally charged negative thoughts, your limbic system (the older, less evolved reptilian brain) takes over. Then your prefrontal cortex which is used for cognitive functioning, empathizing with others and logic has precious energy diverted away from it. As a result, you cannot think as clearly," accessed April 12, 2025, https://pvdpsych.com/5-ways-that-negativity-affects-brain-chemistry-and-what-to-do/#:~:text=When%20you%20have%20emotionally%20charged,you%20cannot%20think%20as%20 clearly.

CH 15: Reflection Questions

1. Unfriend your inner mean girl: Bring to mind one mortifying parenting moment where your inner mean girl was triggered. What was the negative thought she brought to your mind? Rephrase that thought into the third person ("she" instead of "I"; "her" instead of "me") to make it separate from you, and write it down. What words do you need to think to externalize it?
2. Strengthen your inner wisdom: If you think back to a golden moment of your parenting, a time when you were embodying your highest self, what do you notice about her? What generous things does your highest self say about both you and your Spicy One? Write out three compassionate truths for each of you.

16

Welcome Everyone's Big Feelings by Honoring the Body

We've spent many pages shifting your perspective, beliefs, and imagery. But what about shifting how you show up in your body to adapt to the intensity? How to harness your physical power to stay calm amid the chaos?

Your body can sense things unspoken, through nonverbal cues, auditory tone changes, and pressure changes on your skin. For better or worse, your senses are heightened in the presence of someone with ferociously big feelings. Noticing this data and developing a felt sense of safety in your body can help you stay more resourceful in emotional situations that previously overwhelmed you.

A safe body primes a brain to respond with more compassion and creativity (like "Hey, let's try whisper-talking to this shouting child"). Here are some techniques to help you embody the parent you want to be.

Move, Dang It!

Your child is a stressor in your life. But your ability to stay calm (and healthy) comes *less* from handling your child (the stressor) well and *more* from how you handle the resulting stress.

Stress transmutes into trauma when your movement is restricted. Whether you are trapped physically or just mentally, your immobilized body registers the circumstance as less safe. So find your autonomy and move. Move to metabolize stress and anger so they don't build up and metastasize in your body as parenting burnout. According to authors Emily and Amelia Nagoski, movement is the way to complete the stress response cycle.[1]

To understand the stress response cycle, imagine you're on a walking tour of a Kenyan water hole when a mother rhino charges out of the bush. Your body instantly goes into survival mode—tripping its built-in alarm system. Your brain and hormones kick into gear: Adrenaline pumps blood to your muscles priming them for fast twitch movement. Stress hormones keep you powered up, and endorphins help you brush off how uncomfortable this all feels. Your heart races, you breathe faster, your muscles tighten, and you're on high alert—totally focused on the immediate situation. Your senses get sharper, and your memory zooms in on what's most useful right now.[2]

But here's the catch: Your body has to save energy for this emergency mode, so things like digestion, immune system defenses, and even growth and repair get paused.[3] All your physical resources are marshaled to evade that dangerous animal—or whatever the "threat" detected might be. This dramatic whole body and brain shift happens, whether it's a big deal (like rhino tag) or just super annoying (like when it's hot and they won't stop hanging on you and talking incessantly).

So far, only half of the stress response cycle has been initiated. The final sequence happens when you sprint away from the rhino. The pumping of your legs and arms uses up all those extra chemicals and releases you from the terror. The intense movement signals to your body that the threat is gone. The stress cycle has been completed.[4]

If you're not moving as part of your conscious pause, you aren't allowing your body to metabolize the stress of parenting. Your body is essentially still experiencing a ringing alarm for your safety, your organs swimming in a stew of hormones that cause inflammation and compound your stress.

In the book *The Body Keeps the Score*, Bessel van der Kolk illuminates the power of movement with a story. First grader Noam Saul, whose classroom was 1,500 feet away from the Twin Towers on September 11, 2001, ran for his life through the streets of Manhattan, yet he bears no long-term psychological scars.

> At the time the disaster occurred, he was able to take an active role by running away from it, thus becoming an agent in his own rescue. And once he had reached the safety of home, the alarm bells in his brain and body quieted. This freed his mind to make some sense of what had happened and even to imagine a creative alternative to what he had seen.[5]

The opposite of movement is immobilization.

> Immobilization keeps the body in a state of inescapable shock and learned helplessness. Faced with danger, people automatically secrete stress hormones to fuel resistance and escape. Brain and body are programmed to run for home, where safety can be restored and stress hormones can come to rest.[6]

When you can't or don't move, the elevated stress hormone levels essentially turn against you, "stimulating ongoing fear, depression, rage, and physical disease."[7]

Physical activity is the single most efficient strategy for completing the stress response cycle.[8] Emotion requires motion to exit the body. For your conscious pause, try to find your personal gesture of release that helps you metabolize, burn off, and honor your anger.

Try dancing, screaming, or stomping to help you to pump the brakes on your escalating nervous system.

It's important to access movement in the middle of the drama as well as after it, when the Spicy One happily seeks your lap, but you are left contemplating murder. Try different physical actions to see what is right for your body. What gestures cue your body that you are safe and beyond the stressor? Jumping jacks work, but you might also like a hidden isometric exercise like standing with your feet pushed down into the floor while also scraping your legs open. The Spicy One can't see anything, but all your muscles are working. Others prefer a weight-bearing gesture such as standing on your tiptoes like a ballerina.

Allow Controlled Destruction

Explosive kids and their wired mothers need to practice fire drills—agreed-upon action plans for when anger flares. Decide together ahead of time what's allowed. Playfully. Prep the Spicy One with "Soon we will practice what to do when your body feels a burst of anger." Invite a little excitement by whispering, "When I pinch your elbow, pretend you are so angry." Role-play how either of you will respond when you feel the rage boiling up. Maybe it's blowing out pretend birthday candles on your fingers or pushing against a wall or counting one hundred jumps. I suggest controlled destruction.

Controlled destruction is the planned, safe breaking or smashing of objects to help both kids and adults physically release big emotions from their bodies. Think cracking ice blocks with a hammer, tearing up old magazines, or doing wall push-ups until your arms shake. It helps kids work the tension and anger out of their bodies and connects them with their playful, nonjudgmental adult willing to break stuff alongside them.

Controlled destruction can be a helpful activity for an emotionally dysregulated child or their "had it up to here" adult. A child overcome with big feelings needs a physical outlet to move that intensity out of their body. So does a mommy. Tears are one universal way. Door slamming is another. Different methods will be acceptable in different homes. When you were upset as a child, what was allowed in your family? What is allowed now in your house when your child has angry energy to work through? Sometimes a warm, soapy bath isn't violent enough.

Safe expressions of anger are necessary—and different for every unique nervous system. Powerful emotions need to be metabolized through movement in order to process and move them out of the body. We must *give motion to emotion*. Experiment with cathartic movement to cling to when overwhelmed by anger. Harnessed anger is way better than unharnessed anger.

Destroying something together is a creative act of collaboration that lets your intense child feel seen and supported rather than wrong yet again.

It also affirms what their tightly wound body needs while hurting zero people.

Controlled destruction can be "heavy work" that encourages a child to move with or against resistance (like tug-of-war or pushing a weighted stroller). The goal is to engage your child's proprioceptive sense—the internal automatic body system that allows us to locate our body in space and in relation to other objects. It's how you know if you are standing on concrete or grass, or how to walk through a dark bedroom without slamming into furniture. Your child's capacity to calm down and regulate themself is improved by challenges that strengthen their body's proprioceptive sense, like stomping to loud music, sucking on a gumball, or skipping.

Swinging a bat into a pumpkin or slamming a glass jar into a billion bits inside the recycle bin (while wearing goggles) gives strong proprioceptive sensory feedback to our nervous system. A burst of sensory input does wonders to calm and regulate the brain/body. Prolonged pressure applied over a large surface area of our body can also shift the nervous system into a parasympathetic response, inviting the body to "rest and digest." Hello, weighted blankets!

WARNING: The Spicy One under the duress of a meltdown is not going to take direction from you on how to properly channel their anger. In fact, they will likely refuse any alternatives you suggest. So introduce these fierce movements at times when you are both at peace and open. Or let them witness you working through your big feelings (caused by something other than them) using controlled destruction. If they think they are catching you ripping up paper or screaming into the trees, it feels real. So go ahead and build then destroy the snowman or sandcastle together. Smash the ice. You are teaching coping skills.

Monitor the Body Budget

We each respond to the world in our own way depending on countless factors, including how we take in information through our senses, all our past experiences, and the status of what Mona Delahooke calls our *body budget*.[9]

Your best parenting decisions are based on taking into account your child's body and how it processes and experiences the world. Your child's brain is constantly and reflexively scanning their body's resources to see if they are in balance. Below consciousness, your child's nervous system is monitoring and assessing the stability of

MAKE A PLAN FOR DESTRUCTION

Scan the QR code at the end of this chapter to see a list of possible exercises in the Controlled Destruction resource on my website. Read these examples out loud during a calm, connected moment. Let the Spicy One choose the one they will try. Set a context for *when* and *how* it's appropriate to let tension out. Share what it feels like for you when big feelings come and what your body craves to do. Listen without judgment to what your child shares.

their body budget. This includes scanning for energy resources, energy drains, glucose levels, sensations from the environment, and pain.* What triggers a threat response in the body's safety-detecting system is different for every human.

When your child's body budget is depleted (for example, sleeping poorly last night combined with getting in trouble at school, and then not eating their lunch), the brain reflexively reacts with threat-response behavior. Some of that reaction can look like disobedience.

It's crucial to customize your parenting response to account for the current state of your child's body budget as well as your own. You get to make deposits in that budget, such as a meal, a hug, quiet time, firm sensory input or pressure, or the opportunity for deep sleep.

Their body budget dictates whether they behave receptively or defensively.

What if, instead of criminalizing a child's defiance (*"She spit in my face! That five-year-old is a bad girl who's going into time-out!"*), we note that her nervous system is appropriately operating out of a depleted body budget? Nothing to pathologize here. Her body is valiantly trying to protect her from a perceived threat!

In a high-struggle moment, ask yourself:

- How might this behavior be an adaptive response by my child's body or brain to subconsciously protect a body that has been overstimulated, exhausted, and stretched beyond its nutritional, developmental, and sleep reserves?
- How can I see their challenging response as a subconsciously protective stance that I can admire?

* This scanning, called neuroception, is the body's neural circuitry in charge of distinguishing whether internal sensations, situations, or people are safe, dangerous, or life-threatening. This all happens beneath awareness. See Stephen W. Porges, "Neuroception: A Subconscious System for Detecting Threats and Safety," *Zero to Three (J)* 24, no. 5 (May 2004): 19–24, https://eric.ed.gov/?id=EJ938225#:~:text=The%20term%20%22Neuroception%22%20describes%20how,a%20stranger%20as%20an%20assault.

- How can I add back to their body budget rather than get caught up in their behavior?*

You can build up the body budget through nurturing. Sleep is the number one way to increase our body budget. Sleep sets the foundation for successfully managing life at any age.

You can also help by monitoring your own body budget. Your gnawing hunger, elevated heart rate, and other signs of stress are drags on your child's body budget. You know when your child is overwhelmed. Here's some annoying news: They also know when you are overwhelmed, and it stresses them out. Your stress can be perceived by their threat-detection system as their stress, detracting from their body budget. Your depleted body budget affects your child. Boo! I hate that too. It means we parents have to take responsibility for our own microclimate in order to enhance our child's body budget.

Vocalize

At the beginning of my marriage, I interpreted my husband's humming as disrespectful. He would hum when he felt angry with me. We'd be arguing, me coming at him hard with the abrasive, irritated tone I inherited from my mother. Rather than respond harshly or say something he'd regret, he would start humming. I thought he was checking out and not caring. Then I learned that humming is a beautiful way to open up the parasympathetic branch of the autonomic nervous system. My intuitive husband, unversed in nervous system work, was calming his body so he didn't overreact!

Try creating a physical event in your body like humming or singing, which stimulates your vocal cords to calm your nervous system. Eighty percent of the reason I play pickleball is so I can scream and get this primal urge met in a somewhat socially responsible way. If

* These questions are adapted from information I gleaned from Delahooke, *Brain-Body Parenting* and used with my own children.

I swing confidently at the ball but my ball dives into the net, expect me to groan at the top of my lungs, "Aghhhhhhh!"

Yelling does a fine job of releasing frustration. The body gets to physically expel anger in a loud gust of vibrating air. Can we agree it feels delicious to yell? If you are a person with a body that likes to yell at your children, I challenge you to substitute ridiculous words, like "Got dandruff and some of its itches!" or " I will not let orange elephants make me do the two-step tango!"

Or shout some colorful but benign curse words:

"Son of a bee sting!"

"What the freaking shoot!"

"Mother of pearl!"

"Fudge nuggets!"

Cursing and the Spicy One

Recently a Spicy One was heard saying, "Who's gonna cut my *damn* pancakes?!"

In this instance, my friend's five-year-old was trying to get a laugh. But often, when he got angry, his swearing was . . . less than humorous.

I'm not here to judge how individual families approach swearing. That's a very personal decision. But here are some facts:

- Swearing is an advanced linguistic tool for communicating raw, intense emotions—be it anger, joy, appreciation, or sorrow.
- Deploying a few choice swear words has an immediate, visceral impact on the listener, which, when we are in a heightened state and just trying to make ourselves understood, *is actually* a highly effective communication tool.
- Sometimes Spicy Ones swear for their own cathartic benefit. Cursing can relieve tension, increase pain tolerance, and

efficiently intimidate someone we find threatening in the moment. It's a way to access verbal communication when they are feeling too overwhelmed to form thoughtful, kind sentences.

- Research also shows swearing helps make people stronger! In one study, participants who swore were able to keep their hands in ice water longer and had more powerful grips than those who didn't. Cyclists who cursed had more endurance.[10]

I'm not saying, *Eff it! Be a family that swears!* I *am* saying that there are legitimate reasons your intense child may find swearing to be an

CONSCIOUS PAUSE EXERCISE: VUU-ING

Try a therapeutic kind of humming. Vuu-ing* is a lovely (and undetectable to those around you) way to bring yourself back into your body and give your nervous system new information that it is safe. The effect is similar to the relief that singing or the low-pitched yoga "om" gives to the body but less observable to outsiders.

The idea is to make the sound of "vuu" on your exhale, no matter how long or short your exhale is.

Go ahead and bring your attention to your regular breathing. Inhale through your nose. As you exhale, you "vuuu" out your mouth. As your exhale ends, so does the sound. Aim to create a vibration all the way through your body to activate the vagus nerve bundle and balance out inner stress. Close your eyes now (if it's comfortable) and "vuu" three times. Take an easy full breath, and on the exhale coming from the belly make a rumbly "vuu" sound. Try five breaths of vuu-ing. Allow the vibration to resonate down in the belly and up in the chest.

* Made popular by Peter Levine, a pioneer in somatic experiencing. *Soma* is Latin for body. You are bringing conscious awareness to your body's experience.

attractive form of expression in hard times. Which, for someone already wired for intensity and integrity, may feel like *a lot of the time*!

Breathe

Breathing is crucial for cultivating a calm presence. You cannot breathe in the past or the future. Breathing can only happen now . . . in this moment. There's no greater portable technology for mindfulness than breathing. Breath control is stress control.

What do you already know about how you uniquely breathe or don't breathe when you are upset? Many of us hold our breath. We stop the flow of life-giving oxygen in an unconscious desire to get control of ourselves. That's like *not* eating when you need extra energy!

Think back to when you were growing up. What do you remember about the way your parents breathed when they were upset with you? I can picture my mom huffing out air loudly, her red curls lifting from the puff of breath expelled from her constricted lips. Especially when I interrupted her for the fourth time, asking the same question yet again.

Breathing seems so basic. Almost cliché. Yet your breath is the first thing you hold or constrict when you're under stress and need cleansing oxygen the most.

People love to say "Breathe!" or "Just take a deep breath," but that's not always helpful. When you inhale, your heart beats faster. It's activating. Inhaling quickly engages your startle reflex (picture me gasping after my son drops an ice cube down my shirt!). Taking a deep in-breath can rev you up more.

Turns out, the *exhale* is the part of breathing that actually calms you. Our heartbeat slows down on an exhalation. The exhale is when our body softens.

When you are triggered, think only about breathing—not about what initially upset you. If you ruminate on the fact that your Spicy One just did the exact opposite of what you asked them to do—while staring you in the eye—you will not even begin to calm down. There will be time to deal with the causal issues once you have cared for yourself a bit. Your mind's job during breathing is only to count—not to think.

Notice the Clench

The first time I became consciously aware of "the clench," I was in my kitchen, swiping peanut butter across multiple pieces of sourdough for an after-school snack. A gaggle of boisterous first graders were running around my living room. In and out the squeaky front door. The normal commotion of children at play squeezed my lungs tight. My heart hammered like I was in danger. I felt shaky and irritated as the screen door slammed over and over. Each bang jolted through me like a physical blow. Would the hinge break? The dog

CONSCIOUS PAUSE EXERCISE: 4-4-8 BREATHING

By exhaling for twice as long as you inhale, you spend twice as much time relaxing as you do tensing, thereby "doubling" your stress relief.

Here's how to do it: Inhale for four seconds, hold your breath for four seconds, and exhale for eight seconds.

To get the maximum relaxation, inhale through your nose and exhale through your mouth like you're gently blowing out a candle.

On each exhale, let your shoulders relax and sink down farther. And on the inhale, maintain the relaxation you created in your shoulders. Don't let the shoulders rise on the inhale; let the belly expand instead. Then, on the next exhale, let the shoulders melt even deeper.

Expert level: When you inhale, allowing your abdomen to expand (rather than contract), keep the expansion in the belly rather than your chest. Then tighten your belly on the out-breath to expel the stale air.

was barking. Would he bite? A child screamed. Was that happy or sad screaming? Was that glass breaking?

Lurching across the kitchen to grab the jelly, I felt how sucked-in my lower stomach muscles were. How tight my shoulders were. How rigid my jaw felt. My body was locked in a subconscious clench. This posture would have made sense for a "wear your bathing suit onstage" scenario, but I was no Miss America. Why was my body coiled tight like it was at the starting line for a 50-yard dash while I was making sandwiches for nondiscerning eaters?

My inner mean girl had an instant answer: "Because clenching helps us move faster, and hungry kids are upset kids!" But my highest self realized there was no actual need for hurry here. So I tried something new. I intentionally released the clench. I was still able to make the sandwiches but without the sense of urgency that previously bullied my body.

A continuous clench is the telltale sign of negating your body's needs. It makes heading toward your "red zone," or flooded state, difficult to monitor. In the middle of a meltdown (yours or the Spicy One's), ask yourself, "What is clenched right now?"

Bring your attention to that area of the body. Visualize softening and expanding your body to allow and make room for the clench. Then notice how—like most physical manifestations of emotion—it rises like a wave, and then, with some attention, it recedes. You can unclench.

Your upset doesn't come out of nowhere. Generally, there is a buildup—a progression you have been ignoring. The earlier you become aware of your body's internal experiencing (called interoception*), the more likely you can do something about it before

* For some autistic people, interoception development may slow or stop, making it hard to manage emotions and social interactions. Without recognizing emotional signals, responses can escalate—anger becomes rage, sadness becomes distress—appearing as dysregulation or immaturity. On the other end, highly sensitive people may have overdeveloped interoception and become overwhelmed by sensory input. (Like this morning when I retched violently because I smelled a week-old protein drink. My natural gag reflex kicked in despite my being in no danger. I wasn't gonna drink it!)

THE SPICY ONE'S BODY LANGUAGE IS NOT YOUR CONCERN

Many parents have escalated a tense episode into a power struggle by attempting to control their child's reaction to a limit. When you take the visible cues of your child's sour mood personally and command them to hide their upset face or uncross their arms, you invite an unnecessary conflict. Don't try to manage an upset child's body language or assign disrespect to a physical expression of frustration. Assume their gesture is helping them stay calm.

rather than after you've spiraled into dysregulation. Changes in your respiration—such as how deep or fast you are breathing—cardiac activity, and sweating all point to a need for some support. Become an observer of how your body alerts you when you are beginning to be upset or overwhelmed. Consider your jaw, chest, belly, and back. Ask your body, "How are you doing? What do you need?"

Slow Down

I often walk with a friend under the palm trees of Southern California. I can always tell her stress level by how fast she moves. When work is really heating up, she's an Olympic speed walker, darting forward. She's fueled by stress's silent edict that there isn't enough time. When she's just back from vacation, our pace slows to a luxurious stroll.

I'm all about moving fast while exercising. But what about the other twenty-three hours of the day? Your body's speed of movement informs your brain. A slower, relaxed gait gives feedback to your brain that there is no danger looming. Your slower embodiment will inform your parenting.

Moving fast reads as chaotic, not intentional. The Spicy One is taking cues from your speed to see if you are your calmest, most grounded self.

You may be thinking, "Well, that sounds all well and good, but I have so much to get done, I can't afford to slow down." I hear that. Pick a fifteen-minute period each day to experience a lack of rush. Your reduced cortisol levels will thank you.

Rest without guilt!

You do not have to earn your rest. It is not a reward. It is a right.*

Remember, you are the precious medicine for your child. To be a balm, you must protect and care for your body by noticing what it's communicating to you.

S.U.R.F. Your Feelings

In their study of parental burnout, authors Emily and Amelia Nagoski write, "Emotions are tunnels. If you go all the way through them, you get to the light at the end. Exhaustion is what happens when you get stuck in that tunnel."[11] Are you stuck in that tunnel? To get out of that tunnel, you will need to welcome your own big feelings and learn to S.U.R.F.** your emotions.

Emotions are not a problem to be solved. Emotions are sensations meant to be felt. They are biological cycles with beginnings, middles, and ends. You won't be trapped in them if you feel them. Emotional regulation is not about only feeling good all the time. The point is to grow your ability to tolerate and feel and experience emotions and not let whatever you are feeling dictate the immediate action you take.

Physicians Alona Pulde and Matthew Lederman write,

---

* To dive into this revolutionary concept, check out the Nap Ministry at thenapministry.wordpress.com/.

** This concept was developed by Dr. Sasha Heinz, developmental psychologist and expert in positive psychology, adult development, and transformational change. Find her work at DrSashaHeinz.com.

PRACTICE THE ART OF UNITASKING

Unitasking is working on one thing at a time with the intention that that one thing really matters. With the amount of complexity you manage, it's understandable that you stack responsibilities: I wouldn't be surprised if, while reading this sentence, you are also rubbing a child's feet, scrubbing out a couch stain, and doing calf raises. Productivity feels good when so much is out of your control. But multitasking is another way of communicating scarcity and lack to your body.

Embrace the art of unitasking when possible. Enjoy the benefit of a burst of meditation by completely absorbing yourself in one single task. Let each moment bloom with your full awareness. Pause to notice the feel of warm, sudsy water on your fingertips. Focus on the pudgy roll around your baby's thigh. Be here now.

Besides, cognitive science tells us you are never actually multitasking.[12] You are instead switching back and forth between each individual task. Each time you switch tasks, your brain has to reorient itself before it can get back to productivity. That uses a lot of energy you need elsewhere. Humans only have so much bandwidth.

Recharge yourself by bringing all of you to just one thing. It's okay for the Spicy One to be frustrated by your slowed response. Everybody wins when a mom slows her roll.

A difficult emotion like anger isn't in itself dangerous or scary. Anger is a natural emotion—one that carries valuable messages about our unmet needs. However, for many of us, anger was linked to experiences of violence, abandonment, or rejection growing up. As a result, we learned to fear anger and suppress it, believing it was something to avoid at all costs. Suppressing anger, however, doesn't make it go away—it builds up over time. Without a healthy outlet, anger often intensifies and eventually explodes, which can make it feel toxic or harmful. This creates a destructive cycle: suppressing anger until it blows up reinforces the fear that anger is dangerous, leaving little room to connect or express it skillfully.[13]

If we exit the tunnel metaphor and think of emotions as a stormy sea, as Jon Kabat-Zinn says, "You can't stop the waves but you can learn to surf."[14] Try this ten-minute or ten-hour recipe (depending on the space you have in your life): surrender, unfold, recede, and find the name.[15]

Surrender: Stop everything for a moment to let the anger or joy be felt. Pause your conversation. Claim five minutes of inaction to feel, process, and check in with yourself.

Don't try to hold the feelings in. Instead of shutting down, tell yourself you can stop to allow yourself to feel the emotions, and then rest after feeling them. What's your usual signal that it's time to stop? The urge to yell or your eyes crossing? Hearing your heartbeat in your ears? Assign that physical signal as your cue to stop. When you do manage to stop (or pause), build in some celebration!

Unfold: Allow the emotion to exist, expand, and then run its course. To be felt. Anger is not a problem unless you repress it. Tell yourself, "It's okay to feel this." Expand the emotion in your body like a soft red carpet you are unfurling down stairs. Let it be allowed to inhabit your body (rather than fighting or suppressing it). In particular, can you notice and expand the physical sensation of that emotion? What's it feel like to physically be in your body? Check your throat—is there tightness or pressure or aching? Check your belly—is there squeezing or twisting? Put your hand where you feel your feelings. Allow the bodily sensations to shift and maybe even expand for just a moment. Whatever strong negative feelings are rising up, find them and put your hand there. Keep your attention on the physical sensation and breathe into the place you feel the emotion. Investigate the sensations of your anger with gentle attention.

Recede: Eventually, strong feelings mercifully begin to ebb. It might be a solid twenty minutes (or much longer if you make the rookie mistake of rehearsing the reason for your upset). Like a wave that crashes over your shoulders, the emotion will recede. Visualize expelling the last bit of emotion through the bottoms of your feet.

Expand and breathe. Show the emotion there is enough space to hold and welcome it, even as it begins to reduce.

Find the name: This is the last part of the process. Find a name and reason for the emotion. This requires expanding your emotional vocabulary. The typical human can only identify three emotions: happy, sad, and mad.[16] That's like coloring with only red, blue, and yellow dollar-store crayons when there is a box of two hundred artist markers awaiting you. Can you list more than ten emotions? You need the texture and diversity of emotions to fully develop agency over yourself. You deserve nuanced emotional language to help you connect to yourself and other humans in your life. Relationships improve when you can articulate the specifics of your experience.

Part of welcoming emotions is owning your own experience despite the emotional contagion that your child emits. You might be taking over responsibility for other people's feelings if you were trained as a child to worry about your parents' emotional health. One way to start healing this is, when your child begins to show signs of getting angry, frustrated, agitated, or anxious, to ask yourself, "Whose emotions are these? Who is upset here?" The answer is, *they* are. *You* don't have to be. If you are empathetic, your feelings can get twisted up and enmeshed with the feelings of your child.

THE ZIP-UP

When you feel the swell of emotional contagion coming from a disgruntled Spicy One, discreetly take your hand—starting at your sacrum (or pelvis)—and pantomime the action of zipping up your energy all the way to your scalp. Create an intentional emotional and physical boundary—a symbolic bubble that keeps your feelings inside you and their feelings outside of your bubble.

Try it now. Zip up. Your emotions stay inside you; other people's emotions stay inside them.

It's okay—even encouraged—to stay unattached to your child's emotions. You can be present and grounded but not triggered. Try this:

Don't worry about trying all of these techniques at once. Just pick one to work on for a week. Celebrate if you can do it consistently several days in a row regardless of your child's response. This is about you.

CH 16: Reflection Questions

1. When you are overwhelmed, how can your child tell that your body budget is overdrawn? Describe *from your child's point of view* your mannerisms, tone of voice, breathing, and word choice when you are struggling.
2. How were you allowed to express anger in the home you grew up in? What do you wish you could have done to process your big feelings?
3. What physical sensations do you notice when you experience high emotion? Now, as an adult, how does your body like to move, vocalize, or breathe through anger?

For a checklist of controlled destruction options, scan here:

17

Meltdown Magic

What to Do in a Tantrum

Skip to "A Cheat Sheet for Surviving a Tantrum" at the end of this chapter if you are literally in the middle of one and need help ASAP.

Otherwise, let's break this down a bit and learn five ideas that can transform your experience of a tantrum.

First things first.

When your child is going through big feelings, your calm presence is enough.

Humans can get through anything if we aren't alone in it. One of the great ironies of parenting is that your child is more likely to tantrum in your presence because they trust you and feel more secure. "Great," you might be thinking, "I'm a safe person. BUT WHAT AM I SUPPOSED TO DO DURING A MELTDOWN?"

Cast a Conscious Pause

When your child is swirling in on themself, becoming more and more distressed, what is your role? What are you supposed to *do*?

Much of your parental exhaustion comes from resisting your child's upset or trying to head off their anger to make it all better. When you're constantly in a state of resistance, your tank will always be on empty.

When moms ask that question—"What am I supposed to *do*?"—often what they really mean is "How do I stop the meltdown?"

Wrong question.

Hear me now—stopping emotional meltdowns is not your job. Your child's feelings are not yours to fix.

Instead of stopping the outbursts, your responsibility is to grow your tolerance for your child's emotions. To regulate yourself, to stay grounded nearby, to keep them physically safe, and to mentally connect to the humanness of the experience without skipping to judgment or forcing solutions.

Before any heroic action, cultivate your inner calm and unaffected exterior. Connect with your own heart space and sensations in your body.

Slow your breathing by focusing on long exhales. Thanks to mirror neurons, your controlled breath pattern will invite your child's breathing to also slow.

The conscious pause creates space for wisdom to enter the chat. Your calm is the foundation for supporting your child during tumultuous times.

Let empathy be enough. Empathy resides mostly in your silent presence, not in the words you use. Your child needs to writhe, release tension, throw themself to the ground, and off-gas those tough emotions like disappointment. They don't need you to fix it. They need you to endure it with hope that they are getting slightly better each day at regulating themself, to believe that their dramatic reactions in the presence of your calm are changing their brain for the better.

NOTE: If your child is acting physically unsafe, you may need some physical separation during their big feelings. If your child's big feelings often come with hitting, kicking, or biting, read chapter 18 next for assistance.

Choosing to stay present during a meltdown may feel confusing or insurmountable if you weren't comforted as a child. Did adults become visibly uncomfortable or even disgusted with your big feelings? The theory of internal family systems suggests that we learn to dislike the parts of us our parents couldn't tolerate. If no one could accept your emotional, out-of-control parts, when you see those parts in your child, they can feel difficult to love. You might have been taught to fear or even hate out-of-control emotions. You have no practice allowing this guest inside your force field.

If you haven't experienced a calm, loving parent during your grief or anger, don't worry about what you're supposed to *do*. Worry about who you're supposed to *be*: a *non-anxious presence*. When internally disheveled, take a moment to "sit down on the inside," as Emily P. Freeman says.[1] Just being in the same room, doing your own work to regulate, and saying nothing is a gift to your child. Find your calm and then emanate a high positive regard and the healing belief that this too shall pass. Look at you becoming who you needed when you were little!

Call In Your Highest Self

When the pressure builds, ask yourself, "Who is feeling upset?" Notice that it's not YOU! You are OKAY. Your inner wisdom, your highest self, remains untouched by the storm raging around you. Remind yourself of the value of allowing your child to express and work through their emotions and learn the important skill of frustration tolerance. Frustration is part of learning, and everything is learning when you are little. Don't placate your child. They need to reach this peak of not having things the way they like in the presence of a loving adult to develop grit. If you must speak, say, "I believe you" or "It's okay to be upset." Sometimes validating feelings de-escalates them. Often your unaffected silence is the best course.

When I asked my followers to share their epic meltdown stories, Corinna's tale was as upsetting as it was relatable:

TRY STIMMING ON THEIR BEHALF

Stimming, or self-stimulatory behavior, is the neurodivergent impulse to engage in repetitive, often involuntary movements or sounds to regulate your emotions, focus, or cope with sensory overload. Find a voluntary physical motion that calms you, like crossing your hands against your chest while using your fingers to tap on your opposite collar bones. Humming, rocking, muscle contraction, and rhythmic breathing patterns also work. Your body will thank you, and your child may borrow your stim!

> Every time we get to a particular department store, it's like my child hits an invisible force field. He physically can't take another step beyond the security gate. And then the meltdown begins: "No, no, no, I'm not going in there. You come here, Mommy."
>
> I try to gently coax him in: "We can sit in the [shopping cart], and I'll give you cuddles. We will be quick, and then we can go to the playground." As soon as I reach for his hand, he will either get violent and punch, kick, and claw at my face or collapse to the floor like a rag doll. Either way, he's screaming as loud as an air-raid siren and drooling on himself.
>
> I feel heat rise from my feet to my face. I can feel every hair on my head tingle. I go deaf to everything else around me. All I can hear is his screaming. It hurts my brain. It takes all my strength not to smack or squeeze his arms (as my own parents did). I can feel all the eyes on me, and I'm guessing at what they must be thinking. *I would never let my child disrespect me like that. Just give him a good whack and it would be over with. She has no control over her kid.*
>
> All I can do is sit beside him (wherever he's landed) and stare into outer space to let every stranger know that I'm hyperaware that he's disturbing the peace, but also please don't come anywhere near us or look at him or it will send him into the stratosphere.

You've been there. I've been there. It's always worse in public because now there's an added audience to judge both of your behaviors.

You are an unwilling contestant on a haunted game show filled with various ways to get it wrong and be dropped through a trapdoor into what feels like a bottomless tantrum.

It's more important who you decide to BE and what you decide to THINK than what you DO. Once the meltdown is here, the doing won't make much of a difference in the length and intensity of the meltdown. The time for action is mostly *before* and *after* a meltdown. See all the things you can do before in part II and what to do after in part IV.

Since how you THINK determines what you FEEL, and how you FEEL impacts your actions and approach, thinking is a fine place to start. Let's frame your thinking during tantrums and high emotions in a way that resources rather than defeats you.

Embody an Empowering Metaphor

"This child is going to kill me," my client breathed dramatically over the phone the first time we coached together. Teneshia was an actress, so her theatrical communication was lush with flair and gesticulation.

She was at her wit's end with daily physical altercations with her eleven-year-old daughter. Every time her daughter came home from staying with her father, violence erupted. Like when Teneshia told her daughter she couldn't use her iPad for another hour, her wild child hit and scratched her like an animal. It was traumatic for Teneshia. Over and over again in her mind, like an electronic billboard for a heavyweight boxing match, blinked the message, "Parenting this child is going to kill me."

Notice what it feels like just to read that . . . let alone think it. Those are the words spoken by a victim who has lost hope and is weakened to the point of giving up. They are visualizing their demise. "Parenting this child is going to kill me" positions your child as a dangerous *enemy* whom you must do everything *against* in order to survive.

Your child may not do things the way you want them to, but *your child is your curriculum*. You are learning what life is asking of you through staying present to their struggle and yours.

It matters how you *think* about this tough part of parenting. You have a choice of how to frame the challenge. You can think about your child's emotional episodes as a failure—proof that you aren't enough. Or . . . you can decide that everything the two of you do is simply *practice*. You are just two humans failing forward in your souls' attempts to love each other. You have thousands of times to get this right on this side of heaven. It's normal for the same conflicts to happen over and over and for the learning to be slow! This process is not supposed to feel easy, but it needn't be framed as a battle.

In addition to the calming metaphors of the shared scuba tank, seedling, and sloth mom in chapter 13, I'm offering you four more life-giving metaphors to cling to in a tantrum. A perfect metaphor, once embraced, will take you from "hostility to hospitality"[2] and from saving to serving. When you think like a disgruntled villain, you come up with horrific ideas. Choose now how to think during your child's emotional outbursts so you might remember their meltdowns are not done *to* you. They are done in your presence.

Let these fresh ideas percolate in your imagination. Then choose one to visualize during meltdown moments for the next week.

Think Like a Gardener

Rather than a manly carpenter who builds something they are in control of, you are an earthy woman with dirt smeared across your collarbone, humming as you plant seeds. With a contented smile, you are hopeful, imagining the bounty, but you take no ownership of the weather. Professional gardeners must relinquish control since every season is different. So much of the outcome is an experiment.

As a gardener, you tend to the messy process of growth with diligence, tenderness, and care, never focused on perfection. You know you only have so much ability to influence the sprout. Your child's meltdowns allow you to get your hands dirty for the thrill of nurturing wild things. How rewarding is the blessing of a fruitful crop!

Think Like an Oak Tree

Consider the ancient wisdom and strength of an old oak tree, deeply rooted and drinking from the bottomless primordial ground. Visualize yourself ready to pull peace up from the earth.

Your child's oppositional upset is like a summer storm, which your rugged trunk is built to bear easily and even be nourished by. There may be a thousand storms (read: tantrums) in your child's young years. How would you like to weather those rain clouds? Your leaves might shake in the violence of a storm. Your limbs may sway, but you are steadfast, thriving forever. The storm never does permanent or devastating damage to a well-established tree with roots drinking from beneath the nutrient-rich forest floor. Your tree can weather a few twigs breaking off now and then.

In fact, young trees that face harsher weather grow stronger than those never exposed to the wind, as the challenges help them develop a more robust stem and root system. Similarly, your child's struggles, paired with your conscious and warm response, foster a lifelong relationship of trust and co-creation.

When you learn to handle the storms of your young child, you will find the dreaded teen years easier and breezier than parents who were never faced with early childhood squalls. Your mighty oak tree can bend without breaking in your child's emotional storm.

Think Like a Whale Mother

This is a metaphor based on the science of entrainment,* which I first heard when undergoing certification training to become a Simplicity Parenting counselor.

* Entrainment is the synchronization of neural responses (like your child's heartbeat) to an external (or perceptual) rhythm (like your adult heartbeat). With over forty thousand neurons located in the heart, this metaphoric source of deep knowing is worth listening to.

Human beings and other mammals sync their heartbeats with their young through attunement, vocalizations, and good old animal instinct. When baby whales are stressed or disoriented, too far away from Mama, or in danger from a predator, they send out a sonar stress signal. Fast and frenetic. *Ding, ding, ding!*

That signal gets picked up by the mama whale, who then comes a little closer, all the while projecting a calmer, firmer, slower rhythm to soothe her child. *Doooong. Doooong. Dooong.* Mama's physical proximity plus her attuned presence helps the stressed baby whale reorient herself to her mama's big, calm, loving energy. There is power just in the mama whale's presence. No special words or actions are needed.

When you witness the heat rising in your child's cheeks and they begin to groan a warning, it can feel like they grow eight feet tall and you shrink. No longer. Be a giant celestial beast using your body's wisdom as medicine for your child. Even as they mock you or reject your care, be the mythical whale mother oozing unbothered, grounded energy, too primal to be affected by human tomfoolery.

Think Like an Emotions Doula

Anyone who's had the luxury of a doula at her birth knows what it's like to be incredibly vulnerable, messy, and broken while being held in the safety of a doula's intentional care and leadership. (Unfortunately, I only had my husband, who kept saying anxious prayers in my ear like "Lord, don't take this woman from me." Despite his doomed voice-overs, I made it through both deliveries.)

People hire doulas because doulas are trained to *stay calm* no matter how painful or stressful the birth becomes.

- They are **familiar with birth** and **know what to do** when the partner or birthing person doesn't.
- They **encourage** you when things seem catastrophic.
- They **don't judge you or try to take over** because it's not their birth.

- They'll even **customize the way they comfort you** based on your needs. They are **responsive to your requests** and **won't talk if you don't want them to**. They'll rub your back if that's what you want or stay the heck away from you if that is preferable.

Do you see the beauty of an unflappable, warm presence who believes you can do this very hard but natural thing? You get to be the emotions doula for your child when their world falls apart. You are the strong one during this vulnerable and awkward process of growing up gifted while inept at so much. Your Spicy One is "giving birth" to the pain of big emotions and an intense desire to oversee their own destiny while having no actual lived experience. You get to be present for them—respecting their dignity even as they act gloriously undignified.

Your Spicy One needs you to stay hopeful about their emerging skills. To have a vision of their highest self. To believe they are capable of maturing and learning even when you don't see evidence. They need you to trust that beneath their inappropriate behavior is an appropriate human need. When you channel emotions-doula energy during a meltdown, you remember that your child does not want to be destructive. They are wired to fit into the clan and to belong, but they also desperately want to wake you up to the intensity of their perceived need.

Conjure Compassion

My client Sandi has a spicy third grader, Liam, who lost his mind when the lollipop he'd gotten at school and opened carefully at home accidentally fell to the floor. His mama stepped into hero mode because they happened to have another lollipop up high in the pantry. As she moved to get it, Liam went from zero to one hundred, tearfully yelling, "Get it for me, you moron."

[*record-skip sound*]

What now? You and I both know that this is a huge fork in the road. We can either (a) enforce a consequence for disrespectful talk, knowing this could escalate and potentially become a violent afternoon, or (b) continue to hand over the lollipop while feeling like an abused assistant and potentially undermine our child's future ability to cooperate well with others.

The first option is way more painful in the short run, but the second one might have long-term negative ramifications. It feels like a lose-lose. Like the choice between a C-section and six hours of pushing. It's unclear which path is better, and there's no guidebook for it. These are the kinds of high-level emergency-room triage decisions you have to make every day, and it can be downright exhausting.

SIDE NOTE: You may have a limiting belief that their emotional outbursts deplete your energy. I'd like to offer an alternative view—it's actually your *resistance* to their emotions and upset that fatigues you. It takes significant bodily resources to reject reality.

During especially intense moments, repeat a comforting mantra inside your brain, such as:

- "This is not an emergency."
- "I can allow these emotions. I am safe in their storm."
- "This child needs me. It's not personal."
- "I can accept and weather all of this as a form of love."
- "It is more important to be kind than to be on time."

Should Sandi offer a hug? Loving touch reduces fear and pain in the brain center. Except when it doesn't. Unfortunately, some Spicy Ones might get escalated because their body hates containment or their brain interprets the touch as reducing their autonomy. Worth a try.

Hear me on this—their upset is not a failure on your part.

Just like contractions during birth, these outbursts are inevitable. When you are no longer surprised by their intensity, it lifts the fear and anger from your energetic response.

This is your child's developmental process. They will grow out of this. They will mature. But if you expect—and maybe even welcome—the meltdowns, like a doula unfazed by the sticky fluids and anguish of labor, you can see this for the miracle it is. You are witnessing the beautiful and complicated unfurling of a human. Practice welcoming their emotional fever,* knowing it's the pathway to releasing tension. This is your beloved child under the influence of an emotion they can't yet control. Draw close to them with the tender compassion you longed for as a child.

As an emotions doula, you must grow your tolerance for their upset. There's nothing that can make a child more insecure than thinking, "My mom can't handle my anger or sadness." Your Spicy One needs you to stay calm, firm, and loving, no matter their behavior. You get to choose love, even when your child is acting unlovable. You must become comfortable with big emotions so that your decision-making is not clouded by the paralyzing fear of your child's upset. Remember, not only can the two of you get through this; this tantrum could even be something that unites you.

Control What You Can Control

Arrange your body to be on the same team.

When dealing with a tantrum, you can control how you position yourself, your breathing, and the mantras you repeat in your mind. Be a quiet, friendly presence (empathetic facial expression, lowered shoulders, a less threatening, low-to-the-ground posture).

Back to our story.

Sandi could have taken a long exhale and said, "Whoa. Do you want to rephrase that politely so I can help you?" But disrespectful communication was a worrying trend in her house, so she needed to draw a thicker line in the sand this time. She said, "Ohhh, I'm sorry, Li. You may not speak to me that way. You are a kind boy.

* Kim John Payne calls this a soul fever in *Simplicity Parenting*.

You must really want that sucker. Let's calm ourselves a bit and try again in a few minutes."

What do you notice there?

- Empathy: "You must really want that sucker."
- A limit: "You may not speak to me that way."
- Affirmation of his higher self: "You are kind."
- And lastly, an invitation to calm down: "Let's try again in a few minutes."

Guess what? Liam did not calm down.

He escalated. He dragged a chair into the pantry and groaned and cried while calling Mom stupid. It was a loud twenty minutes of him going from angry to desperate to wailing about the sucker. He hurled soup cans onto the floor, looking for the lollipops.

Sandi's inner mean girl began to flare up, chirping, "A good mom's kid would never act like this." She externalized those thoughts ("My inner mean girl wants me to think this isn't normal") and focused on her breathing, allowing her highest self to comfort her by saying, "I am doing the best I can. And that is enough." Meanwhile, her child continued to wail.

When your child is acting physically or verbally abusive, there's not a lot for you to do. The middle of a tantrum is not a time for teaching. No education is happening when a child is losing it. Sometimes the tantrum just needs to run its course. A mammal in a state of distress unconsciously scans your face and posture for threat. Their nervous system is asking, "Are you friend or foe?" Adjust yourself. Soften your eyes. Look away if they are prone to embarrassment. Stay near but keep yourself and them physically safe.

Being an emotions doula does not mean you have to be a robot or caretaking zombie. You are being attacked by someone with a brain impairment who is in emotional distress, but their words hurt. The squall of a tantrum is deflating. It's okay to be human. To notice that. A doula might match energy, mirroring the intensity in her loud voice as a sign that she sees and believes what the patient is dealing with. Or she may say softly, "I hear you screaming and in pain. I'm going to get you ice chips," to give herself a needed break. You, after being called a stupid poo-poo head, can say, "I need to step out of the room and let my body come down, but I will be back!"

Remember that this is not the time for logic or teaching. Compassion means staying nearby or allowing yourself to leave the room for a break if you're overwhelmed. Use your voice sparingly and only to project safety. If compelled to speak during a meltdown, say with a reassuring, slow, deep voice, "It's okay to be upset. I'm here." Then allow kind silence.

When the Spicy One is sending off sparks, take physical action to slow everything down and care for yourself. It's a lot. Sip some ice water to change the temperature inside you and to stall while you choose a measured response.

Their yelling is often them looking for connection, your attention. A lifeline. Responding robotically may feel disconnected to your child. You are allowed to match their passion: "Your anger is fierce! I can see how mad you are. Would you like to squeeze my hand?" If your child uses physicality to express their anger, learn how to block, contain, and step out of the way while saying, "I will not let you hurt me or yourself." (More on that in the next chapter.)

Remind yourself in this storm, "I am safe. My child is learning to handle a limit. I can stay in my loving. Nothing is wrong here."

Each experience of your child losing it while you attempt to stay calm brings forth a new collection of synapses in their hyper-elastic brain. Experiencing your co-regulation when they are in emotional overwhelm is growing their brain and shifting their biology. The meltdown can be the moment you are building toward rather than avoiding.

Every time your child melts down but you stay calm, you've helped them safely release stress and tension. It's another trust knot in the tapestry of your relationship.

Plan with your child what you will do if they get stuck in a loop, asking something over and over that you have already answered. During a connected moment, ask, "What can be our signal when you ask the same question over and over again?" Let them know, "Next time, I will answer you once. If you ask again, I'll ask you to repeat what you already heard me say. And then if you keep asking, I'll put two fingers to my lips, and you will know it means I love you and I'm done talking."

You, the parent, are allowed to have boundaries that help you through the big feelings!

Now to the end of Sandi's story . . .

Only after the twenty-minute tirade—where he did *not* get a replacement lollipop (go, Sandi!)—did Liam finally become calm. Sandi and Liam snuggled on the couch.

He had reached that place past resistance into acceptance of his plight. He confided in her that the lollipop was a prize for scoring the highest points possible on his classroom's behavior chart. This boy who tends to struggle in class had triumphed and exercised all his self-control at school, and that lollipop was physical evidence of his personal success.

Sandi put her hands on each of her little boy's cheeks and looked deep into his eyes, acknowledging his disappointment. "I understand how that must have been hard for you. I am so proud of you!" she said. Despite the violence of their afternoon, she meant it.

To be an emotions doula, begin by cultivating your own calm. Lean into empathy for both of you and curiosity for what the need is behind this intense reaction. Stay kind and openhearted even as you stay firm. This is an art, not a science. There will be times when you look at the situation and choose to give in because it's for everyone's best interest at that moment, and there will be other times when holding the predetermined boundaries feels deeply important. Only you can do this mental math.

Are you wondering if Liam ever got a replacement lollipop? Here's where I remind you that there is not one right way to parent in this scenario.

What would you have done, knowing your own child? I approve!

An emotions doula asks herself, "What does *this* unique child need from me at *this* moment?" Do they need me nearby or far away? Touched or left alone? Your child will signal what they need. As we conclude this chapter, I hope you are taking away the concept that your child's blowups are normal and there is a large array of ways to respond. You will find success when you are calm and not judging your child or yourself.

CH 17: Reflection Questions

1. How do you want to think when the Spicy One is losing it—like a gardener, an oak tree, or a whale mother? What about your chosen metaphor will be helpful during a tantrum?
2. What part of the emotions doula description could help explain how you will practice being the next time your child is upset? Where can you lean into your role of comforter rather than resister?
3. What part of the following cheat sheet feels most important for you to try? Why?

A CHEAT SHEET FOR SURVIVING A MELTDOWN

Your quest: Pick a single point of focus to practice during tough moments (for a week).

CAST A CONSCIOUS PAUSE

- ☐ Cultivate your inner calm and unaffected exterior before any action.
- ☐ Connect with your own heart space and sensations in your body.
- ☐ Slow your breathing by focusing on long exhales.

CALL IN YOUR HIGHEST SELF

- ☐ Ask yourself, "Who is feeling upset?" Notice that it's not you! You are okay.
- ☐ Remind yourself of the value of expressing emotions and learning frustration tolerance.

EMBODY AN EMPOWERING METAPHOR

Gardener   Oak Tree   Whale Mother   Emotions Doula

CONJURE COMPASSION

- ☐ Think of your child in the throes of an anxiety attack, an involuntary seizure, or a soul fever. Give grace for the limitations of their immature brain.

- ☐ Repeat a comforting mantra inside your brain, such as
  - "This is not an emergency."
  - "I can allow these emotions. I am safe in their storm."
  - "This child needs me. It's not personal."
  - "I can accept and endure all of this as a form of love."
  - "It is more important to me to be kind than to be on time."

CONTROL WHAT YOU CAN CONTROL

- ☐ Arrange your body to be on the same team. Be a quiet, friendly presence (empathetic facial expression, lowered shoulders, a less threatening, low-to-the-ground posture).
- ☐ Use your voice sparingly and only to project safety. If compelled to speak, say with a reassuring, slow, deep voice, "It's okay to be upset. I'm here." Then allow kind silence. This is not the time for logic or teaching.
- ☐ Stay nearby to hold space for them, but leave the room for a break if you're overwhelmed.
- ☐ Choose a physical motion that calms you, like tapping, rocking, humming, muscle contractions, or chewing on ice.
- ☐ If your child can tolerate it, engage in a wholesome distraction (that signals safety for you), like crocheting, applying hand cream, or lying on the floor in happy baby pose. Do not use your phone.

Download your own copy of the cheat sheet for a quick reference guide with your Spicy One here:

18

When Things Get Violent

This chapter should be read along with chapter 17.

Jennifer still sweats thinking about the meltdown that erupted at the end of her daughter's playdate. It started with harmless stall tactics like begging for "one more hug" from her little friend as they walked to the car. Next, her child tried to push past her to run back inside, biting and scratching. Jennifer felt suffocated by dread when she realized how big the tantrum was going to be. She was embarrassed and afraid of getting hurt.

It's confusing and scary to be the leader of a child you cannot control. And when that child regularly has violent emotional episodes, the chasm between your private family life and the perceived blissful experience of other parents is wide and lonely.

Even a veteran hostage negotiator may have never had to hold an infant safely while fending off a seven-year-old trying to kick them or tear up all the family scrapbooks. I'm not talking about a classic tantrum. I'm talking about a full-scale physical and emotional meltdown that includes attacking you and their siblings and/or trying to harm physical belongings.

Congratulations! Your family deals with *impulsive aggression*.[1]

That's a phrase psychologists use for reactive, overt, explosive responses that exceed appropriate levels of emotion for the situation. Impulsive aggression is not a planned response but rather a heat-of-the-moment reaction resulting from strong emotions mixed with a bold temperament and an underdeveloped brain. Impulsive aggression is a big part of your life when children have neurodivergence or trauma in their background.*

Impulsive is the key word. You must remind yourself that *your child does not premeditate their attacks*. This is not an aggressive child but rather an overwhelmed kid who can't yet calm themself.

Hanna has a son who used to impulsively melt down in a way that scared her. She described it this way:

> He will hit, kick, intentionally throw [things] at us. Even though he's eight, he's a pretty strong, little dense dude, so he can really enact some pain, or he can get catastrophically destructive. So not just throwing pillows on the ground or harmless moves like that.
>
> We've tried things like a crash pad in his room. We have a trampoline. We have sensory spaces. We've tried to give him alternatives like "You can feel really angry, but we can't hurt people or other things or yourself. Do you want to punch a pillow? Do you want to go for a run?" or "Let's go outside." We've tried these things, but a lot of times, he is already in blackout rage. So we have to ride it out. His therapy team has advised us, "If you can, physically move him into a safe space." And for us, a lot of times that's his bedroom, where we've had to flip the lock on the door because, if not, he will grab hard items and try to hurt us.
>
> And then we just kind of close the door and sit outside it to tell him, "You're not alone. We're right here, but until your body is safe, I can't come in there."
>
> So even a lot of times when the rest of the family is safe, it just feels really *ick*. I feel like we're isolating him. I feel like I don't have

* Fifty-four percent of children with ADHD also exhibit aggression; see Raman Baweja et al., "Artificial Intelligence and the Future of Psychiatry: Insights from a Global Physician Survey," *Digital Psychiatry* 2, no. 1 (2023): 100025, https://doi.org/10.1016/j.digip.2023.100025.

> the tools. He's a big guy. Like, I can't physically pick him up and bring him up the stairs if he's gonna grab the side rail of the stairs. I don't think he intended to throw us down the stairs, but I don't think he realized how much it was gonna throw me off balance and put us in a dangerous situation.

Let's pause here. Breathe in and out the emotions that this intense testimony might have awakened in you. If you recognize some of this scene, you're not alone. This is typical in the private homes of many young Spicy Ones.

I've been there, on the other side of the door from a tornado. My oldest turned twenty-one this year. Years ago, when I first taught the Moms of Spicy Ones group program,* she overheard me talking about choosing respectful consequences. She said, "I remember when I was little and you used to lock me in my room. Was that respectful?"

Gentle reader, please know I wanted to say, "How much can I pay you not to remember that? That's not part of my brand." Instead, I asked, "Tell me more. What do you remember?"

She said, "I would be trying to hurt you, and you would hold the door, and I couldn't get out. I'd be so mad." We spent some time repairing—meaning I expressed empathy and remorse for the fear, loneliness, and anger that I could guess she must have felt being physically alone in the room during her emotional storm.

Since we were going there, I asked, "Do you remember me trying to hold you?" As a young parent, I had read that Susan Stiffelman of Hand in Hand Parenting recommended "loving restraint." This meant holding your child with a calm body as they moved against you to release their anger.

She remembered. "Yes, I would scream, 'You're hurting me!'"

I asked, "Was it hurting you?"

She admitted, "No, it just felt really not good. But no, you weren't hurting me."

---

* Join the waitlist for the next session at MaryVanGeffen.com.

I share some of this personal journey with you now to make the point that parental moves you aren't proud of can be a part of your story, and it doesn't mean it's beyond repair.

Locking your child in a room and sitting on the other side of the door is not going to be in the steps I teach you. Yet sometimes you are engaged in serious risk mitigation, knowing people are going to get hurt if you stay in physical proximity. Physical separation might be all you've got. Trust yourself, especially if you are following a plan you made outside the stress of a meltdown.

Please know there is so much you can do *beforehand* in a child's environment and in your leadership approach to reduce the inflammation that contributes to aggression. That information is covered in the rest of this book. Let's assume you've done all that prework to create a more emotionally sensitive and cooperative environment. You've been observant of the signs of your child's body that show they are headed toward meltdown, and you've tried distraction or reflective listening or firm, assertive limit setting or feeding (because sometimes it's a blood sugar situation, and kiddo needs a cracker). You've done *all the things* to attempt to evade the impending distress, short of lying down and playing dead.

None of it has worked, and "the kicking horse is out of the barn." Your child is either twitching and growling (indicating an emotional tornado is coming), or they're already in full-scale dysregulated meltdown mode. Now what?

The ideas I share here are not necessarily sequential. Some of these tips will resonate deeply with you, and others won't match your style. You are the boss of your home. I don't know the particulars of your child, their background, and their abilities.

What irks me is when the advice for parents dealing with violent meltdowns is "Call 911 if things escalate." That is such a loaded recommendation. First, if your child is Black or brown, there is a risk that police or even emergency medical intervention will escalate the conflict and put your child in more danger.

Second, regardless of your situation, bringing police or emergency services personnel into your home can shift a sweaty meltdown into a traumatic event. Obviously, request emergency services help if your gut says this episode is beyond your family's ability to contain, but there are more than a few things to try first.

DISCLAIMER: I am not a licensed psychologist or healthcare professional. Reading this book does not replace the care or assessment of psychologists or other healthcare professionals that could help support any mental illness your child is battling.

All right, let's get into it.

Be the Calmest in the Room

A meltdown is an existential crisis of sorts. This child has reached a limit they can't negotiate or bully their way through. Their body is interpreting their rising emotions as a threat, and all the autonomic nervous system coping mechanisms are taking over. The prefrontal cortex, where rational thought and empathy live, has temporarily closed, a big handmade sign in the window that says in illegible handwriting, "Out to lunch."

Your goal in this scenario is to communicate a felt sense of safety so their body signals their brain that they're not in danger. You, the adult, staying unbothered is part of this. None of the rest of these ideas can work without your measured, grounded "I've got this" vibes. To de-escalate this situation, your body must emanate calm—the physical embodiment of safety. You are the adult and the safety in the room.

You are our only hope, Obi-Wan Kenobi.

The least helpful move is you or your co-parent getting worked up (see chapter 21 for help on this). We need you generating a peaceful heartbeat and low blood pressure.* Think of yourself as that dependable lighthouse consistently sounding its horn while a ship caught in a storm tries to find its way back to shore.

* See "entrainment" in the "Think Like a Whale Mother" section in chapter 17.

Your number one job is to get yourself calm, not to stop your child's undoing. Check in with your heart rate. Allow yourself to disassociate from them for a moment as you assess your own body. They're already off to the races, right? Comforting and collecting yourself is the crucial first step. "Actively work as your own caregiver," as neuroscientist Andrew Huberman advises,[2] noticing your own distress and saying kind, comforting things to yourself.

Staying at peace during your kid's aggressive episode is postgraduate-level parenting work! To make it easier, aim for affective calmness.[3] Affective calmness is demonstrating an exterior of peacefulness you don't feel inside. Don't respond to negative words or behaviors with emotional reactivity. Instead, fake it until you make it. What would that look like for you? A soft face. Droopy eyebrows. Deep, slow exhales. Likely no talking. Slow movements. Nothing frantic.

Practice Self-Compassion

Show up for yourself. Don't abandon your inner child who's terrified by the Spicy One and what they might be capable of. Dealing with a confrontational or aggressive person is shocking. It's normal to feel intense overwhelm. To be flooded with stress. Notice and acknowledge the bodily sensations that come with these feelings with a kind internal observation like "I'm feeling hot anger in my body." No judgment needed.

Emotions aren't right or wrong. They just are. Naming them helps them move through you rather than get stuck like shame-fueled secrets.

Fear might be the first emotion to welcome and S.U.R.F.* Fear stops us from leading well. According to Bruce Perry, a renowned child trauma expert, "When we feel deeply frightened we can no longer think. We can no longer access our prefrontal cortex, the seat of reasoning and judgment in our brain."[4]

* See "S.U.R.F. Your Feelings" in chapter 16.

This being locked out of our prefrontal cortex is happening to you. And it's also happening to your child. When either of you is in a state of fear, Perry says brain scans show that there is virtually no activity taking place in your thinking brain. So you respond with the basic mammalian response to feeling threatened: You fight, flee, freeze, or fawn.

Address the fear in your body by noticing it with tenderness, maybe even placing a loving hand on your chest and abdomen. Whisper to yourself, "You are feeling fear. It's going to be okay. We've been here before. It always passes."

Learn Self-Defense

Is there a small, scared part of you that is worried for your safety? The part of you that wants someone else to save you. I get it. But the person doing the saving needs to be you. One concrete way to save yourself when the Spicy One starts growling is to lean on your familiarity with self-defense.

The obvious first line of protection for parents of kids who blackout rage is to grow your ability to keep your body safe. I'm not advising you to get in a physical altercation with your struggling child. I'm telling you that if you tend to freeze under stress or don't know how to block a swing or move your body out of harm's way, you have some important homework. If you are terrified that your body or your other children's bodies are in danger, it's time to make sure you get comfortable using your full faculties to protect yourself. Growing your competency to defend yourself and others will turn down that fear.

If you have no history of trauma or are blessed with an assertive "get out the way" personality, you may already be able to perform basic defensive gestures. Good on you, you beast! But if you weren't lucky enough to take a basic defense course in college like I did and practice daily reps of basic blocking, you may not have the muscle memory of what to do when attacked. Feeling equipped to swipe your palms left or right to deflect a strike transforms a tough interaction to be less fear-based. And we already talked about how fear impairs your thinking.

Even though you may only have to use these skills a handful of times with your passionate child, the inner knowing that you can de-escalate aggression rather than fall into a prey response will ease much of the charge your helplessness contributes to the scene. When your physical fear is gone, you can create a safer space to let the meltdown unwind and dissipate.

Specifically, do you know how to block a punch or dodge a kick? I know you didn't think these were things you would have to know to parent well. I am sorry about that. And yet this is your reality. It's time you felt confident in your body's ability to keep you both safe.

Self-defense means learning to properly and safely restrain someone. It means noticing the patterns in your child's aggressive reactions. Do they tend to kick so you need to have a knee raised to protect your groin? Or are they more of a puncher? Or a biter? When you observe and note their physical reactions, you can be more prepared. For instance, if little Sophia likes to face punch when she learns screen time is over, you must set that limit ready to bend your arms in front of your face to protect yourself from predictable swipes.

I want to name the elephant in this padded room. If you were treated physically rough or abused as a child, a local parks-and-rec defense class will not be enough to help you protect yourself at a basic level. You will need to work through the ways your child reminds you of how it felt to be mistreated in the past. Exploring somatic therapy can help.

BOTTOM LINE: If you allow yourself to be hit because you don't know self-defense, that's not okay for either of you. Your child needs you to be empowered to protect both of you from their impulsive aggression. Not to mention, the Spicy One also excels within the structure of a martial arts weekly class.

Find the Most LOVING Interpretation

Reframe what's happening here for maximum resourcefulness. Do you tend to joke that you are witnessing a murderous rage? Do you whisper to yourself that your Spicy One enjoys hurting you? That kind of victim-like thinking is not helpful.

Reframe this episode as something with less intention or malice. Notice how holding one of these other interpretations below might land in your body. Write one down in the spot where meltdowns happen since it's impossible to recall new ideas during an onslaught.

- ☐ This meltdown is an involuntary nervous system activation.
- ☐ This meltdown is an anxiety attack.
- ☐ This meltdown is a brain on fire.
- ☐ This meltdown is an uncontrollable emotional seizure.

This meltdown is not happening to you. It's happening to the Spicy One—with your support. See what finding a less combative story can do for you. After a violent episode, some Spicy Ones do not remember what happened. That sounds seizure-like, doesn't it?

Know that their body's ability to come back to nervous system equalization is expanding with each meltdown where you stay calm yet the limit does not change. You are buying time as they grow the part of their brain that can tolerate being upset. They're doing the best they can with the tools they have, but their tools suck right now. Remember that their anger is a state, not a trait. This is not an aggressive child but rather an immeasurably effervescent[5] kid who can't yet calm themself.

You are witnessing impulsive aggression. Don't mistake it for what therapists call predatory or instrumental aggression, which is an entirely different universe. Why am I bringing this up? Predatory aggression is a planned act of harmful behavior toward another individual where the aggressor gets themself in a more advantageous position than their victim. Meanwhile, impulsive aggression (which is what your kid does) occurs spontaneously and is not preconceived.

It often does not result in personal gain on behalf of the aggressor.[6] Your child does not gain from losing their mind and melting down and destroying their own artwork. It's easier to find your empathy for your child when you see how they are, in some ways, at the mercy of their own response.

Finding the most loving interpretation is believing that there is a legitimate reason for your child's upset.

Ask yourself, "If my child was suddenly articulate and mature and could explain what's happening from their perspective as well as what they wanted and how they were suffering, what would they say?" If that leaves you flabbergasted because you don't know, I'll ask another question: "What would you have wanted from your mother if she'd witnessed you acting this way at the same age as your Spicy One?" Acceptance, trust, and compassion are usually the answer.

Something your child desperately wants or doesn't want led to this upset. Being curious about that underlying need or desire does not mean you move your boundary or change the rules for them. But it does mean you cultivate an understanding of how their fiery disappointment makes sense in their brain. This increases your capacity for compassion, which helps everyone involved.

Set the Stage for Peace

Put away that beloved clay sculpture you made in school and that expensive glass candy dish. Embrace this period of your life where you must remove everything fragile from the places you hang out as a family. Anything that can be used to harm people or that would bring you great grief if broken needs to be stored for a bit. Let your home support you in this season.

When you realize you are headed into a meltdown, look around at what could be used as a weapon. Before things boil over, move that glass of water or fork out of eyesight and reach. Designate a safe place in the home to be physically angry. A place you both agree on ahead of time to go to—or [*cough*] be taken to—when things get out of control. That can include soft places to struggle, like pillow forts, beanbags, punching bags, or crash pads in the hall.

Practice "give us space" drills with the other little people in your home so they know how to exit the area and move to a safer location. Where should they go? To your bedroom or across the hall to the neighbor's apartment? What's the code word or prearranged signal? Figure out these logistics up front so everyone is more prepared for the inevitable, and the number of people involved is reduced.

Gather sensory input tools, like balled-up socks that feel good to throw, a scream pillow, exercise resistance bands, and fidget toys into a calm-down box for use only in these special moments. Try wrapping your child in a stretchy or weighted blanket to provide deep pressure stimulation. A lavender-filled pillow or menthol inhaler stick to sniff helps. Cold packs and ice cubes are a godsend.

De-escalate with Your Body

In their fight-or-flight state, a child can't hear or interpret your words. However, they are still taking cues from your body. Your gritted teeth, held breath, or fisted hands signal danger. In emotionally charged situations, nonverbals are your primary tool for transmitting empathy and understanding.

Become aware of what your body's posture communicates. For instance, standing tall may come across as looming and threatening to a dysregulated child. Or it may be the perfect show of force they need to stand down. Only you can know this through trial and many errors.

Kneeling or sitting cross-legged on the floor may be the sign they need to know you are not scared by their big feelings—or it may invite them to deck you. Maybe it's you lying face down in a child's pose and humming. Calming yourself helps calm them.

Your approach will depend on the child and on your skills, background, and physical and emotional capacity. No outside expert has the answers for you. You are a mammal with great natural instincts. Check in with your animal-knowing to determine if it is best to keep as much distance as possible between you and your upset child. Or would it be a balm to move toward them as warmly as the situation will allow?

Make nonverbal "I come in peace" gestures. These are the safety signals that their hijacked limbic system is craving. Try positioning your palms facing your child and your fingers reaching up for that international gesture of "I mean no harm."

Speak from your chest with the deepest rumble you can muster to help vibrate your calming vagus nerve and theirs. Think majestic lion, purring itself awake and ready to put a firm paw on anxious kittens. Or try letting your voice get quieter and slower. Whisper so they must quiet down to hear you. Tiny humans might unconsciously try to match their body to yours. Use that instinctual response to your advantage by slowing things down.

If there is more than one adult in the house, try asking your co-parent to position themself across from you so you are on either side of the child. A psychologist who works with combat veterans with post-traumatic disorders shared with me that adult patients undergoing a psychotic episode are more likely to strike out at a vulnerable target—the physically smaller person—unless there is a "show of force." At a hospital, this might mean muscle-bound men standing behind an elderly doctor. Since you don't have that luxury, maybe in your home a "show of force" means your co-parent or a neighbor (whom you covertly text) comes over to be with you. Multiple calm adults can help a wild child feel contained and assure them that attacks will not be tolerated.

Some will read the last paragraph and say to themself, "Heck no! The more people witnessing my kids' meltdown, the more agitated my kid gets." Nice work. You know your people best. Every child/adult combination will be different and require a different technique. Do what works in your situation and leaves you less shaken and more pleased with your composure and generosity.

TOUCH

Don't touch your child during a meltdown unless they like to be touched. Some kids long for deep hugs and containment. Like a weighted blanket, these full-body sensations help bring them to the present. For others, touch or close proximity is too activating. Everybody is different. When Spicy Ones are unsure of their emotions and in a state of emotional confusion, many don't like to be touched.[7]

SIDE NOTE: Even if your kid doesn't like being contained, it still gets to be a part of your family's response to unsafe body movements on their part. You are the benevolent queen of this home. Let physical restraint be an option only if you can use it with great tenderness and when it is necessary to keep everyone safe.

WARNING: If you find yourself squeezing or clutching a child harder than is necessary in a fiery moment, containment is not a tool for you. Be honest and assess the emotional weather within you before touching them. If you're gently telling yourself, "I can keep us both safe," with a tender voice, that is a very different experience for your child than being touched by someone who is thinking, "That's it. I'm so sick of this kid." Using restraint requires you to cultivate a nonviolent energy. If not, their mammal body is going to interpret your touch as an attack.

Maybe staying in their line of vision is the most you can do to physically support them. Holding space and bearing kind witness. Let it be enough. Later, during a connected moment, brainstorm with your child. Ask, "What would feel better than being held when your body is lashing out? What might I do to help keep everyone safe?" In their right mind, a child does not want to hurt us or another child. When they do hurt loved ones, that adds *shame* on top of the other emotions driving the aggression. You can normalize your plan (if it involves restraint) by saying, "It is my job to keep everyone safe, and sometimes that requires gentle containment."

It's important to clearly verbally redirect your child with a firm "You may not hit me." I could make an argument for either raising your voice to communicate the importance or whispering, depending on your unique child. Always start with verbal redirection. If it's making things worse, try silent, warm communication instead.

Find a low, rumbly register that's nonthreatening but assertive. Let this voice emanate from the immense well of respect you have for you and your child. Only you know if it's time for words or if verbal communication will further infuriate them.

If you must speak, try short phrases like:

- "I'm here to help."
- "It's okay."
- "Take your time to feel your feelings."
- "I believe you."
- "You aren't in trouble."
- "We'll talk afterwards, when we are both calm."
- "You're a good kid having a hard time."[8]
- "This is just what it's like to be human."
- "I'm not going anywhere. I won't leave you."
- "It's okay to be upset."

Lower the Stakes with Humor

One mom stalled out a category 5 meltdown by asking in a whiny Pixar character voice, "What was that window thinking? How dare that window not open? I'm gonna write something nasty on that window with my dry-erase markers." Suddenly there was a way out of the meltdown for the child. Laughter.

Try an unexpected Broadway song or funny face and see if it might snap your child out of the emotional spiral. Each episode will be different. This may make your kid giggle and redirect their attention, or it might accidentally insult them. Sometimes humor aimed at the ridiculousness of the scenario, but not at them, can help. Other times it wakes up their shame monster.

Blame an inanimate object: "It's the LEGOs' fault that you got upset. Those stinky orange LEGOs. I knew we shouldn't let orange LEGOs in the house." Begin to look with crazy eyes to the left and right. "Or-aaaange LEGOs. I'm coming for you!"

Your kid can't access reason. So do things that only his limbic system—the social center of his mind—can understand. Initiate warm, playful physical contact.[9] Be a buffoon and "accidentally" walk into the door (do the ol' kick the bottom of the door but then grab your head like it hit the door trick). Trip over the rug or get confused by gravity. Anything to give your child a way to laugh. Mr. Van Geffen used to harness a silly voice and a mischievous wink and say, "Now you've done it. You've summoned Scissor Grip." He'd move toward our angry child to give them a "vigorous snuggle"[10] with his legs while swearing, "It's not me! It's Scissor Grip." Laughter is a more socially acceptable way to move through big feelings. It's worth a try.

Recover and Repair Rather Than Punish

What would you do if somebody just suffered a seizure? Do that thing. Help your kid recover by bringing them an ice pack or a glass of water. Try something sour like Warheads or half a lemon so a sensory experience becomes the body's bookend of the meltdown. Instead of punishing, let there be compassion and a firm belief that every time you go through this and you stay in your loving, you are teaching them a little more about *how* to regulate (see healing apologies steps in chapter 22).

Track Your Progress

When I was trying to lose a little weight around my midsection, I joined a weight-loss app. Each day I entered every item I ate. It was a pain in the butt, not just because it was time-consuming but because it made my magical thinking visible. Before joining the app, I would have told you I ate lots of fruits and vegetables. The app would tell you that was not reality.

The same happens with tantrums. We overestimate how often it's happening because it's such a painful experience. Upsets overshadow the everyday good. Start tracking the meltdowns. Create a spreadsheet with the date and duration of each meltdown moving forward. Without capturing these metrics, your brain is going to tell you that "it's bad; it's always been bad." But that's not necessarily the case. Write down the start and stop times, the date, and what the trigger and difficult behavior were.

But also document what you are most proud of. Did you notice their disorientation earlier? Did you breathe out before responding? Did you bravely cut the playdate short even though it caused an explosive reaction? What can you celebrate? Doing so primes your brain for making changes and sticking to them.

Involve Other People Who Love Your Kid

Last, don't isolate yourself in this experience. Keeping a secret like this can begin to feel like an abusive relationship rather than the day-to-day struggles of parenting a chaotic human with an underdeveloped prefrontal cortex. If violent meltdowns are wrecking your family, seek out professional support from your pediatrician, an occupational therapist, or a child therapist. It also helps to choose a person who is beloved to your child to be their unofficial sponsor in this effort to bring more respect and calm to their episodes.

This requires that person to invest some quality time into hanging with your kid in the good times, building up some relational capital so that after a violent meltdown, this auntie or uncle figure has the right to stop by the house and say with tenderness, "I heard you had a tough day yesterday and hit your mother. That must have been tough for both of you. Is there anything I can do to help?"

Involving some accountability without shame can help drag your family struggle out of the shadows and into the spotlight of community. The Spicy One will not like it. But that's okay. You are the adult, and if your intent is to choose someone who is very much *for them* and not out to judge or ridicule them, call in the reinforcements with peace of mind.

CH 18: Reflection Questions

1. **Find the loving interpretation:** Which way of framing your child's aggressive behavior feels most helpful for you and why: nervous system activation, anxiety attack, brain on fire, or emotional seizure?
2. **Recover and repair:** What's a violent interaction between you and your child that still lingers in your memory? Describe it in detail. How would you do it over if you could? What needs to be said or done to move forward with repair? (See the "repair recipe" in chapter 22.)
3. **Track your progress:** What's everything else that you are not noticing that's not so hard? What stories and memories can you gather to prove that there is indeed progress here? What tales can you tell of how you worked through very sticky moments and lived to walk the earth another day? How have those hard situations been part of the instrumental growing process for both of you?

PART IV

FIND YOUR FIRM TO KEEP AWAY BURNOUT

You know in your bones that your Spicy One has enrolled you in a lifelong boot camp for boundary setting. Your little spitfire pushes every limit. Their public displays of emotion and brazen defiance ignite the fear and judgment in anyone unfortunate enough to witness the drama.

There is a temptation to avoid their upset and bend over backward to keep them content. Unfortunately, your Spicy One won't adapt to the struggles of real life or evolve their coping skills without first experiencing many disappointments. Often, you must be the disappointing wall they cannot knock down. They need what you both fear: situations where negotiation is useless. Times when Mom calmly refuses to bend the rules. When the inconvenient facts are not going to change. A moment where resistance is futile.*

* "Resistance is futile" was first said by the Borg, bad-guy cyborgs in the *Star Trek* TV franchise, who used it to warn their targets before assimilation. You are welcome for the nerdy reference.

Only when they realize there is nothing they can do to get what they want can they move past their anger and bargaining to grieve about their powerlessness. You, dear mama, must be both "an agent of futility and an angel of comfort."[1] It is the irony of your position. To help them learn to adapt, you must "dance the child to [their] tears, to the place of letting go, and to the sense of rest that comes."[2] Help them build frustration tolerance by allowing them to experience frustration early and often (in the presence of a warm caregiver). They'll still wake up the next day alive and beloved.

This last part of the book explores scripts and considerations for confidently enforcing limits with the Spicy One. We zero in on the cost that siblings and spouses pay for the ride with your tiny terrorist and what you can do to support them. There's a bonus chapter on surviving the judgment of others, accessible when you scan the code on the next page.

We'll end this journey together with a lesson on how to apologize when you've messed up, which we are all bound to do as we parent these wild, incredible humans.

Let's get to it.

BONUS CHAPTER

Judgment from Others

Respectful Responses to Criticism that Reshape How Others See Your Spicy One . . . and Your Parenting

Some of our worst parenting happens when other people are watching. There's something about the perceived judgment from others that gets in the way of staying true to your path. Unfortunately, your child's turmoil encourages others to invite themselves into your business. People can't help but share their unwarranted advice—be it grocery store lookie-loos, friends with a sparkling Mild Child, or even your well-meaning mother-in-law.

For scripts on what to say when folks have opinions (which pushed this book over the acceptable word count), access the bonus chapter here:

19

Disciplining the Spicy One

My Southern mother tells vivid stories of being the oldest of five kids in a small house in Augusta, Georgia. When my grandmother grew weary of the unending fiddle faddle* between siblings, she would wipe her hands on her apron and say ominously, "Wait until your father gets home."

Later that evening, once he sipped his martini and loosened his tie, he would line the children up in the hall. One by one they would come into the bathroom to be spanked. Oldest last. She says the fear was worse than the actual beating.

When my mother grew up, she didn't want to spank. But without a wise mentor or healing parenting book, she slapped instead. Or she delivered long, withering lectures using character assassination. Many parents today have made talking the new hitting. We drone on, waiting for some new awareness in our child's eyes or contrite tears to signal us the message has hit its target.

* Tara Bremer's delicious Southern phrase for the unexpected nonsense your child loves to get into when bored.

THE ORCHID EFFECT: WHY POSITIVE PARENTING IS THE WAY

Research consistently shows that strong-willed children are more significantly impacted by parenting approaches than their easygoing peers.[1] Like revived orchids, they thrive with reasoned explanations and collaborative problem-solving rather than punishment-based approaches,[2] while showing pronounced negative reactions to punitive discipline.[3]

The good news: Strong-willed children outperform their peers when raised with positive, responsive parenting![4]

How do you discipline a strong-willed child if you want to move away from harsh punishments like hitting, shaming, yelling, or lecturing? That depends on what you mean by *discipline*. Let's start with a shared understanding, because the meaning of that word has shifted over the last couple of generations.

Discipline used to mean punishment and control tactics to get desired behavior from small people. That's not going to be the vibe we practice here. In your home, discipline becomes a synonym for teaching.

The word *discipline* derives from the concept of *disciple* or *student*. To disciple someone and bring them into line with your philosophies, you must teach. Great parenting and great discipline are teaching. Our baby humans are brand-new to this planet and need repeated guidance and instruction even as they reject it.

Great discipline is not about punishment. And yet most parents wonder [*read in an evil witch voice*]: "How can I make this hurt enough that it won't happen again?!" We are the dour pharisees demanding that someone atone for their sins.

Sometimes parents go to punishment because they feel out of control or out of ideas. But sometimes they mistakenly think it's the proper thing to do. It isn't.

Think of punishment as the nuclear option used by overwhelmed adults who can't see an alternate way forward. A destructively blunt power tool.

Punishment lets everyone know just who has power and who is lowly and should feel shame.

When administering a punishment, our face is usually twisted in disgust. The problem is, when a Spicy One picks up on your disgust or feels powerless and ashamed, they act out. When they smell anger on you, they give it back double time. They are not learning the lesson. Their brain can't defend and welcome new information at the same time. Luckily there are more effective techniques you can use for teaching.

Recently, my client Kayla scheduled a coaching session because her eleven-year-old daughter was screaming at her every morning. No matter how gently she woke her or how much time she gave her to get ready, each day began with crying and yelling as they tried to leave the house on time for school. Kayla's husband, frustrated by the repeated drama, was becoming increasingly angry. He yelled back at their daughter. This made things worse.

Kayla was wondering, "How do I get my child not to scream at me for doing my job? How do I get both kids off to school every morning without feeling exhausted just by what we had to go through to get there? Is there a consequence that might work?"

It makes sense that parents want to know what comes *after* their child ignores a limit. Limits without consequences are bluffs that erode your leadership and contribute to unhealthy expectations. I answered her question by sharing the following techniques. Circle the one you want to try first.

Keep Your Eyes on the Prize

Stop focusing on the *behavior* you don't want, and use your mental faculties to determine what *skill* you are trying to *build*. It is important to limit yourself to *one* important lesson, despite the hundreds

WHAT'S THE DIFFERENCE BETWEEN PUNISHMENT AND CONSEQUENCES?

Punishment is designed to make someone hurt or feel ashamed for what they did and is often delivered in anger or frustration with the goal of preventing future behavior through fear. Consequences are the automatic result of cause and effect. They are delivered calmly, without emotion, to instruct, keep everyone safe, and build accountability. Consequences can be either natural or imposed. *Natural* is when your child faces the real world result of their choice (e.g., the Spicy One slices his finger even though you asked him not to use the knife). *Imposed* are limits you set ahead of time and follow through on calmly. As in, "You can use the knife to cut the strawberries if you keep your eyes on the cutting board. Oops. Okay, we will try this tomorrow because you are not following the cutting rule." An imposed consequence is most effective if determined and communicated up front.

of possible corrections you could make. In this case, the primary lesson was "We leave for school on time." There are likely a bajillion lagging skills Kayla also wants to help build in her child, but you overwhelm and shut children down when you present all of them at once. The idea here is to get some momentum and success with one skill before adding another. So you ignore other problematic behavior for a bit to build this new skill.

The skill Kayla is trying to teach is waking up and getting out of the house on time. The lesson *cannot* also be "We don't cry and scream." The attitude and upset are not within your control. That can come later, after this basic skill is solidified.

Do not trip over attitude while you are building a boundary. Doing so dilutes your teaching. Think of attitude as a short garden wall between you and the beautiful landscape of following through on the primary lesson. One thing at a time. Stay centered on the original skill. For now, ignore their reaction to the discipline.

It's your right to set a limit, and it's your child's right to grieve that limit.

Turns out school is a hostile place for Kayla's child. Her daughter uses every ounce of self-control she has just to eke out decent grades and keep away from the bullies. Every morning, her daughter wakes up remembering that she is once again heading into a dismal place she does not want to be.

Her resistance makes perfect sense. In this family's situation, Mom isn't able to change the school situation, and she doesn't want to accommodate the Spicy One's school refusal. (Often, parents make accommodations to protect a child from their anxiety, but this unknowingly strengthens the anxiety. Kids can interpret this support as validation that the phobia is founded, that in this case, school is too scary for her to handle.) So Mom doubled down on making home a safe space to grieve. Her child was *off-gassing* her emotions. You know when you bring a new carpet into the house and it emits that plastic smell for a few days? Off-gassing is normal.*

It's not personal. Think of it like a dog that barks all morning until you take it for a walk. Just part of their process. After many practice opportunities, once the new behavior is more habitual, you can switch to working on the attitude. Don't try to do too many things at once.

Know Your *Because***

Knowing your *because* helps you keep your eyes on the prize. Say to yourself, "I am setting this limit *because . . . why*?"

Ask yourself, "Why is this boundary important enough to enforce?" Answer yourself, and maybe go one level deeper. "Why does it really matter to me?" If the answer is "meh" (as in, "I guess I don't

* Especially *after-school constraint collapse*—that dramatic falling apart after being in an institutional setting all day.

** A phrase from Carolyn Gatzke, a parent coach I hired when my kid was impervious to punishment.

really care if she makes her bed before school"), then don't make that request of your child.

But if your *because* is indeed important to you (as in, "I want her to brush her teeth so her breath doesn't stink and cause more social exclusion"), then you can own your reasons and follow through.

Allow Natural Consequences Rather Than Punishment

We've all wrestled through getting our circus monkey someplace on time, but any show of urgency only immobilizes them more. It's natural to want to hurl an ultimatum: "If you don't get out of that bed right now, no iPad for a week!"

Punishment, like a scathing lecture or removal of privileges, does not offer your child any real solutions on how or why they should achieve the desired or appropriate behaviors. Plus, punishment feels arbitrary to the Spicy One. It puts you on opposing teams and sets you up as the adversary.

Natural consequences don't need to be added by a parent. They are part of what happens automatically. When you let go of a balloon, it flies out of reach. When you rip your posters off the wall, your wall is bare. Mom does not need to fix it.

In Kayla's example, to get to school on time, they must leave home by 7:45 a.m. The natural consequence of the Spicy One's refusal to leave on time? Being late to school.

As it turns out, Kayla's daughter happens to be a kid who does not want to walk in late. So Kayla let her daughter know that from now on, Mom was going to leave no later than 7:45 a.m. in order to get little brother to school on time. If her daughter wasn't ready to leave by then, Kayla would come back after dropping brother off, and they would drive to school late.

NOTE: Do not make these pronouncements if you haven't done the soul-searching to investigate whether you really mean it. Are you sure you are ready to follow through? Is this nonnegotiable for you? Then proceed. Is this a hope, but you might fold if the Spicy One gets upset? STOP! Do not communicate it yet.

The hard part for Kayla is following through with this policy and then allowing for the extreme discomfort both of them will feel when she leaves at the time she said she would. Plus, Dad (or a trusted friend) has to agree to be home on that morning.

Consequences almost always inconvenience the parent. There will be a reaction from the Spicy One when the unwanted thing happens. There will be pleading and bargaining. That's hard to sit through for a parent. It's not fun for anyone. But it is crucial that they experience disappointment repeatedly (in the confines of your unconditionally loving presence) and get to that grief. You are building their frustration tolerance through good ol' exposure therapy.

Much parental suffering comes from avoiding the limit or information that will upset your child when in fact you could be guiding them to the boundary faster and more often.

When you know in your bones that what you have said must happen, let them realize more quickly that they are dealing with a boulder they cannot move. Beware of sending unconscious signals that there is still wiggle room. Confidently guide your child into the rich territory of grieving a limit. To the place of underlying tears. All the while staying on the same team, being for them rather than against them.

Practice being compassionately unfazed by their reaction. This child is not your raging parent (if you had one). Don't be afraid of angry tears that eventually turn sad when you hold a loving boundary. Tears are a symptom of a soul learning resilience and wisdom, especially when shed in the presence of a calm, loving adult.

There are natural consequences of your child's aggressive episodes. You may need space and some time to recover. It's okay to walk away—to put a physical boundary between your child and you when you feel flooded. You can calmly tell them that you would like to stay and listen but that you need to go drink some water or visit the bathroom. Go splash water on your face, text your bestie, breathe, or move your body.

This is not abandonment. This is co-regulation.

Never Kick Someone When They Are Down

Don't lecture a child who has already endured a consequence. When your daughter is playing too roughly with a toy, you can ask her to keep the item on the table and warn her that dropping it might break it. But if she doesn't change her rough handling, it will stop working. And when it does, *nothing needs to be said.* The natural consequence has occurred.

Through this real-world experience, she has realized that she must be more gentle if she wants to keep her toy. When it breaks, she may be sad. She may be angry at you. You do not need to say, "Well, I told you not to play with it so roughly." That is your ego talking. It isn't helpful, and it isn't kind. You also don't need to replace the toy or take away the sadness. Instead, be a warm, safe place where your child can grieve about their failures. Say something like "I can see how sad you are that your toy broke. I've got hugs if you need them." May you calmly and kindly set boundaries without your need to be right creating more conflict.

Focus on What You Can Control

In Kayla's situation, her child may be yelling because that's the only way she knows how to process her disappointment and fear. We can't physically stop her from yelling. We aren't allowed to remove her voice box. Burying her in blankets to reduce the sound seems dangerous. Those are ridiculous examples, but I want you to get the point that we need to be sure we can insist upon whatever we command.

Each time you demand something you can't enforce, you reduce your credibility with the Spicy One.

You can't enforce a limit that's dependent on someone else's bodily behavior. In this case, the boundary Kayla can set is with how she, the adult, will personally respond. When a child reaches a certain size, that's all you have control over.

Another boundary Kayla can set in this situation is with her partner. His reaction to the spectacle is exacerbating the morning misery. She needed to have a frank conversation with him. She asked him to muster up an encouraging morning energy, especially when the drama swelled. If he was unable to do that, he had her permission to walk away.

Do you need to have a heart-to-heart with a partner who might be making things worse?

Kayla's difficult conversation with her spouse took unnecessary pressure off these tough mornings. Their shared understanding of the plan shifted the energy of the drama. While the mornings themselves didn't magically get easy, the changes Kayla and her husband made gave her daughter less to resist and more space to be upset at the tough situation rather than at her parents.

Control Your Nonverbals

Notice the tone of voice you use with your Spicy One. That plus your posture, your body movements, and facial expression convey way more than your actual words do. Nonverbal communication can either support your message or refute it. Nonverbals tell your child if you like them or if they are a burden. Watch your body posture when setting a limit. Find your inner royalty and stand like a leader (see chapter 8).

It's your tone of voice that unhooks conflict from anger. Practice adjusting your voice to be friendly, slow, and grounded* even when your chaotic child is once again rocking the family boat. Your friendly, slow, and calm emotional energy does not come *after* your child complies. It comes *before*, during, and regardless of the compliance.

If you unconsciously think your child needs to earn your friendliness with their good behavior, I'm so glad you are here!

As the leader, the emotional weather starts with you. It's not a reward.

---

* Like the narrator for the *Charlotte's Web* movie or the narrator (Red) from *The Shawshank Redemption* movie.

PATTERN INTERRUPTUS!

When your child is headed down a habitual, reactive path you've seen a million times before—the whining that is building, the stiff body language signaling a breakdown, the maniacal laughter that precedes predatory behavior inflicted on someone less powerful—it's time to *interrupt that pattern*!

How? Do something you don't usually do. Break out of the usual role you play. Find a way to change the atmosphere. Ditch your entrenched response. It just may shortcut their brain's well-rehearsed sequence!

They squeal in frustration.

You narrow your eyebrows in disapproval.

They get louder.

You breathe out loudly and use a fake, placating voice that broadcasts your fear.

Your fear makes them more anxious . . .

You get the idea.

Instead, do something different and out of character to change things up, like

- Squat down low or lie on the floor in a child's pose (when you'd usually tower over your child with arms folded).
- Drop your voice to a lower register (when you normally would go higher into your pleading voice).
- Sing a command with operatic flourish.
- Whisper to showcase how chill you feel in this situation (fake it till you make it).
- Raise your hands above you and lean on a doorjamb while yawning loudly.
- Strut your stuff in an impromptu solo dance party.

These are all physical shifts that stop both of you from getting into the habitual swirl.

SHOUTING WHILE DRIVING

Do you have a child who shouts out rude words or makes annoying, high-pitched sounds while you are *driving*? The only thing you have control of is the car. Try pulling the car to the side of the road and waiting. Eventually, the Spicy One may quiet down to ask, "Why aren't we moving?"

Say, "I'm waiting for there to be quieter, respectful talk. I can't drive safely when there are harsh words happening." You may have to stop the car a couple times, but once the Spicy One knows you are serious, they may settle down.

It's tricky to fix your tone of voice because you are probably unaware of it. Especially if you have been on the receiving end of a belittling voice while growing up. Try this: Imagine you are talking to someone new—*a potential friend*. You would not dare show irritation or disdain for a fellow adult you wanted to impress. How would you tell that new friend that you have to cancel the coffee date you set up last week? *"I'm sorry, but I can't meet for coffee until next week."* Now apply that tone to "I'm sorry you're upset, but you may not pull my hair." Give your child the same respectful tone.

Or pretend it's someone else's child at your house. When you welcome a playdate into your home, wouldn't you be mortified if that child went home and told their mom you were mean to them? Your child deserves the same patient, welcoming tone you muster up for guests. Take the "We are glad you are here" tone and apply it to "Daughter, you may put your plate back in the sink now. We are cleaning up." No anger needed.

You can also adjust the register of your voice to better enforce a limit. Vocal coaches divide the human voice into three registers: chest, middle, and head voice. You can modulate your voice and choose where in the body it comes from. For leading a distracted kiddo, use your most rumbly lower chest voice. The low, grounded tone. Try saying, "Only parents sit in the driver's seat. Come out of the car," while holding your hands over your lungs and feeling a vibration. Now try it while placing the sound at your forehead. Very different textures.

Notice whether you tend to speak in a higher-pitched voice that comes from your head (think Kelly Kapoor/Mindy from *The Office*, or even Mike Tyson). In our patriarchal society, higher-pitched, more feminine-sounding speakers can unknowingly communicate anxiousness and a lack of confidence. (Hate the game—not the player!) We want to choose a deeper chest voice; this voice feels close to a rumble. It's a warm, low-pitched tone from your belly, not your head. There's no question being asked in the chest voice. It does not end directions with a question mark or the word "okay?"*

Notice if you tend to speak faster when anxious. Slow it down.

Kayla had to practice setting boundaries in her deepest, slowest voice rather than her naturally high-pitched and fast cadence.

It will help to have a mentor, someone whose voice you literally mimic when disciplining your child. Who comes to mind?

Create Physical Proximity (2 × 2 × 2)

One error that parents of Spicy Ones make is to lob commands from half a room away while multitasking. There you are at the sink, cleaning a cup, shouting, "Hey, get your coat on while I get the dog's leash on." It seems logical. Let's divide and conquer. You have way more to do than they have, so can't you be moving things along as you coach them to get their crap done? No. Reasonable requests from far away do not work with Spicy Ones (or teenage boys, unfortunately). Even threatening countdowns like "3 . . . 2 . . . 1" stop working when your child outgrows the fear of what comes next.**

---

* The Spicy One takes any command that ends with "okay?" as a choice. And they will choose "No, thank you." If you need a capstone phrase, try "Do you understand?"

** Conversely, positive countdowns to hoped-for actions from the child's point of view are invigorating. "I will help you tie your shoe in 3 . . . 2 . . . 1. Boom! Here I come."

From now on, you are going to give direction using the 2 × 2 × 2 method of physical proximity.[5] Invitations to cooperation are always made within two feet of the listener, with the speaker's two feet planted, and maintaining eye contact with two eyes.

If you're going to ask your kid to do something—assuming you've first connected—you need to be in their physical bubble, within *two feet* of them. Not downstairs yelling upstairs to them, "Hey, clean up your room." Instead, close enough to whisper in their ear, "It's time to clean your room." Your solid, palpable presence helps to see it through. The atmosphere changes when a parent asks you to do something within hugging distance. Not threatening. Just close and present.

The next 2 is *two feet planted*. Your two feet. This is hard. You have so many responsibilities. But if you are in the middle of folding clothes, trying to find keys, and picking up blocks, do not bother issuing a command to your child. You will not get compliance. They are a poker player, and your tell is multitasking. You being distracted means the Spicy One is going to take their chances because your attention seems too divided. They're unconsciously betting you won't enforce this. According to their child logic, you don't really mean it.

From now on, bring your full presence to whatever you ask for. Kayla started taking a moment to feel her toes and heels rooted into the floor. She slowed down to get close enough to touch her child's shoulder, stand stationary, and smile. Taking in her child, she commanded, "It is time to brush your teeth." Do you feel that power? Sometimes it worked!

The last 2 is your two eyes looking at their two eyes. You might come really close to me, but if I'm staring down at my Magna-Tiles stacked into a shining star, you don't have my attention. I might be quiet, but I can't hear you. You haven't neurologically connected with me because I am currently connected with my creation. Try saying, "Can I see your eyes, please?" Better yet, you start looking at their Magna-Tiles too until they become aware that you have entered their world.

If you can't see their eyes, they likely can't hear you. However, receptive listening looks different for different neurotypes. Some kids need to repeat back your words to indicate they are tracking with you.* Others, like those with ADHD, need to fidget or doodle to hear best.

The 2 × 2 × 2 method is a game changer because limits with children need physical proximity. They might understand what you are asking them to do, but it doesn't mean they have the brain maturity or the impulse control to follow through on it. So you have to bring your adult body to setting the limit.

Instead of lobbing the command across the room, "Don't play with that record player," you have to come over, put your hand on the device, and say, "No sir, we may not play with this. What you *can* play with is this . . ." No more sitting on the couch, holding your computer open, and saying, "You better not make me get up." You have to get up.

Get up, come close with a calm energy, and use your body in a nonthreatening way. That is effective parenting.**

Years ago, when I heated up dinner and served it at the table, no one would come to eat it. I singsong shouted several times, "Dinner is ready. Come to the table, please." Each announcement got progressively shriller but still ignored by my child. So I exhaled loudly to get the tension out of my body, and I went to him. I crouched down next to where he was lying on his bedroom rug and said, "Dinner is served, and I have called you several times."

* According to the Cleveland Clinic, *echolalia* (or *echophrasia*) is the action of repeating what someone else says. The repetition could be words or phrases. This behavior is automatic and nonvoluntary (you don't mean to do it). It's common among toddlers who are learning how to talk and people diagnosed with autism spectrum disorder. See https://my.clevelandclinic.org/health/symptoms/echolalia.

** If your partner is new to this style of parenting, model for them what it looks like to get up and move toward your kids. Practice physical proximity, and it will inspire a change in your house. You might warn your partner by saying, "I've decided I am not going to shout commands anymore. I'm going to be respectful, especially when our kid is not being very respectful. Will you hold me accountable?" That's the kind of vulnerability that helps an entire family shift.

"I know. I'm coming," he replied, dreamily stroking his dog's fur. He still wasn't moving.

Me: "I want you to come now. It's getting cold." I stared into his eyes.

He looked at me, finally taking in the fullness of my presence. I could see him do the mental switch from dreamland to dinnertime. "Arghhhh. Fine, let's go." He exhaled.

It was only after I brought my full presence to the ask that it was fulfilled.

Practice the Do-Over[6]

This next technique doesn't apply to Kayla's five-alarm morning fires. This is your go-to teaching approach for when things aren't that heated.

Imagine you are volunteering in your child's elementary school classroom. The teacher asks little Lauren, "What is two plus two?"

Lauren guesses, "Three?"

The teacher replies, "Nope, head to a time-out at the back of the class." Some time goes by and the teacher says, "I'm going to give you a second chance, Lauren. What is two plus two?"

Lauren still isn't so sure. "Five?"

The teacher escalates. "Nope, wrong again. You are out of here—go take a time-out and come back when you know the answer." If this happened, what would Lauren learn about math? She would learn to hate it.

This kind of discipline seems outlandish, but we have used that same logic with how to handle kids who are rude. Politeness is a skill. If time-outs aren't going to teach a child the skills of addition and multiplication, they won't work for skills like courtesy and good citizenship and chores.

What would help Lauren learn math?

- Showing her the concept.
- Doing it together with her several times.

- Once she can do it on her own, locking in the skill by reviewing it with her every once in a while.
- Keep celebrating every time she tries.

That is how you teach someone to love math or fill the dishwasher or learn whatever skill they lack. We learn best by practicing, not punishing. We grow by trying something and failing and then adjusting until we understand how to do it. We learn from a calm, kind, and firm leader insisting, "Hold on, let's try that again. This time, ask me politely for a new fork. There you go!"

Your assignment is to take on a new habit of saying, "Try again, please," or "Let's try that one more time." Give your child a chance to be successful. Then celebrate when they get it right. Human behavior is learned by practicing over and over again. "Experience, not information, is the key to emotional development."[7] Each time you do something, even if not perfect, it becomes more a part of you—something you remember and can do later when a parent is not there standing over you.

Behavior that needs to be learned first needs to be taught. If something is important in your home, then commit yourself to teaching it. And some kids, like the Spicy One, need to be taught it eighteen times before it is in their body and they are ready to do it on their own. The act of doing a task correctly creates a muscle memory. The Spicy One viscerally experiences what it feels like to go with the program. Or they remember, "Mom's going to make me do it all over again, so I might as well do it the way she wants the first time."

The do-over doesn't have to be done with anger. You don't need to make your child feel bad for a lesson to stick. That's old programming. No anger is needed. There is so much research that shows that the parts of your brain that do the most rational thinking—the learning you are engaged in right now—shut down when there is shame or fear present. The very lesson you are trying to teach when you yell is not being received. Your child's brain and nervous system get flooded by your anger. Blood flow goes to the survival brain's operation, making them unable to grasp the basic principles you are so adamant about. If your child is once again ignoring what you want them to do, you don't need to up the intensity, you need to insist they try it again the correct way.

WARNING: The do-over is not convenient. Unfortunately, as with all great parenting, it's neither efficient nor quick. But it is effective.

My favorite part of the do-over is that it ends with your child doing right! So much of old-school parenting is "I'm disappointed in you. You will need to earn back my trust." (Today's employees quit when their boss pulls that power trip.)

A punitive interaction ends with everyone feeling bad and disconnected. The child feels like a failure. You feel discouraged. Conversely, the do-over ends with your child performing successfully! It gives your kid a chance to shine and impress you as the last moment in the conflict.

When my boy was ten years old, I was working on him learning to hold the door for people in public. I must have said it thirty times: "Please hold the door for me," and "A gentleman holds the door for people behind him." It took a while. I remember going to Chipotle, where he busted in past me as we neared the front door. He zipped into line and started thinking about his order.

Meanwhile, I stood outside the restaurant, my face very close to the door that had slammed on me. He gestured at the buffet line: "I'll take beef and cheese and . . ." Then he looked around for me, the person paying, and saw me still standing at the front door. Yes, people were indeed walking around me, wondering if I was having an aneurysm.

Yet I persisted.

Finally, he came back to the front door and asked, "What are you doing, Mom?" I replied, "Oh! I'm waiting for you to please hold the door for me." He shook his head and did so grudgingly. I walked in proud, head held high like a queen. I announced for all, "It is good to have a son. Thank you."

That was all that needed to be said. Not "I can't believe you didn't hold the door again! Why won't you hold the door?" or "We've been over this!" You don't need to harp on the negative. Instead, celebrate when the skill you are teaching happens (even if it's coerced and sloppy). You hold the space for it to happen by insisting on (inefficiently but effectively) repeating the behaviors you say are important.

Another example: If you are walking your child to school and they dart across the road but make it safely across by the grace of God, you don't need to yell or spank. You also can't shrug, do nothing, and walk home muttering to yourself.

You insist on a do-over. Not convenient at all. You cross the street, collect your child, kneel down, and say, "I know you are excited to see your friends, but we need to go back and practice crossing the road safely." Then you walk back to the original place on the street and say, "Show me how we cross the street."

Your kid racks their brain and remembers what you taught them. "Uh, we look left and then we look right."

"YES!" Together you cross the street again after they have looked both ways. You hug them and say, "You are a safe kid. Have a great day at school." End the skirmish on a positive note with everyone succeeding.

The do-over is great for teaching manners. If your Spicy One grabs a toy impatiently out of your hand, saying, "Give that to me!" you can slow things down and respond, "Oh, no, thank you, hold on a second. Let me have that back, please. Ask me again politely." The Spicy One might groan but then mutter dejectedly, "Can I have it, please?"

"Yes, you may," you can respond, beaming.

You are not going to flip out about the poor attitude your child often brings to the do-over. Remember, don't trip over attitude when you are trying to teach a skill. That's your kid acclimating to you keeping them in the discomfort of trying again. That's their frustration that they are not yet done with this interaction and on their merry way.

HEADS-UP: Do-overs apply to you too. When you catch yourself acting like Scary Mommy, say out loud, "Let me try that again!" You are creating a culture where messing up is seen as human rather than grounds for shunning!

Collaborate on Boundaries Ahead of Time

If the Spicy One repeatedly freaks out around a certain activity (swim lessons!) or a particularly cantankerous time of day, sit down with them when things are feeling good and describe what's been happening. With no judgment. Ask them how *they* would like things to go instead. Listen and try to verbally reflect what you are hearing. Brainstorm a better plan together.

Sometimes this conversation can serve as an emotional inoculation. They get the opportunity to think about—and on some level experience—the possible emotions ahead of time while they are still calm. This helps them be better prepared to roll with the issue in the future.

In Kayla's case, this sounded like a chat over Saturday pancakes: "You might cry when I remind you that it's Monday morning and a school day. You're allowed to cry and be sad. Do you want to tell me now what might help you during that time?" You can provide some ideas if they can't think of anything, but best to wait patiently for their input. Planning and strategizing now for an intense future feeling can help reduce its impact when it comes.

Paint a picture of your future together.

On a tough morning, you could say, "When I pick you up from school, I want to eat yogurt in the park and hear about your day." This moves your child's focus from the current struggle to a positive future moment together. It tells them subconsciously that your relationship is solid and things will work out—without lecturing about their behavior.

Stay on the Same Team

We've all been at youth sporting events where teammates brutally fight over a ball. Fans shout, "Same team! Same team!"

You need to conspicuously choose your child's team, especially when you are setting a boundary. You do this by differentiating the bad behavior from the inherent lovability of your child.

Let's say the Spicy One is hitting their sibling. The problem isn't the urge to hit—we've all felt that. The problem is the missing conscious pause between the urge to hit and the action. When we yell, "We don't do that. What are you thinking?!" we introduce shame, which doesn't help unstick behavior.

You must explicitly differentiate your kid's crummy actions from their inherent lovability. Use a firm tone and set the boundary while reminding yourself of this child's goodness. Assure them that their behavior is not too much for you to handle. This looks like putting your arm around a squirming Spicy One and saying, "You are a gentle person. I will *not* let you hit. I know you are working hard on *not* hitting your sister. Look at your sister's face—that didn't feel good. Come hit this instead." Then head on over to that beleaguered ottoman that feels so good to beat up.

It's crucial to share the fact that the urge to want to strike out at someone is normal! Tell your child, "I remember that feeling" or "Your uncle John felt that way all the time."

Get underneath the behavior to the feeling. Ask them (if you're able to be calm and genuinely curious), "I wonder . . . what made you want to hit? [*pause*] I get angry when people take my things too. I've felt like hitting before. And I know that in your calmest heart, you don't want to hurt your sister's body."

Separate the behavior from who your child is. When they feel like a bad kid, they make bad choices. "I know that situation upset you. You are a good kid. I am going to help you stay safe. We are going to get through this."

Then prime their brain by visualizing together a different choice for next time. Role-play! "I wonder if, next time, you could use your outside voice instead of hitting. Let's practice together. Try to take my toy." (Call on your high school theater experience if you've got it.) "'HEY, I DON'T LIKE THAT! Give it back!' Now, I'm moving my body away, so I don't hit you."

When you can, intervene before the urge becomes action. When you hear your child screech, "I want that seat!" you know what generally comes next. If you are able, get in there and interrupt the sequence. Break their habit by being there, using your body as a barrier between children, and saying neutrally, "I hear two very upset kids. What's going on?"

Give yourself mercy when it isn't possible to drop what you are doing in time to short-circuit the aggression. Shoot for three times a day to give them a sense of being supervised and protected from their antisocial inclinations.

The goal is to help them be safe *before* the problematic behavior, not *after*. Show them how to move away from the other child to get their big energy out. Assure them, "I am going to work with you to practice this." Demonstrate that you aren't scared of them by declaring, "I won't let you kick. You are learning to be a safe kid. Let's go help you calm down." Stay levelheaded, like an ER nurse attending to a patient with a missing limb.

Design Your Home to Communicate Your Limits

Your home sends signals to your kids about what is expected of them. In Kayla's case, she used to keep the blackout shades drawn throughout the morning, working in the half dark like a hobbit. After our call, she started raising the blinds fifteen minutes before she actively woke her child, letting the natural light do its work.

- Want shoes off at the door? Put a basket in the front entranceway.
- Want a peaceful bedtime routine? Begin to dim the lights an hour before bed and play soft classical music.
- Want homework time to be less contentious? Clear off a designated spot at the table next to you and have sharpened pencils and other supplies nearby.

- Tired of fights over what to wear every morning? Enact a nightly ritual of choosing tomorrow's outfit and laying it out dramatically on the bureau.
- Want your kids to play independently for a bit in the morning? At night, arrange their stuffed animals in a mysterious circle while they sleep.
- Want your kids to treat their things with more respect? Create a toy-rotation library with most of their toys put away in opaque bins, leaving out only a few beloved items for use.
- Want them to start helping with chores? Put plates and cups and silverware at their height where they can easily reach the items needed to set the table and empty the dishwasher.

As we close a topic we could spend days on, let me normalize that your Spicy One needs to hear limits multiple times to believe they are real and to grow their capacity to cooperate. Don't give up! Setting a boundary is not a one-and-done situation with a Spicy One. I encourage you to make these numerous limit-setting occasions cordial and connecting.

CH 19: Reflection Questions

1. Which of the tips for disciplining the Spicy One will you practice this week? What about this one feels attractive or important to you?
2. Whose tone of voice can you copy as you learn to find your low, slow chest voice?
3. What idea do you have for switching things up in your home's physical setup to make parenting easier?

20

Protect the Sibling

Moment of silence for the overlooked *sibling* of the Spicy One, who has to live with a human yo-yo of emotions who blames everyone else for their upset.

Moms of Spicy Ones are haunted by our inability to create a safe space for every child. You can't help but wonder if the sibling of the Spicy One has been traumatized by what they witness and the aggressive behavior they deal with.

Unfortunately, you cannot guarantee a tension-free environment for anyone. Every family is filled with complex humans who say and do things that occasionally hurt each other.

In your family, everybody gets what they need but not always what they want. This looks like different disappointments for different people. Maybe your Spicy One needs physical touch when they are screaming, while your Mild Child wants quiet to help them decompress from conflict.

Someone loses.

Everybody gets what they need, but not always *when* they want it.

Quiet time might have to be on a date with Mom or once the Spicy One is set up with a video. Tell yourself, "Everyone cannot get their needs met at once. It's okay for people to wait." In your family, you can choose to acknowledge when harm happens and pause to talk about how we reconcile and what each person needs in order to feel cared for. (We will go into the art of repair more in chapter 22.) If there is more conflict in your home than you want, this is a good time to exhale. Real intimacy is born from hurting each other and then sticking around to understand your part in the harm and how to make things right.

A common question: "What should I do about the nasty things my Spicy One says to their siblings?"

I remember a long season when every dinner was interrupted with asking our Spicy One to excuse herself because her anxiety was aimed at her little brother in the form of put-downs like "He's disgusting!" or "Ew, why does he have to eat like that?" or "I don't want to hold his gross hand while we pray!" It was tough to have those words said in this family I wanted to make supportive and gentle.

I had to remind myself of the good news:

The Mild Child looks to you—the parent, not their sibling—to feel safe and treasured.

Put another way, a child's self-concept comes from their parents, *not* their out-of-control sibling.

Double down on empathetic witnessing and parental validation to help the Mild Child develop a healthy sense of self no matter how many times the Spicy One takes up more than their share of the family's oxygen. Be the upstander when action is needed but don't discount the value of your listening and reflecting back their lived experience. Work on your own calm and verbalize to the sibling what's happening. You don't have to protect them from another's big feelings, but you can equip them.

Amid the big, intense emotions, help your child feel safe with verbal and physical reassurance. Rest in knowing that your Mild

Child is learning how to be with difficult people. This skill will serve them well in all kinds of adult relationships.

Beware the Glass Child Syndrome

Glass child syndrome refers to the experience of being a child whom parents look right through and past in order to tend to a sibling with more acute and obvious needs.

The "glass child" gets labeled as strong, capable, and independent despite how they might be crumbling inside. In their chaotic home, they feel invisible. Glass children grow up too fast since they caretake for overwhelmed parents by striving to be perfect and problem-free. They are conditioned not to have or be a problem. This charade leaves wounds they spend years picking at as adults.[1]

When I asked adult siblings of Spicy Ones what advice they had for you, the glass children stepped forward to describe their experience:

sensitivesara22 commented: They still say that I'm "not sensitive". No, I am very sensitive, I just didn't feel as though I was allowed to have emotions, but the more spicy sibling was. Now in adulthood I'm treated as though anything hurtful said will bounce off me 😐 (spoiler...it doesn't). 18m

♥ Reply Message

chillgirl101 commented: My parents also didn't know how to deal with my spicy sister. I became compliant and "easy" to ease the burden. I saw how hard it was on them. My mom thought I was great and basically didn't have needs since I never voiced them. I wish they knew I still had needs and needed to be checked in on and guided. 24m

♥ Reply Message

hazzhandsmom commented: Because of my sister, I had to become the clown. I made it my mission to avoid any yelling by making people laugh. No one knew how desperately sad I was inside. It was so lonely 1h

♥ Reply Message

responsible.riley commented: I became overly responsible (and was encouraged in that) and felt a lot of pressure to be the good child. I am naturally more compliant and I was always called the easy one, so I succeeded, but there have been difficulties in my adulthood because of that. I wish I had been given latitude to make some decisions and even mess up without incurring the grave disappointment of my parents, and I wish they had not asked me to be responsible for so much. 2h

♥ Reply Message

bottledup34 commented: Unfortunately my parents only made things worse. They had no idea though. All their energy and mine ended up just trying to keep my older sister from upsetting constantly. I was celebrated only for my lack of emotional outbursts, which really just were happening on the inside, by 5th grade I started developing an eating disorder, along with extreme protectionist behavior and depression. 3h

♥ Reply Message

These are the nightmares of exhausted parents of Spicy Ones. It's understandable to allow the needs of the quiet, easy one to drift away in the shuffle of dealing with the boldest, most outspoken child.

But there is so much you can start doing and stop doing to avoid the glass child syndrome and help your Mild Child feel supported, seen, and protected.

The difference between a chaotic childhood with parents who can't see your needs versus an upbringing where a loving adult pursued you and allowed for your imperfections is everything!

You do see them, which is why you feel guilty about their lot in life. Look at you literally reading a chapter on their plight! That's a perfect example of you making space for their hidden feelings and unspoken needs, even if they are communicated with nuance and a slight shoulder shrug.

You care well for the Mild Child when you allow them to have difficult days, when you slow things down to give them time to find their voice. When you circle back to a topic and assure them you want to hear the good, the bad, and even the ugly from them, you are dodging the glass child syndrome.

Well done.

Protect Them

Maybe it goes without saying, but protect your Spicy One's siblings! Yes, your Spicy One is just a child, and lashing out doesn't make them a bad kid, but fielding physical abuse is damaging to your other children. It is your job to prevent it, *not* to make the easy one more understanding about enduring physical harm.

This may mean separate bedrooms or no unsupervised play for a season.

Give the Mild Child consistent opportunities for peaceful and conflict-free times each day. A fifteen-minute reprieve they can count on. Allow them to wear earplugs in the car if it's loud.

Ensure their emotional safety by treating the careless, aggressive words from the Spicy One as a big no-no—an unfortunate event you are willing to stand firm on even though drawing attention to it may escalate things. Let the family be late to school to address unkindness. Let the peaceful dinner be capsized by escorting the Spicy One away from the table if their words are bullying.

For example:

SO: "Tanner is a fatty. Tanner is a fatty!"

You [*stopping everything you are doing and coming within touching distance*]: "Oh, no, thank you. We use encouraging words in our family. We don't make comments about someone else's body. What are you needing right now, Derrick?" [*You are looking for an appropriate need beneath the inappropriate behavior.*] "Are you wanting Tanner to chase you or play with you?"

SO: "No! I'm wanting him not to be fat."

You: "That's name-calling, Derrick. You are a kind boy." [*to Tanner*] "Come with me, please, Tanner." [*using your body to lead the child out of the room*] "It's important when someone chooses unkind words to walk away from them or to say 'Stop. That's disrespectful!' in your biggest outside voice. Derrick, let me know when you are ready to use kind words so you two can play together again. You are a kind person. I'm here when you want to talk about what would make you angry enough to name-call."

Be Okay

Your sturdiness as a parent in the face of crying and combustion is everything to your Mild Child. If you are not okay, they certainly won't be. When faced with Spicy One ridiculousness, slowly exhale, lower your shoulders, and smile bravely as a sign to them that everything is going to be all right. Don't put siblings in the position of having to caretake for you.

The good news is that the Mild Child is less affected by the Spicy One's big feelings when you are grounded and sturdy. The Mild Child is looking to you, their trusted adult, to know if they are okay, if they are worthy. They are not creating their self-esteem based on how the salty Spicy One responds to them. That's more of a risk when you are missing from the equation.

One wounded adult sibling shared,

> When my sister would storm out after their fights, I was the one seeing mum sobbing over the table. So I swore never to cause trouble. What that meant was that I learned to never express feelings/thoughts/problems with my parents, so I learned to never need them.
>
> —Flora

Take care of you so you can be the tone setter who doesn't fall apart in front of your kids. Sure, your kids will be better off for witnessing some authentic tears along the way. And they also need to experience the grace of a healing apology when things inevitably fall apart. But the norm needs to be "Mom and/or Dad has this covered. It's hard but handleable." Occasionally insist that they refuse to roll over to let the Spicy One have their way once again. Assure them, "It's okay that your sibling is upset. You get to tell us what you need, and you are not responsible for their response."

To be okay, you will need your own access to warm validation and a place to be heard. You deserve to process the heaviness that comes with this life.

Share your shattered innards with other sturdy adults. Not your kids.

That can look like a weekly coffee date with a friend willing to listen, journal writing, hiring a therapist, or joining the Moms of Spicy Ones group program.*

---

* If you need community to feel more confident, calm, and centered amid the chaos of a strong-willed child, join my Spicy One Society or get on the waitlist for Moms

When you are okay, the Mild Child is much more likely to be okay in the long run.

Notice and Correct Your Bias

Do you tend to force more responsibility for resolving conflicts on the Mild Child because you know they will comply rather than you-know-who, who will turn every argument into a telenovela?

> It would have been so much more bearable if I had been invited to take up more space in our family. Our whole family seemed to orbit my sister. I knew they wanted me to be the peacemaker.
>
> —Angela

Have you assigned a role to a child that they shouldn't have to carry, like the responsible one, the comforter, the dependable one, or even the faithful companion to the Spicy One?

> I was told by our (bad) family therapist that I was both of my parents' favorite child because I was "low maintenance."
>
> —Brittney

strongsally789 commented: My twin was the spicy one. I was told at a young age that I needed to look out and take care of her. I was always the "strong" one and things like my severe depression was not even acknowledged. I wish I could have just been a kid and not felt this responsibility for her. 52m

♥ Reply Message

Try this: On Sunday, announce that the Mild Child will be picking Tuesday's dinner (or whatever choice seems to get abdicated to the Spicy One). This helps the Spicy One practice being disappointed and the Mild Child experience their own value in the family.

---

of Spicy Ones, my eight-week group coaching program for parents like you, at www.MaryVanGeffen.com.

Gently ask yourself two tough questions and share your answers with another parent.

1. ***Are your expectations for the Mild Child age appropriate?*** Do not yield to the temptation to let them become the therapist or the arbitrator of the family. Parentification happens when you lean on a child to play an emotional support role.
2. ***Are you secretly grateful that that Mild Child doesn't need more from you because you are exhausted?*** If the answer is yes, let that be an indication that you need more support and your quieter child may be masking their needs.

There is no blame here. You didn't create these circumstances. Much of this dynamic is beyond your control, especially if you parent alone. Don't let this information capsize the beauty of your efforts.

When you have more capacity, assess the responsibilities you have given each child. Make tiny adjustments to elevate each of your kids' needs to be a kid.

Pop the Emotional Zits

Jenna remembers clenching the steering wheel and recoiling when her thirteen-year-old Mild Child announced to the family, "I don't want to have kids when I get older because I don't want to have one like her [his seven-year-old Spicy One sister]." This confession happened in front of the Spicy One. Tears streamed down his sister's face as Jenna felt defeated once again in the fruitless effort to help them like each other.

NEWS FLASH: This kind of outburst is a sign of a healthy Mild Child who hasn't gone silent. This ain't no glass child!

Like a pimple that needs popping and its pus extracted in order to heal, your Mild Child needs to tell you all the gunky, toxic thoughts filling their resentful little body. It may feel scary to give airtime (without the Spicy One in earshot) to this kind of talk. But don't fall for the lie that voicing a sad makes it more potent. It's actually the opposite!

The sibling needs to talk about how hard this is. To realize that their desires and preferences are as important to you as the Spicy One's. Create a routine venting space (AKA emotional pimple-popping session) even though it's hard to hear. Try a feelings check-in with the Feelings Emojis PDF on my website. Find the QR code at the end of the chapter.

How to pop an emotional zit: ask → listen → validate → brainstorm

Ask

Wondering if your Mild Child has been inadvertently socialized not to be a problem? Don't interpret their silence as a lack of internal upheaval. Ask them how they are doing. Listen to their experience of your family without defensiveness. Wonder aloud what it must be like to have the brother or sister that they have by asking, "How does it feel to have a sibling who needs so much adult attention?" You can even ask the taboo thoughts like, "Do you wish your sibling would go away to camp for a week?" Assist them in mentioning the unmentionable so it can be processed. So they can move on. Don't let the answer to "How are you doing?" be "Fine." Let them know you have capacity for and interest in their emotional needs.

Listen

Listen more than talk. Don't shush them or try to gaslight them by pleading ("You've got to love your brother!") or deflecting ("It's not his fault; he has a disability"). The Spicy One has brought a lot of loud into the Mild Child's quiet little life. Let them try on dramatic words to capture the suffering they endure. Encourage them to voice their irritation and grief while you nod with a neutral expression. Manage your face while they share. Especially those eyebrows of yours that like to travel north when you feel anxious.

Validate

As Alicia Maples says in her "Recognizing Glass Children" TED Talk, "The sibling is experiencing the same stress, conflict, and trauma that you are experiencing but without the wisdom or coping skills of an adult."[2]

Validation helps them cope better. You could say something like:

"You know what? You are right. It's not fair."

"It's okay not to be okay."

"We love you unconditionally. You don't have to take care of your sibling or us!"

"We have space for your sadness and your mistakes and your anger."

"You go be a kid. I will be the adult."

"You are allowed to be upset with your sibling."

Part of validation might be taking accountability for your own neglect or permissiveness:

"You are absolutely right. I shouldn't have made you give him the remote control. It was your turn. I will do better about protecting your turn to choose the show."

Be a safe space by communicating that their big feelings are valid (and don't faze or wound you). The opposite of validation would be comments like "That's your brother! You shouldn't say that," or "Please be positive. I'm dealing with a lot."

Your Mild Child is hurting if you are hurting. Nobody has to feel wrong for that.

Brainstorm

Ask how you can better support them: "What do you need from me next time your brother is dysregulated?" Brainstorming ideas comes *after* the more important steps of ask, listen, and validate. There may not be a fix for this scenario.

Nurture a One-on-One Relationship with Your Mild Child

Families give us a sense of belonging, but it's alone time with another human being where real intimacy develops. The conversation is different. There is less need to compete to be heard. Nonnegotiable weekly time with you away from the chaos is everything to this child! The Spicy One will not like it, and that is okay. Let them know they will have their own time with you as well. (See chapter 7 for more details on special time.)

Cheryl Cardall from the *Fight Like a Mother* podcast invites us to think, "What if [time with your Mild Child] is not another drain but a way to fill you with joy? What if this was the break you needed?"[3] Let time with this easier child be part of your self-care. Finding a thing you do together can be as fun for you as for them. Maybe it's walking through a quiet Japanese garden or attending a loud concert that the Spicy One could never handle.

ATTENTION: Do not talk about the Spicy One or your parenting problems on your one-on-one dates. Enough of their life is dedicated to their sibling's issues. Focus only on the kid in front of you. On connecting and laughing.

FEELING FLOODED BY THIS CHAPTER?

If having these kinds of conversations is beyond your capabilities right now, find the Mild Child a therapist or counselor they can be open with. Or ask an adult you trust to be their sounding board. It helps to expressly invite the Mild Child to share their experiences of being a sibling with someone else. They may be withholding to protect you. Check out the Sibling Support Project, which creates local opportunities to gather with other siblings who get it.*

* Thanks to Jessica Patay, founder of www.wearebravetogether.org for sharing this group with me, found here: SiblingSupport.org.

Remind them often that their dreams and hurts matter to you. This is a lifelong process—a marathon, not a sprint. One long-suffering adult Mild Child explained,

> As an adult, I still desire my parents' effort to maintain a relationship with me even though I don't "need" them in any financial, logistical ways. And if they've made plans with me, barring an actual emergency, I need them to follow through with me even if one of my sister's chickens goes missing or my brother whines about something.
>
> —Ava

WARNING: The Mild Child may use special time to vent if there is no other pressure-release time with you in regular life. That's a good thing.

> I wish my mom had the bandwidth to show me care. The most damaging thing for me wasn't when my spicy siblings were being a lot. It is the fact that she was so exhausted by it that the care for me NEVER came. It didn't come until I was an adult, and it came in the form of her regrets and apologies. But the damage was already done. It's hard to be the forgotten sibling.
>
> —Tara

Other ways to communicate that you care for the Mild Child's needs:

- Give them a gift or physical object to let them know you are always thinking of them. A feather, flower, or secret note will do just fine!
- Voice words of affirmation that have nothing to do with how they have endured or cared for the Spicy One.
- Start a mother/child journal to write letters back and forth to each other. Slap a photo of the two of you on the cover. Write a note on the first page telling them the purpose of the journal is to hear what's on their heart and have a space

to share. Include a light story or joke. End by asking them to write back. Leave it on their bed.

- Skip school one morning to have a secret day together they'll never forget.
- Show up at school with takeout and spend their lunch break being alone together in the car.

Name the Elephant

Don't ignore the big, hairy pachyderm in the room that everyone can see and smell. Everyone feels the impact of the needs and limitations of the Spicy One. It's confusing if you don't discuss it. Avoiding the topic makes it seem taboo or shameful.

Give siblings the words for what's happening in your family. Name the yuck. Voice a repeated age-appropriate phrase for what's happening in the family, along with your commitment that you will keep them safe and can work through this.

The best phrases serve both to illuminate the challenge and to point to the hope of the future. Write out a description that feels both respectful to the Spicy One (consider how they would feel hearing you say it to the neighbor once they are an adult) and specific enough to capture the heaviness it can bring to your family experience. Some examples:

- "Your sister struggles to regulate when she is disappointed. Her nervous system is not *yet* developed enough to handle setbacks, so she sometimes acts out. We are working with her to help her find appropriate ways to control herself. In the meantime, always come tell us when you need a break."
- "Your sister is diagnosed with ______. You didn't cause it, and you don't have to fix it. Everybody has different abilities and challenges. There just happens to be a medical name for this one."

- "Your brother can't calm his emotions *yet*, but as he learns, you deserve peace and care too."
- "Your sister's ADHD makes staying flexible difficult for her. It's understandable to feel stressed when she screams."
- "Your brother's highly sensitive body feels things very deeply. We are working on teaching him coping skills to help him keep calm even when he's uncomfortable. Let me know what you need during the hectic times."
- "Your sister's impulse control is delayed. When she's agitated, her brain does not yet slow down to understand the effects of her behavior. That doesn't make her behavior okay. We are working on it."
- "It can be hard for you to share your own stress or needs because your sibling seems to take so much of our energy . . . but we want to know what's on your mind."

Debrief with siblings after a particularly stressful event. Putting words to a confusing interaction is so helpful. When Megan's Spicy One unbuckled his car seat at 50 mph to climb up and slap her. . . while she was driving . . . she started a conversation the next day with her Mild Child. "That was scary when Tony got out of this car seat and hit Mom. I'm glad I'm an experienced driver and could pull over until he was calm enough to get back into his seat. What was that like for you?"

That is so much better than leaning on your child like a peer to admit, "I don't know what to do about Tony. He's so violent. One of these days he's going to cause an accident!"

PRO TIP: Do not give them a speech about all they are learning from this hardship. Yes, it's true that siblings of high-needs children learn compassion, self-reliance, and sensitivity to others. But that long-term gift is irrelevant to your suffering child right now. Treasure that in your heart, but don't say it. It may feel condescending right now.

Teach Self-Care and Boundaries

Little eyes are watching how you walk through this season. Know that modeling self-care practices like basic hygiene, daily movement, unearned rest, and silly recreation helps all of you. Show them how you invest in your own mental, emotional, physical, and spiritual health without guilt. Look into respite care to refresh your spirit.

Empower them to speak up for themselves:

> "Can you say, 'Don't touch me like that' in your loudest voice? Good! Try it again with your chest puffed up and your hands in front of you."

Assure them that their needs are not inconvenient:

> "I don't always notice the things you need, so I want you to feel comfortable to ask for what you need. Come to me. Tell me when something is bothering you. I can handle it."
>
> "I never want you to suffer in silence. If I am having a day where I can't attend to you in the way I want to, I still want you to tell me about what you need."

If they tend to isolate themselves or live in their "cave" (room), they are hiding from the noise and should be affirmed (not teased) for taking care of themselves.

Create Community

The Mild Child might hear from grandparents and other well-meaning folks, "You need to be a good kid for your parents. They have so much to deal with because of your sibling." Counteract this harmful message by playing matchmaker. Seek out another adult and point-blank ask them to ask the Mild Child about their situation and give empathy and validation. Let your Mild Child know that it is more than okay to share their truth. No secrets needed.

Let the Mild Child hang out with other families that have a more typical dynamic. Lives can be changed for the better just by having a weekly dinner date with a family not struggling so much. Join a parent/child group, Girl Scouts, Boy Scouts, or some other structured meeting that is just about you and the Mild Child.

As we close this chapter, notice any judgment you have for yourself and lean into your holy imagination.

- Imagine your Mild Child appreciating that you would read this chapter and work to protect them from getting lost in the chaos.
- Imagine your Mild Child having robust words and understanding for their experience because you made space for them to process their feelings and talk about the impact of their sibling's explosiveness on them.
- Imagine your Mild Child's healthy self-esteem because you saw them and named the goodness with words of affirmation. You stayed calm and set a cool temperature even when their spicy sibling was red hot.

Well done for making it through a whole triggering chapter giving you MORE TO DO. You are a generous parent.

CH 20: Reflection Questions

1. After reading this chapter, what loss or sadness are you becoming aware of for your Mild Child—and for yourself as their parent? What dreams or expectations about family life are you grieving that need to be acknowledged before you can move forward?
2. How would you describe the challenges of your Spicy One in an age-appropriate manner to their sibling?

3. This chapter asks a lot of an already stretched parent. What is one realistic way you can create space for your Mild Child's needs without completely depleting yourself? What support or boundary do you need to put in place to make this sustainable?

....

To download my Feelings Emojis PDF that you and your kid can use to name your feelings, scan here:

21

When Your Co-Parent Is Triggered by the Spicy One

You might be totally sold out for attempting conscious, positive parenting. Every day you wake up and throw yourself into it. You are committed to the journey.

What do you do if your partner overturns, undoes, or actively works against the work you do to respectfully parent? What if they actively ambush the whole process by running in and escalating things with their own unprocessed anger? You want to be a united front, but meanwhile they haven't read a parenting book or spent a minute reflecting on their own upbringing. Do you just sit back and let them do it their old-school way? It feels disjointed when both adults aren't playing by the same rules.

One of the most challenging parts of modern parenting is navigating a partnership with another human offering a drastically different parenting style! This has to be the number one fight among couples with kids aged two to ten. Navigating parenting *and* your marriage are two areas of life that seem intertwined to some degree.

Ahem! [*taps mic to make sure it's on*]

First let's name the male elephant in the room . . . AKA the bull. The most prevalent challenge is usually trying to get *a man* to join the effort. Some of my wording below is going to feel too gendered and mired in traditional roles. For ease of communication, hang with me for a moment.

It's not his fault. Many men living in a patriarchal society—like the US, where male behavior must fit into a narrowly acceptable range—have been raised with no support in understanding their own feelings of helplessness, rage, and sadness. When these painful emotions overtake their child or themselves, they don't have the skills yet to tolerate it. They weren't allowed to feel and act that way, so it feels wrong in their body. They have no lived experience of being protected and working through this pain. They can't yet handle the chaotic nature of a child's big feelings or defiance.

Here's the good news:

One single lone ranger of a mom can change the entire trajectory of a family.

Especially when the motivation is love. I've seen it time and time again with hundreds of clients. When a mom in a family system stops following the old scripts and instead branches out to a new set of beliefs and behaviors, everyone must adjust. Like an ocean liner with a wheel at the helm that tugs just a half inch due north, eventually the entire ship sails north.

Modeling works. You doing the thing you wish your husband would do is powerful. Didn't Gandhi say, "Be the change you want"? As you choose respectful, calm ways of responding to your children, your partner is marinating in this goodness. He is experiencing firsthand the difference even if he can't articulate it. Your self-control is expanding his understanding of safety and home. Trust the work you are doing and the culture-making impact you are having. *Positive change is contagious!*

One husband of a MOSO graduate said, "I noticed that she's more Zen now. She's being calm and not reacting and understanding that our child has a need and not just a desire. . . . She practices things like scuba breathing and being the oak and not listening to her inner mean girl and trying to emulate the role model she wants to be."

Your partner is healing by experiencing and witnessing the love you are giving. And part of that healing process is getting him big-time triggered. He can thank you later.

Here are some tips for making this voyage easier on everyone.

Discern the Danger

Ask yourself, "Is my husband attempting to discipline with a clunky and awkward approach that is a bummer to witness? Or is this actually abusive behavior?"

If you think abuse is happening, seek help immediately.

Insist on family counseling. Don't stop speaking up. But if the scenario is safe but far from optimal, assure yourself your child can have a different relationship with each family member. It's their journey. They need to come to terms with who their other parent is—warts and all. You can be a buffer, coaching the child how to talk to authority and helping them advocate for themselves but there will be conflict you can't fix. One child said to his dad, "You are talking like you don't like me." They were words his father needed to hear.

Pick Your Title for This Parenting Journey Carefully

Many people struggle with the efficacy of a concept called gentle parenting. Faced with the power of a Spicy One, the word *gentle* can feel flaccid (are you imagining what I'm imagining?) or permissive. Plus there is not enough research on "gentle parenting." It's too new a concept.

Instead, call your approach "authoritative parenting."

Authoritative parenting is high warmth and high demand. It is setting clear, reasonable expectations and monitoring behavior in a respectful and loving manner. Mistakes are used as a chance to teach important lessons rather than a trip wire for certain punishment. Authoritative parents balance freedom with responsibility and give limited choices based on developmental ability. The goal is for children to be self-regulated, self-determined, cooperative, and socially responsible.

This is different from *authoritarian* parenting—with its high demand and low warmth. Authoritarian is giving orders ("Just do it, or else . . .") and focuses on control. You are also not advocating for permissive parenting with its low demand and high warmth—AKA giving in ("Just do anything you want").

You are Goldilocks walking the middle of two extreme styles. Nice work!

Establish a Positive Learning Environment

When my kindergartener was learning how to read and write, I made the heinous mistake of circling every wrong word on her homework. I wanted her to spell things correctly if she was handing this work in, right? Thankfully, the teacher told me to stand down. I learned that at this early learning stage, the goal is to instill the love of reading and writing. Not accuracy. This is not the time to notice misspellings

YOU ARE THE BOSS

I love me some *child-centered* parenting, but I reject *child-led* parenting. Your young child is brand-new to earth. Too many choices and too much ambiguity about who is in charge leave them feeling insecure and grumpy. Only give choices between options you, the adult, are happy with. Be clear about when it's their choice and when it's parent's choice.

or wonky grammar. Similarly, don't micro-correct your partner as they muddle through a new way of communicating.

Whether you are a kid or a parent, remedial skills are learned best in a positive, celebratory environment with shared objectives. Look for the bright spots—acknowledge what your partner does well and bring attention to the wins. Try to catch your co-parent doing all the things they already do so well. That might sound like "I saw you holding your tongue when Brevin talked back to you. You were a ninja, staying above his attitude to deliver the more important message that he needs to follow through on his commitments. Nice work!"

Struggle is a part of learning. Make it okay to fail by using phrases like "I'm still learning" or "Daddy's still learning" or "We are still learning." This helps us acknowledge our partner's actions without judgment or blame. Everyone gets multiple opportunities to figure this out.

Ditch fighting words like *always* and *never*, which wake up defensiveness in anyone.

Use "I" statements rather than "you" to keep defensiveness at bay. A nonthreatening script might sound like one of the following:

"I noticed . . ." (Just the indisputable facts.)

"I think . . ." (My interpretation of those facts.)

"I feel . . ." (Insert emotion word here.* This will require vulnerability.)

"I want . . ." (How you would like things to go next time.)

Bravely ask for accountability and encouragement from your co-parent.

Focus more on what you are going to do—not necessarily what you require of your spouse. As in, "I've made a commitment never to look at our son over a screen. So when he tries to get my attention,

* To expand your emotional vocabulary, check out Brené Brown's list of "87 Human Emotions and Experiences" at www.brenebrown.com/resources/atlas-of-the-heart-list-of-emotions/.

I'm going to close the computer, breathe, and give him eye contact. Can you help me stay accountable?"

Did you catch that last sentence? I want you to ask them to monitor changes *you* are trying to make. Ask them to keep you accountable. This moves them out of contender and into the teammate spot. Share your case studies in progress. Be open about your frustrations with your pace.

There is quiet power in communicating your own work and journey with your partner.

Share what you may be trying or struggling with personally and invite your partner to brainstorm and use their inborn fixing skills.

Equip them with the exact words you would like to hear to keep you motivated. This could sound like "Honey, I'm working so hard to keep my cool. When you notice me not contributing to the madness and being a safer person than I have been, will you encourage me? I'm learning that when humans celebrate the little changes, we prime our brain to take on more change. Your opinion of me matters a lot to me, so I'd love any positive affirmations you can muster to help me keep going."

There is powerful magic in "cleaning up your side of the street" first. Wait until you are doing everything in parenting the way you want to before you spend energy correcting your partner. You'll find this rule keeps you doing the work rather than looking for flaws in others.

Be Curious and Compassionate with Your Partner

Don't be mad, but . . . your partner needs the very same tenderness you are patiently trying to give your Spicy One.

Take time to ask him how *he* feels, and make space to process "intense" interactions, as in, "Honey, that meltdown was epic—how are you doing after that?" When he has a safe place to complain and unburden himself, he will be more apt to cooperate (just like the Spicy One).

Ask him the deeper *whys* behind his opinions on parenting. What was it like to be little in his home? How did he wish his parents would have handled his spiciness? Ask if he is content with the relationship he has now with his parents. Is that what he wants thirty years from now with his own kids? Include your partner in the unconditional love and growth mindset you are cultivating for the Spicy One. This is a learning laboratory where no one is the expert. Everyone has a voice.

Model the skill of encouragement by highlighting your partner's positive efforts, no matter how minor, with the phrase, "I respect how you . . ."

Share Your Stories

Talk about what it was like to be little and how the past has shaped your longings about the kind of family you want to be a part of. Describe the formidable experiences that defined how you want childhood to look in your home.

For instance, I told this story to explain why I didn't want our kids in the "Clean Plate Club":

> When I was seven years old, I had my first spend-the-night at a neighbor-friend's house. The morning after, I was pouring cereal in a plastic bowl when the mom of the house said, "Mary Leigh, in this house, we drink all the milk we pour." I side-eyed her as I covered my Frosted Flakes in delicious cold milk. Five minutes later, when I went to clear my dishes, she cooed, "Uh-oh. Remember, we drink all the milk we pour." I looked down at that beige room-temperature liquid and balked.
>
> She pointed to the chair and said, "Why don't you sit at the table for a few minutes more and see what you can drink? We finish what we pour here." I was mortified and wanted to go home. I sat there memorizing the Tony the Tiger info on the cereal box for what felt like an hour. Finally, she acquiesced, announcing, "You may leave the kitchen, but from now on you drink what you pour here."

Not a problem for this Spicy One because I never went back to that house again.

That experience informs why I don't require my kids to finish food. I don't want them to feel that humiliation and lack of autonomy. Notice that when I share my personal story with you, you might be more open to my beliefs than if I lecture you on the academic theory behind Ellyn Satter's food division of responsibility.

Ask your husband to share his stories of growing up. What moments did he appreciate most about his parents' approach, and when did he resent it? Awakening these memories helps your partner access his awareness of the powerlessness of childhood, which just may increase his empathy for your Spicy One.

Point to the Research

Focus on cold, hard scientific data to pull parenting strategy out of the realm of debatable opinion. Point your partner toward illuminating parenting research by googling phrases like:

- Attachment theory[1]
- Influence of parenting styles (autoreactive vs. authoritarian)[2]
- Relationship dynamics[3]
- Resistant temperament / differential susceptibility[4]

Try reading sections of this book aloud that inspire you. Share Instagram stories that you find helpful. Never give up!

Develop a Shared Values List

In a weekend marriage course I took with Mr. Van Geffen, the teacher from the Gottman Institute told us 69 percent of repeated disagreements with your spouse are considered nonsolvable arguments.[5]

Often what causes these relational impasses are the deep and meaningful core values of each partner contrasting against each other. Other times the disagreement is born out of your partner's unrequited dreams: "I wanted us to be a family that made music together, but the Spicy One won't practice his piano!"

Your job is to find common values and normalize different ways of getting there. (Scan the QR code at the end of this chapter to see a list of 500 Possible Values.) The conversation could start like this: "Let's say that we get this parenting thing right—we each become the best parent we could ever be. What is your hope for our child because of our parenting success? How do you hope our parenting efforts are evidenced in their adult life? Can we each come up with three phrases to describe the kind of person or life we hope they lead?"

Perhaps you find you are united in wanting your child to be a strong self-advocate: mission accomplished! Whatever you uncover, put your shared vision up on the fridge! Refer to it often and be willing to change it as you change.

Welcome Some Counterbalance

When a shift happens in one member of a partnership, it's common for the other parent to counterbalance that shift. Imagine a mom is starting to soften her vocal approach to tantrums. Not yelling. Just humming to herself because she knows disagreement is not disrespect. Dad wonders if, as a unit, "Aren't we being a tad too passive?" To restore equilibrium, he ups his volume, yelling more than he used to. That's a typical short-term response.

The long-term goal is to decide as a couple how you will respond in unison instead of having to balance each other out. But opposites do tend to attract.

Couples work well when a partner has traits that we ourselves don't yet possess. Core values can be the connector.

Counterbalance plays out when Mr. Van Geffen is irritated by our dog's barking. I am upset too by the constant interruption, but something about my spouse's out-of-character frustration compels me to go the other way, explaining how sweet this dog is. I accuse my husband of being negative. But if he wasn't as upset, then I would likely step into the role of most disappointed in this dog. (Have I mentioned that I'm no longer a fan of soft-coated wheaten terriers?)

The core value is we both want a quiet house.

Be Willing to Be Influenced . . .

Are you allowing your partner to have a different point of view and share it with you? Who better to notice our blind spot than our co-parent? Sometimes in a valiant climb to become a conscious, respectful parent, we may find ourselves teetering on the ledge of permissive parenting. Maybe you are overcorrecting for your own parents' harsh approach. Maybe your partner can see something from their distant vantage point.

What might you have to learn from your partner?

. . . But Clear on Roles

If you find yourself on the defensive when it comes to how you parent, you might say something like "I realize you have lots of opinions on proper parenting. We both do. Do you have the time and/or interest to read some parent education research and join me in learning about what mental health professionals recommend? If not, and I'm the only one who will be doing the work to educate myself on parenting, I'd like to take the lead on the strategy setting, with your support. It won't work for you to take a passive role in the learning but an active role in evaluating my approach."

Let Them Learn How They Learn

Your partner may take in information very differently than you do. They may even require a very different teacher than who works for you. (More than one dad has complained that my videos seem too woo-woo for them. It's okay!)

Here are some resources that seem to resonate well with male partners of MOSOs:

- *The Anatomy of Peace* by The Arbinger Institute. This book explains the leadership results you get when you cultivate a *heart of peace* rather than a *heart of war* toward someone you are trying to impact. The *heart of peace* sounds like "I will treat you like you matter. I respect that your voice is just as important in this conversation as mine." It's Golden Rule, authoritative leadership—treating people like you would want to be treated. Meanwhile, a *heart of war* causes us to "other" someone, making them an object in the way of our success. When your heart is at peace toward someone, you get a better version of that person.
- Adam Young's website offers short free PDFs on the science of attachment and what children need from their parents (adamyoungcounseling.com/free-resources/). My favorite skill he mentions is "Be Strong Enough to Handle Your [Child's] Negative Emotions." Can you imagine if every parent was sturdy enough to do that?
- *How We Love* by Milan and Kay Yerkovich is helpful if your partner is ready to dive into how their own childhood drives their relationship style. This book helped my husband and me see our harmful patterns in marriage and parenting. It includes quizzes that divide people into five different personalities based on how your upbringing impacted your communication approach: Pleaser, Avoider, Vacillator, Victim, and Chaotic. I'll never forget Mr. Van Geffen's teary eyes when he read the description of the insecure and lonely thoughts of a Vacillator (my style). Meanwhile, I was able to understand more why he retreats in an argument (his style is Avoider).

- Mr. Chazz (@MrChazz) on Instagram. He's a gentle, modern Mr. Rogers sharing the breakdown in brain functioning that happens in both a parent and child during conflict.

CH 21: Reflection Questions

1. What do you appreciate most about your co-parent's approach? What is their unique gifting in parenting? Go tell them!
2. What childhood story gives some texture to why you want to parent respectfully and intentionally?
3. What core values do you have in common with your co-parent (even if you have different ideas of how to honor those values)?

For my list of 500 Possible Values
to peruse together, scan here:

22

Healing Apologies

I wish I could hug every mother reading this who thinks she's already blown it. The chronic yellers. The unsupported single moms. No one can manage a sensitive sour-patch kid without blowing up from time to time. I should know.

One day when my Spicy One was three years old, I made the mistake of letting the sweet potatoes touch the hot dogs on her lunch plate. It was supposed to be her younger brother's nap time, but my Spicy One's screaming and kicking became so loud and chaotic that the toddler stumbled out, sleepy-eyed, to watch us fighting.

I had just read that restraining your child in your arms (if you could stay calm) was a great way to help them move more quickly through a tantrum. Heads-up: This did not work for my kid. I wrapped my arms around my daughter tightly and said brightly over the yelling, "I'm holding you." She screamed, "Let me go, I can't breathe!" I kept repeating, "It's okay. It's okay." But it didn't look or feel okay.

We struggled against each other for what felt like an eternity. My three-year-old's upset was a thrashing earthquake while my anger boiled under the surface like rising lava. She gasped for air between screams and twisted her body against me. Then she kicked me in the tummy.

My Puppet Mistress inner mean girl swelled up to two hundred times her regular size and hissed, "You aren't a respectable mom if your child treats you this way."

I dragged her to her room, yelling, "Enough!" like a classic Disney villain. I shoved her in there, slamming the door and locking it. I slid down against the wall and cried. I could hear her doing the same on the other side of the door. My no-longer-sleepy baby didn't move toward me. Would you have? I was acting unsafe.

What do we do when we mess up? Extra ice cream for dessert? Avoid eye contact for a day? Go buy them a toy and never discuss the incident again? No.

When a rupture happens, we repair it.

We all have a fear of losing connection with our Spicy One when they grow up. How could a healthy relationship have its roots in so much drama and conflict?

The parent of a Spicy One must make room in her heart to fail hard and often. The clash of your child's ironclad will and delicate heart against your high-stakes duty to govern the ungovernable creates excruciating turbulence. Your clunky shows of force will hurt them. As will your flippant teasing or dismissive exhaustion. You will disappoint yourself and your child many times. And yet you must begin again each day knowing a bit more of what does not work. Mistakes don't make you broken or wrong. That familiar twisted knot of shame in your stomach is simply a reminder to embrace the power of a restorative apology.

So often we make the mistake of pretending it never happened and hoping time heals wounds. This leaves our child to process the hurt alone and make assumptions that aren't helpful, like "I'm a kid who drives adults to rage."

Moving on without talking about it brings no resolution and misses the opportunity to let the hard times bring us closer.

Causing harm and being harmed are unavoidable parts of being in relationship, especially with a sassy, feral child like yours. The goal is not to stop messing up with your child. In healthy, securely attached relationships, caregivers and their babies are only in sync 30 percent of the time. The other 70 percent, they're out of sync—making repairs and coming back together.[1]

One study says,

> Appropriate parental responsiveness does not mean that parents never make mistakes. Rather, it implies that even after . . . misreading a child's cues, or after moments of inevitable conflict, a parent can acknowledge the rupture and successfully re-engage with the child. . . . Patterns of disruption and repair may actually foster the child's trust in the parent as a reliable figure.[2]

Another study notes,

> What we know from the attachment research is that it's not the absence of rupture that predicts security of attachment, but the presence of repair. In fact, these ruptures in connection, when followed by successful repair, can actually strengthen the attachment relationship.[3]

Your attachment is strengthened by the work of repair.

Feeling shame is unnecessary. It depletes your motivation to do the sacred work of repair. The intimacy that comes after an apology and the heartfelt reassurance that things will be better bring healing like nothing else in a relationship.

Here are five ingredients for successful *repair recipe*.

1. Initiate the Conversation

Moving toward your child to initiate a conversation might be a grand departure from how you were raised. The end of gaslighting and pretending.

Once I calmed down, I went to my daughter, gathered her up with all her sweat and tears, and said, "I'm sorry Mommy treated your body roughly."

You might say, "I think I hurt you yesterday. Could we talk about it?"

Speak in a way that matches their age. Don't burden them with adult information or emotional baggage that you must deal with, but do say the words "I am sorry." Give an explanation but not an excuse. Young children need this conversation on the same day as the offense.

As Carlos Whitaker said in a reel on Instagram, "The goal of an apology is not to defend yourself. It's to heal someone else's pain."*

Bravely say the words "I'm sorry" without including "but" or "if you would just . . ." As tempting as it is, do not blame the Spicy One for your behavior. Your child did not "make you mad."

2. Invite Your Child to Share Their Feelings

Encouraging your child to say what it felt like for them when you hurt them is the step most people skip. It's natural for a child to say "That's okay" because they can't tolerate the knowledge that you, their protector, would do anything cruel. Without your intervention, they may even blame themself.

Perhaps you say, "No, it's not okay. I was rough and hurt you. You deserve to have your body treated gently."

If they're too young to articulate their experience, give them words to make sense of what happened to them. Narrate what happened in a story: "Mommy was rushing bedtime and didn't take time to be gentle when you wanted extra melatonin gummies. I had a scary look on my face and a mean tone when I grabbed the bottle. It probably made you feel afraid."

Then pause. Allow space for them to integrate and respond.

3. Confess Specifically and Apologize

Confess and apologize using words describing exactly what you did: "I'm sorry I hurt your hand," not "I'm sorry we fought," nor the invalidating phrase "I'm sorry you feel that way."

* Follow him on Instagram @loswhit.

Don't coax them to share the blame for your behavior with discounting language like "If you hadn't yelled in my ear, I wouldn't have hit you." You've lost the opportunity to teach whatever skill or behavior contributed to your poor response. Now you are teaching the skill of repair! As you own and rectify harm, be conscious of your nonverbals. A "sorry" without the matching body language and tone of voice causes more confusion.

Include a proclamation to counter any false belief that the incident may have spawned. In my example, I held my daughter's face and spoke slowly and gently: "You are worthy of being treated gently, especially when you are upset."

Affirm your child in who they are and what they deserve. This reminds them they deserve love, especially when they are acting unlovable (so do you, by the way). It is healing to hear this truth, for both of you. Plus it becomes a boundary for the next moment of upset.

4. Prioritize Atonement, Not Your Child's Forgiveness

Don't require forgiveness from your child. When you pout and ask expectantly, "Do you forgive me?" you put the child in the position of having to relieve your adult guilt.

You, the adult, need to forgive yourself.

Try a phrase like "I hope you will forgive me." This is not a demand; it's an invitation. Allow your child to sit with it a bit. *The response to causing harm must be victim-centric.* Think about what would help the child, not what would make you, the one who messed up, feel better.

Atonement is doing what is necessary to make things right. Atonement acknowledges the need to repair what was broken. Focusing on this active making of amends equips your child for the inescapable future times they will also harm others. You are humbling yourself to model what to do after you inevitably screw up.

Ask the Spicy One what they need from you in this moment. I'm crossing my fingers it's just a hug. No need to buy them something.

TRY HEALING STORIES

One way to solidify relational repair is by telling a healing story together.

Putting basic words (and maybe hand-drawn pictures) to the confusing experience of an out-of-control parent can help a child make sense of a hard moment.

On the day I described above, I wrote a storybook for my daughter with stick figures on orange construction paper that I folded in half. It read,

> Gigi was frustrated. She didn't want her sweet potatoes to touch her hot dogs. Her anger boiled up inside her and made her head hot.

I wanted to help raise her body and emotional awareness by exploring what it might have felt like in her body.

> Mommy got angry at Gigi's loud crying and tried to hold her too tight. Gigi didn't like it. Gigi kicked Mommy by accident because her body was so mad. Mommy was rough with Gigi and dragged her to her room and left her all alone.

We want the story to end with the child reconnecting with you, their caretaker, and a promise of a different future, as in:

> Later, Mommy calmed her own body down and hugged Gigi and told her, "I will never hold you too tight like that again or drag you. You deserve to feel safe." The next time Gigi ate lunch, the sweet potatoes touched the hot dogs again. But this time when she got sad, Mommy stayed calm, speaking quietly and kindly until Gigi felt better.

Reading this story turned a light on in my daughter's eyes. Like an energized magazine publisher, she instructed me what to draw on each page. Then she commanded me to read it to her every day for a week.

Days later, she would read it to her little brother with great authority. The sting of it was gone. Now she owned the story. She especially loved the last part, which read,

> From then on, Mommy and Gigi treated each other with care and kindness, especially when they were upset.

Healing storybooks can be especially helpful when working through disturbing healthcare memories, adoption attachment anxiety, and other terrible incidents and behavioral blowups.

Years ago, I did not offer atonement, but if I had to do it again, I might ask if she would like me to massage some moisturizer into her arms to care for her skin better than I did during our violent encounter.

5. Make a Promise for the Future

Make your apology real by expressing what will be different next time. "I'm going to do three exhales instead of yell next time." Or "I'm taking a class to help me be calmer.* If I feel angry again, I'm going to walk away and cool off a little." This builds reassurance in your child that this situation will not happen again. They need not fear future repeats of the pain because you are committing to a new way forward.

Normally I tell people the sixth step is to get support to make changes and become a safer person. But you are already doing that! You are doing the work to own your triggers, practice the missing skills, and engage in the healing needed to be the person your child needs . . . and the person you needed when you were little.

Support may come in a parenting book like this, a group program, or sharing memories of your childhood with a trusted friend. Commit yourself to practicing this repair recipe and trying and failing at this new way of parenting. Each time it gets easier.

Restorative apologies and retelling a difficult event in story form are miraculous practices for redeeming a poor parenting moment. May you practice bringing vulnerability and connection into the equation when you inevitably mess up.

---

* For a parenting class that teaches you how to stay calm in the chaos of your child, go to MaryVanGeffen.com.

CH 22: Reflection Questions

1. What step of a restorative apology is most important for you?
2. What were apologies like in the home you grew up in?
3. For parents of young children: What experience has your child been through that might be relieved in part by creating a book together?
4. For parents of older children: What story of the past could you tell that might bring a nonjudgmental explanation and needed empathy to a difficult memory?

PRAYER FOR MOMS OF SPICY ONES[4]

O Lord, I confess,
I am tired and angry at myself,
at this larger-than-life child,
and maybe at you.

Why didn't you give me one of the easy ones?
The kids who pine to wear matching outfits.
The ones who dutifully ask for
permission to cross the road.
The mild children who can run
more than one errand without a tantrum.

Forgive me, Lord,
for my eye rolls, my heavy sighs,
and the conditional love that I sometimes direct
at this sparkly human.

Give me grace where I feel contempt.
Give me mercy for the meltdowns.
Burn away my fear for their future.
Remind me today that difficult children
can make the most brilliant adults.

But most of all,
give me deep delight in this storm of a child.
Let me love them like you do, God.
Extravagantly, recklessly, and unreasonably.

Open my eyes to the precious ways my Spicy One
bears your image and echoes your creativity,
love, and power.
Amen.

To listen to this prayer,
visit maryvangeffen.com
/bookresources or scan here:

CONCLUSION

Inspiration for the Road

As I write this final chapter to you next to a glittering Christmas tree, my young adult Spicy One is scream-giggling and shriek-running as her Mild Child brother chases her around the loop of our kitchen and living room. She's paying the price for shutting down his phone in retaliation for him not pausing an episode of *The Office* when she went to the bathroom. It's a wild contrast to our quiet days when she's away at college. I welcome this lovely chaos. My Spicy One is at a top university, flush with friends and earning great grades. There is fierce loving trust and unbridled silliness here in this family.

My rumpled heart has swelled with pride and contracted with hurt throughout her life:

> [*Swell*] She's fifteen and the first of her friends to get a job. She works the bakery's cash register with confidence while her married adult coworker leans on the counter complaining unprofessionally about her impending divorce.
>
> [*Swell*] She's sixteen and welcoming in her shy forty-year-old small group leader before any kids arrive for Bible study. I can still hear her asking questions to draw out the adult—essentially leading the leader.

[*Contract*] She's twenty and calling her dad a cuss word because he won't let her use the front room to entertain her friends.

[*Swell*] She's twenty and warmly greets each of my adult friends, asking them about their lives.

As your heart vacillates from hopeless to empowered, and sometimes back again, let your effort be enough. Celebrate your imperfect leadership and your commitment to compassion over competency. You pour time and attention into your parenting, and it shows.

This is still the beginning of a long expedition. We have gone over the map together at the visitor center, but now you must hike the mountain . . . alone.

Just knowing things doesn't make them easy to do. No one expects you to stop yelling forever. You will mess up many times on this journey, but as you grow, your attention to sacred repair will become quicker. Remember—the apologies and the mending *are* the work. You don't need yourself or the Spicy One to be perfect to lavish love on the both of you.

May you see the Spicy One's loyalty to their own soul as inspiration rather than competition.

Trust your gut because you know your kid and what they need. Fade out the noise of everyone else's opinions about your child or about you.* You know your values and the skills that are still a stretch for you, so you can draw on your intuition. Parenting by formulas doesn't work. This is an art, not a science.

As I release you into the wild world of parenting this incredible human who has all dials turned up to 11, your homework is to remember that healing happens in a helix. It winds around—two steps forward, one step back. Keep circling back to compassion.

"Be with the child you have."[1]

It can be scary to open the aperture of your heart to take in the full panorama of your glittering child—their eccentric perspective,

* For guidance on caring less about what others think, check out the bonus chapter, "Judgment from Others," at www.maryvangeffen.com/bookresources.

their unworldly knowing, their unfettered potential and refusal to be anyone but themselves, and the way they see through your adult nonsense. And it's scary to meet the full grandeur of ourselves, unencumbered by what society expects of us! I believe in you.

Embrace the fact that you are uniquely designed for this child. Treat these techniques and perspectives as tools to experiment with, knowing you alone are the best source of wisdom for how to implement them. Choose to parent from love rather than fear. Actively live in the most positive outcome possible for your child, believing the affirmations you cast over them. Your Spicy One will grow up to be an awesome human—capable of contributing passion and positivity to the world!

Finally, please forgive the past version of you. The woman who shouted so hard at her child that her throat was sore later. That out-of-control, unsupported version of you deserves love too. What you cannot accept in yourself will be difficult to allow in your child. Give mercy to past you. Allow her to start again each day anew with your grace. Treat yourself like someone you are in charge of helping. How would you support you if it was your responsibility to do so? May you whisper this blessing over the Spicy One when they are finally fast asleep:

> I help myself to help you
> I heal myself to heal you
> I hold myself to hold you[2]

Well done, you thoughtful and generous mother, you!

APPENDIX

Profiles of 9 Inner Mean Girls

Perfectionist · People Pleaser · Star Performer
Martyr · Logical Learner · Anxious Auntie
Impatient Princess · Puppet Mistress · Escape Artist

#1 THE PERFECTIONIST

Your strengths being misused: Attention to detail, high standards, dedication.

What she does: Makes you obsess over getting everything exactly right instead of focusing on connection. She turns every mistake into evidence that you're failing as a parent.

How you'll know it's her: You feel anxious when things aren't organized perfectly and criticize yourself constantly.

The Perfectionist makes you think:

- ☐ "I'm not parenting well enough. Other mothers wouldn't lose their cool like that."
- ☐ "If I can't get my child to behave, I'm a failure."
- ☐ "Everything needs to be done the right way or it's not worth doing."
- ☐ "My child's room/behavior/grades reflect poorly on me."

- ☐ "I should be able to handle this without getting overwhelmed."
- ☐ "Other families have it all together. What's wrong with us?"
- ☐ "If I make a mistake, everyone will see I don't know what I'm doing."
- ☐ "My child needs to meet these standards or they won't succeed in life."

When the Perfectionist takes over, you might:

- ☐ Redo your child's chores or homework because they're not done "right."
- ☐ Focus more on appearance (clean rooms, good behavior in public) than emotional needs.
- ☐ Criticize your child's results instead of celebrating their attempts.
- ☐ Avoid activities where you or your child might fail or look messy.

How this affects your Spicy One: Your child becomes afraid to try new things or make mistakes. They may become anxious perfectionists themselves or completely give up trying because nothing they do feels good enough.

The Perfectionist Reframe: "Progress, not perfection. My child needs a loving, present mom—not a perfect one."

#2 THE PEOPLE PLEASER

Your strengths being misused: Empathy, harmony-seeking, consideration for others.

What she does: Makes you abandon your own needs to gain acceptance from your child and others. She convinces you that love must be earned.

How you'll know it's her: You feel guilty saying no and constantly worry about what others think of your parenting.

The People Pleaser makes you think:

- ☐ "It's my job to help manage other people's feelings."
- ☐ "If I can help people stay happy, life will be easier."
- ☐ "If there is conflict or my child is discontent, I must be failing."
- ☐ "What can I do as a mom to earn love and acceptance?"
- ☐ "They should know how to care for me since I do so much for them."
- ☐ "I have less value if my children don't need me or won't let me help them."
- ☐ "The Spicy One is selfish and doesn't think of my needs."
- ☐ "How can my child not appreciate all that I do? I give so much!"

When the People Pleaser takes over, you might:

- ☐ Give in to your child's demands to avoid their disappointment or anger.
- ☐ Apologize excessively when you set necessary boundaries.
- ☐ Say yes to avoid conflict when you want to say no.
- ☐ Sacrifice your own well-being to keep everyone else happy.

How this affects your Spicy One: Your child learns that love is conditional on performance and that their emotions control your decisions. They lose respect for your leadership because you're inconsistent with boundaries and rules.

The People Pleaser Reframe: "My child benefits when I also consider my own needs. It's okay to disappoint my child and others as I stay true to myself."

#3 THE STAR PERFORMER

Your strengths being misused: Drive, goal-orientation, leadership.

What she does: Turns your worth as a parent into a performance where you must constantly prove you're successful. She makes you see your child's struggles as a reflection of your failure.

How you'll know it's her: You feel like you're competing with other parents, and your child's behavior feels like a report card on your parenting.

The Star Performer makes you think:

- ☐ "My child's success is my success, and their failure is my failure."
- ☐ "I need to have the best-behaved, highest-achieving child."
- ☐ "If my child isn't excelling, I'm not doing enough."
- ☐ "Other parents must see me as the mom who has it all together."
- ☐ "My child's struggles make me look incompetent."
- ☐ "I should be able to fix this problem quickly and efficiently."
- ☐ "My parenting methods need to produce visible, impressive results."
- ☐ "If I can't handle this child, what does that say about me?"

When the Star Performer takes over, you might:

- ☐ Push your child into activities to make yourself look like a devoted parent.
- ☐ Feel embarrassed by your child's meltdowns instead of responding with compassion.
- ☐ Compare your child's development to other kids' constantly.

- ☐ Focus on quick fixes and results rather than long-term relationship building.

How this affects your Spicy One: Your child feels like a project to be managed rather than a person to be loved. They may become performance-oriented themselves or rebel against your expectations entirely.

The Star Performer Reframe: "My child shines with their own light and walks their own path. My gift to them is consistent love, support, and gentle guidance as they become who they're meant to be."

#4 THE MARTYR

Your strengths being misused: Sensitivity, emotional awareness, creativity.

What she does: Keeps you stuck in "poor me" mode instead of taking charge. She uses guilt and emotional breakdowns to avoid taking responsibility or moving into action.

How you'll know it's her: You feel powerless and want your child to comfort *you* during conflicts.

The Martyr makes you think:

- ☐ "Why have I been dealt this child? Nobody else has it this hard!"
- ☐ "What did I do wrong to have a child treat me like this?"
- ☐ "Once again I'm stuck sacrificing my happiness for this kid."
- ☐ "Nobody ever listens to me or understands what I go through."
- ☐ "I don't get a choice. Things just happen to me."
- ☐ "My child needs to understand how they're making me feel."

- ☐ "I never get what I need. I'm always considered last."
- ☐ "What's wrong with me that this keeps happening?"
- ☐ "I am alone in handling the hard work. I have no resources."

When the Martyr takes over, you might:

- ☐ Cry or have emotional breakdowns in front of your child during conflicts.
- ☐ Say things like "Look what you've done to Mommy" or "You're making me so sad."
- ☐ Withdraw affection until your child apologizes or comforts you.
- ☐ Share adult problems with your child to get sympathy.

How this affects your Spicy One: Your child feels responsible for your emotions and starts walking on eggshells. They learn to suppress their own big feelings to take care of yours, which can create anxiety and people-pleasing patterns that follow them into adulthood.

The Martyr Reframe: "My child isn't responsible for my emotional needs. I'm the adult here, and I can handle this situation with strength and wisdom. I will remember my belovedness."

#5 THE LOGICAL LEARNER

Your strengths being misused: Problem-solving, calm under pressure, analytical thinking.

What she does: Keeps you emotionally disconnected from your child by making everything a problem to solve. She treats feelings like inconveniences that should be reasoned away.

How you'll know it's her: You feel uncomfortable with big emotions and try to logic your way out of messy situations.

The Logical Learner makes you think:

- ☐ "If I just explain it the right way, my child will understand and comply."
- ☐ "Emotions are getting in the way of solving this problem."
- ☐ "My child should be able to control themself if they just think about it."
- ☐ "Crying and tantrums are manipulative and illogical."
- ☐ "I need to stay detached and unemotional to be effective."
- ☐ "There's a logical solution to every parenting challenge."
- ☐ "My child's feelings don't make sense, so I should correct them."
- ☐ "I don't have time for all this emotional drama."

When the Logical Learner takes over, you might:

- ☐ Give lengthy explanations when your child needs comfort.
- ☐ Dismiss your child's emotions as "overreactions."
- ☐ Focus on behavior modification instead of understanding underlying needs.
- ☐ Avoid physical affection or emotional conversations.

How this affects your Spicy One: Your child learns their emotions aren't welcome or valid. They may shut down emotionally or escalate their behavior to get the emotional connection they need.

The Logical Learner Reframe: "My child's big emotions signal important needs. I choose to be curious about what's underneath their communication rather than rush to fix or dismiss how it is expressed."

#6 THE ANXIOUS AUNTIE

Your strengths being misused: Protective instincts, awareness, responsibility.

What she does: Fills your mind with worst-case scenarios and keeps you in constant worry mode. She makes you parent from fear instead of confidence.

How you'll know it's her: You are hypervigilant, believing danger lurks everywhere and you must control everything to keep your family safe.

The Anxious Auntie makes you think:

- □ "If I don't keep my family close at all times, someone will get hurt."
- □ "The world is dangerous and something bad will happen if I'm not vigilant."
- □ "If I don't think through everything, it's going to go very wrong."
- □ "My child's behavior means they might become a broken adult."
- □ "I am ruining these kids, and the stakes are life or death."
- □ "Making mistakes will expose us to punishment and harm."
- □ "Trying new things is generally not safe."
- □ "When is it all going to go wrong again?"
- □ "Everything is up to me to protect my family."

When the Anxious Auntie takes over, you might:

- □ Hover and micromanage instead of letting your child learn independence.
- □ Catastrophize normal childhood behaviors as signs of future problems.

- ◻ Avoid new experiences that might be beneficial but feel risky.
- ◻ Transfer your anxiety to your child through constant warnings and worry.

How this affects your Spicy One: Your child absorbs your anxiety and becomes fearful or may rebel against your overprotectiveness. They miss out on building confidence through age-appropriate challenges.

The Anxious Auntie Reframe: "I don't have to carry the weight of every possible outcome. I can trust myself to handle whatever comes. I am safe to imagine a positive future."

#7 THE IMPATIENT PRINCESS

Your strengths being misused: Enthusiasm, flexibility, imagination.

What she does: Keeps you constantly looking for the next better thing instead of being present with your child. She makes ordinary moments feel boring and insufficient because she believes you need constant stimulation to feel alive and fulfilled.

How you'll know it's her: You feel restless and distracted, always thinking about what else you could be doing or what more exciting activity could replace this mundane moment.

The Impatient Princess makes you think:

- ◻ "Parenting is the opposite of fulfilling. I need work or volunteering to feel successful."
- ◻ "Why can't my child keep up with all the fun things I have planned?"

- ☐ "I should say yes to every opportunity, even if it overwhelms my child."
- ☐ "I need to do many things at once to feel alive."
- ☐ "It's going to be more fun when the kids reach a different age."
- ☐ "It's boring to be with my child without adding distractions."
- ☐ "I can't follow through on discipline or routines."
- ☐ *"There's so much I'm missing out on while dealing with this tantrum."*
- ☐ *"I am trapped by these repetitive parenting tasks."*

When the Impatient Princess takes over, you might:

- ☐ Constantly check your phone during family time.
- ☐ Overbook your family's schedule with activities.
- ☐ Start projects with your child but lose interest quickly.
- ☐ Feel bored or trapped during one-on-one time with your child.
- ☐ *Plan the next activity while still engaged in the current one.*
- ☐ *Rush through the bedtime routine to get to your "more interesting" evening activities.*

How this affects your Spicy One: Your child feels like they're not enough to hold your attention. They may act out to get your focus or become anxious about your inconsistent presence.

The Impatient Princess Reframe: "This moment with my child is enough. I don't need to be anywhere else or doing anything else right now. *Presence creates the richness I'm seeking.*"

#8 THE PUPPET MISTRESS

Your strengths being misused: Decisiveness, leadership, protective care.

What she does: Convinces you that everything will fall apart if you're not controlling every detail. She makes you micromanage instead of teaching your child independence.

How you'll know it's her: You feel irritated when things don't go according to your plan and hesitate to let your child make their own choices.

The Puppet Mistress makes you think:

- ☐ "If I don't dictate this situation, everything will go wrong."
- ☐ "My child can't be trusted to make good decisions."
- ☐ "I usually know what's best for everyone."
- ☐ "If I let go of control, chaos will follow."
- ☐ "My child should do things the way I would do them."
- ☐ "I can prevent most problems if I just manage everything properly."
- ☐ "Other people don't understand my child like I do."
- ☐ "I need to fix my child's problems for them."
- ☐ "It's either I control my kids or they control me."

When the Puppet Mistress takes over, you might:

- ☐ Do things for your child that they can do themself.
- ☐ Make all decisions without including your child's input.
- ☐ Feel anxious when your child is with other caregivers.
- ☐ Rescue your child from natural consequences.

How this affects your Spicy One: Your child doesn't develop confidence in their own abilities and may become either overly dependent or rebellious against your control.

The Puppet Mistress Reframe: "I can support my child without controlling them. My child needs to learn from their own experiences, even when it's hard to watch."

#9 THE ESCAPE ARTIST

Your strengths being misused: Self-preservation, adaptability, boundary awareness.

What she does: Helps you avoid difficult emotions and conversations by encouraging you to check out or run away. She keeps you from staying present during your child's hardest moments because she believes conflict will destroy the connection and inner peace you desperately need.

How you'll know it's her: You feel the urge to distract yourself or leave when things get emotionally intense to preserve harmony and avoid witnessing the escalation.

The Escape Artist makes you think:

- ☐ "Their intensity feels like it will consume me if I stay."
- ☐ "This is too much. I should just shut down until it passes."
- ☐ "I'll deal with this later when I feel better."
- ☐ "Maybe if I ignore this problem, it will go away."
- ☐ "I need something to numb this overwhelming feeling."
- ☐ "I'm not strong enough to handle my child's big emotions."
- ☐ "This conflict is too hard. I should just give in."
- ☐ "There's no point in repairing. It's better to pretend it never happened."
- ☐ "If I engage with this conflict, it will escalate and ruin our relationship."

When the Escape Artist takes over, you might:

- ☐ Withdraw emotionally, even when physically present.
- ☐ Avoid bringing up difficult topics or setting boundaries.
- ☐ Give in to demands just to end the conflict quickly.
- ☐ Use substances or activities to numb difficult feelings.

How this affects your Spicy One: Your child feels abandoned during their most vulnerable moments and learns that big emotions make people go away. They may escalate to get your attention or shut down emotionally themself.

The Escape Artist Reframe: "I can stay present during my child's hard moments. This feeling will pass, and my presence matters *more than avoiding temporary discomfort.*"

ACKNOWLEDGMENTS

Thank you to those who have mothered me:

- Alicia, Andrea, Anne, April, Barb, Beth, Bleema, Brenna, Bronwen, Carolina, Carolyn, Casey, Cheryl, Dana, Danielle, Devi, Donni, Elissa, Emily, Erika, Erinn, Gail, Griselda, Holland, Indy, Jacquie, Jen, Jenny, Jill, Judy, Karen, Kathy, Katie, Kayla, Kelle, Kelley, Kelly, Keri, Kimber, Kirsten, Laura, Lauren, Lisa, Lorie, Louise, Mandy, Maria, Megan, Melanie, Melissa, Nici, Nora, Rachel, Rebecca, Shelly, Sophie, Susan, Tara, Tessa, Tracy, Yvette

Thank you for reading early drafts and giving feedback that made this book so much better:

- Amanda, Barbara, Carrie, Chelsea, Elizabeth, Harrison, Heather, Jillian, Julie, Kate, Katie, Kayla, Kelle, Kendra, Laura, Lucy, Maria, Mel, Meredith, and Todd

Special thanks to:

- The 1,700+ graduates of the Moms of Spicy Ones group program who taught me as much as I taught them.
- Todd, for the way he looks at me like I'm special, his patience during the writing season when he had to feed me, his pearls

of wisdom, and his unsinkable efforts to focus on the good about both his Spicy Ones.

- Keith, for his disarming tenderness that I swore I didn't need. Thank you for not looking away as I gulped down your affirmation.
- My family—Bob, Chad, Charlie Rose, Danielle, Esme, G-Dad, G-Mom, Joey, John, Judy, Katie, Lila, Louise, Melanie, NJ, and the entire Bouma nation.
- Jill, for tracking my writing, providing firm executive function when I wanted to chase squirrels and lie in the grass, and admitting my last-minute ideas are usually good.
- Lisa, my agent, for flying to my house to make me write this book.
- Kelsey and Kristin, my editors who made this ADHD explosion of ideas more decipherable and reader friendly.
- The Spicy One Inc. team—Alex, Giulia, Jill, Karen, Keri, MaryKate, Rachel, and Rae.

NOTES

Introduction

1. Lisa Miller, *The Awakened Brain: The New Science of Spirituality and Our Quest for an Inspired Life* (Random House, 2021), 7–10.

Chapter 1 Is Your Child a Spicy One?

1. Quoted in McKenna Princing, "What's Neurodiversity and Why Does It Matter?," *Right as Rain by UW Medicine*, accessed January 20, 2025, https://rightasrain.uwmedicine.org/mind/mental-health/neurodiversity-or-neurodivergence.

Chapter 2 Name the Hard So It Can Get Better

1. Chapter 10 in David Erickson and Amanda Erickson, *The Flourishing Family: A Jesus-Centered Guide to Parenting with Peace and Purpose* (Tyndale House Publishers, 2024), 173–90.

Chapter 3 Are You Also a Spicy One?

1. See stevecusswords.com.
2. Sharon Hodde Miller, *The Cost of Control: Why We Crave It, the Anxiety It Gives Us, and the Real Power God Promises* (Baker Books, 2022), 116.
3. Emily P. Freeman, *How to Walk into a Room* (HarperOne, 2024), 126–28.
4. E. N. Aron and A. Aron, "Sensory-Processing Sensitivity and Its Relation to Introversion and Emotionality," *Journal of Personality and Social Psychology* 73, no. 2 (1997): 345–68; Jenara Nerenberg, *Divergent Mind: Thriving in a World That Wasn't Designed for You* (HarperOne, 2021), 9–11.

Chapter 4 What Do You Hope for Your Kid?

1. This quote is commonly attributed to Henry Kissinger, though the exact source is unclear.
2. H. Brevy Cannon, "U.Va. Study Identifies Four Family Cultures in America," *UVA-Today*, November 15, 2012, https://news.virginia.edu/content/uva-study-identifies-four-family-cultures-america.
3. Brett and Kate McKay, "Fathering with Intentionality: The Importance of Creating a Family Culture," *The Art of Manliness*, July 22, 2013, https://www.artofmanliness.com/people/fatherhood/family-culture/.

Chapter 5 Are You a Good Enough Mom?

1. This quote is commonly attributed to Jill Churchill. The original source is unclear.

Chapter 6 Listen to Your Inner Child

1. Terri Apter, *Difficult Mothers: Understanding and Overcoming Their Power* (W. W. Norton, 2012), 175–77.

2. Daniel J. Siegel and Mary Hartzell, *Parenting from the Inside Out: How a Deeper Self-Understanding Can Help You Raise Children Who Thrive*, 10th anniversary ed. (Penguin, 2013), 134.

3. James Baldwin, "The Creative Process," in *The Price of the Ticket: Collected Nonfiction, 1948–1985* (Beacon Press, 2021), 324.

4. Esther Goldstein, "What Is An Inner Child and What Does It Know?," Integrative Psychotherapy, accessed June 20, 2025, https://integrativepsych.co/new-blog/what-is-an-inner-child.

Chapter 7 Connect Rather Than Control

1. Research conducted by Bath Spa University found several positive outcomes for families trained in emotional coaching, such as parental reports of a 79 percent improvement in children's positive behaviors and well-being. Rebecca Digby, Eleanor West, Sarah Temple, Rebecca McGuire-Sniekus, Olivia Vatmanides, Antoinette Davey, Stephanie Richardson, Janet Rose, and Richard Parker, *Somerset Emotion Coaching Project: Full Evaluation Report*, Bath Spa University Institute for Education, July 2017, https://www.bathspa.ac.uk/media/bathspaacuk/education-/research/attachment-aware/Emotion-Coaching-Full-Report-July-2017-(1).pdf.

2. Heather S. Lonczak, "What is Positive Parenting? 33 Examples and Benefits," PositivePsychology.com, May 8, 2019, https://positivepsychology.com/positive-parenting/.

3. NBA teams that touch each other more (fist bumps, head slaps, chest bumps, low fives, full hugs, team huddles) win more games. Michael W. Kraus, Cassy Huang, and Dacher Keltner, "Tactile Communication, Cooperation, and Performance: An Ethological Study of the NBA," *Emotion* 10, no. 5 (2010): 745–49.

4. Mel Robbins, "When Nothing Seems to Be Going Your Way, Here's Exactly What to Do," *The Mel Robbins Podcast*, episode 259, January 14, 2025, https://www.melrobbins.com/podcasts/episode-259.

5. Inspired by the quote widely attributed to Erick S. Gray: "Whatever you give a woman, she will make greater. If you give her sperm, she'll give you a baby. If you give her a house, she'll give you a home."

6. "The Satter Division of Responsibility in Feeding," Ellyn Satter Institute, accessed June 30, 2015, https://www.ellynsatterinstitute.org/how-to-feed/the-division-of-responsibility-in-feeding/.

7. Gordon Neufeld and Gabor Maté, *Hold On to Your Kids: Why Parents Need to Matter More Than Peers* (A. A. Knopf Canada, 2004), 74–85.

8. "Make the Most of Special Time with Your Child: How-To Checklist," Hand in Hand Parenting, November 2014, https://www.handinhandparenting.org/2014/11/make-special-time-child-checklist/.

9. Kim John Payne with Lisa M. Ross, *Simplicity Parenting: Using the Extraordinary Power of Less to Raise Calmer, Happier, and More Secure Kids* (Ballantine Books, 2009), 150.

Chapter 8 Find Your Inner Royalty

1. Kim John Payne, *The Soul of Discipline: The Simplicity Parenting Approach to Warm, Firm, and Calm Guidance—From Toddlers to Teens* (Ballantine Books, 2015), 54.

Chapter 9 Aim for Curiosity and Delight

1. Serena, SLP, and Kylie, OT (@play_spark), "In education and in pediatric therapy . . . ," Instagram, November 1, 2023, https://www.instagram.com/play_spark/p/CzGnv7pukNP/.

2. This idea is based on the "fascinated anthropologist" from Shirzad Chamine, *Positive Intelligence: Why Only 20% of Teams and Individuals Achieve Their True Potential and How You Can Achieve Yours* (Greenleaf Book Group, 2012), 87.

3. Toni Morrison, "Does Your Face Light Up?," OWN, November 2, 2011, originally aired on *The Oprah Winfrey Show*, May 26, 2000, https://www.oprah.com/oprahs-life-class/does-your-face-light-up-video#:~:text=One%20of%20Oprah's%20greatest%20lessons,Clips.

4. Based on Rachel Held Evans's discussion about reading Scripture "with the prejudice of love" in *Inspired: Slaying Giants, Walking on Water, and Loving the Bible Again* (Thomas Nelson, 2018), 56.

5. This wording comes from Rachel Nielson, creator of the *3 in 30 Takeaways for Mom* podcast, who offers a three-year motherhood journal called *Flecks of Gold*, which you can find at https://shop.3in30podcast.com/.

Chapter 10 Speak Words of Warmth, Not War

1. *We Bought a Zoo*, directed by Cameron Crowe (20th Century Fox, 2011). This is my romanticized version of the scene. It may be different watching it ten years later.

2. This technique was taught to me by Kathy Salazar via the Parent Talk system in 2010, https://practicalparenttalk.com/.

3. John E. Bates, Alice C. Schermerhorn, and Isaac T. Petersen, "Temperament and Parenting in Developmental Perspective," in *Handbook of Temperament*, ed. Marcel Zentner and Rebecca L. Shiner (Guilford Press, 2012), 425–41.

4. Grazyna Kochanska and Ross A. Thompson, "The Emergence and Development of Conscience in Toddlerhood and Early Childhood," in *Parenting and Children's Internalization of Values: A Handbook of Contemporary Theory*, ed. Joan E. Grusec and Leon Kuczynski (Wiley, 1997), 61–65.

Chapter 11 Sprinkle In Rhythm

1. Ursula K. Le Guin, *The Lathe of Heaven* (Scribner, 2008), 159.

2. Kreshnik Burani et al., "Longitudinal Increases in Reward-Related Neural Activity in Early Adolescence: Evidence from Event-Related Potentials (ERPs)," *Developmental Cognitive Neuroscience* 36 (2019): 100620, https://doi.org/10.1016/j.dcn.2019.100620.

3. Chris Voss and Tahl Raz, *Never Split the Difference: Negotiating As If Your Life Depended On It* (Harper Business, 2016), chap. 4, under "Key Lessons," http://livre2.com/LIVREE/E1/E001005.pdf.

Chapter 12 Teaching Life Skills to a Hellion

1. Brenda Smith Myles, *The Hidden Curriculum: Practical Solutions for Understanding Unstated Rules in Social Situations for Adolescents and Young Adults* (Future Horizons, 2004).

2. My condensed description is based on the work of Northern Illinois University Experiential Learning Center, https://www.niu.edu/citl/resources/guides/instructional-guide/experiential-learning.shtml.

Chapter 13 Stop Yelling

1. See Dr. Dan Siegel, "Daniel Siegel Hand Model," July 23, 2015, YouTube video, https://www.youtube.com/watch?v=qFTljLo1bK8.

2. Stephen R. Covey, *The 7 Habits of Highly Effective People: Powerful Lessons in Personal Change* (Free Press, 1989).

3. I learned this exercise from Shirzad Chamine in the Positive Intelligence course and app, Positive Intelligence Inc., 2021.

Chapter 14 Identify Your Inner Mean Girl

1. Lewis Howes (@lewishowes), "What's more important: less negative thinking . . . ," Instagram, July 20, 2024, https://www.instagram.com/reel/C-ERReSPgaM/?igsh=MWNwZjI5MW15d2Zqcg==.

Chapter 15 Unfriend Your Inner Mean Girl

1. Janet Jackson, Jimmy Jam, and Terry Lewis, "Nasty," *Control*, performed by Janet Jackson (A&M Records, 1986), vinyl/CD/digital.

2. Based on "the five sage powers" in Chamine, *Positive Intelligence*, 83–98.

3. Quote from Gregory Boyle, *Tattoos on the Heart: The Power of Boundless Compassion* (Free Press, 2010), 20.

Chapter 16 Welcome Everyone's Big Feelings by Honoring the Body

1. Emily Nagoski and Amelia Nagoski, *Burnout: The Secret to Unlocking the Stress Cycle* (Ballantine Books, 2019), 5.

2. Nagoski and Nagoski, *Burnout*, 5.

3. Nagoski and Nagoski, *Burnout*, 5.

4. Nagoski and Nagoski, *Burnout*, 5.

5. Bessel van der Kolk, *The Body Keeps the Score: Brain, Mind, and Body in the Healing of Trauma* (Viking, 2014), 52.

6. Van der Kolk, *Body Keeps the Score*, 54.

7. Van der Kolk, *Body Keeps the Score*, 54.

8. Nagoski and Nagoski, *Burnout*, 15.

9. Mona Delahooke, *Brain-Body Parenting: How to Stop Managing Behavior and Start Raising Joyful, Resilient Kids* (Harper Wave, 2022), 20.

10. Allison Davies, "The Swearing Workshop," Allison Davies: Music and the Brain, accessed April 1, 2025, https://allisondavies.com.au/the-swearing-workshop.

11. Nagoski and Nagoski, *Burnout*, xiii.

12. Paul Atchley, "You Can't Multitask, So Stop Trying," *Harvard Business Review*, December 21, 2010, https://hbr.org/2010/12/you-cant-multi-task-so-stop-tr.

13. Alona Pulde and Matthew Lederman, "Navigating 'Pink Tote Lid' Moments: Turning Parental Anger into Connection," *webe kälm*, accessed April 13, 2025, https://webekalm.com/blogs/dear-webe/navigating-pink-tote-lid-moments-turning-parental-anger-into-connection.

14. Jon Kabat-Zinn, *Wherever You Go, There You Are: Mindfulness Meditation in Everyday Life* (Hachette, 2005), 30.

15. Dr. Sasha Heinz, "S.U.R.F.," accessed July 22, 2025, https://drsashaheinz.pages.ontraport.net/s.u.r.f.

16. The average number of emotions respondents could identify in Brené Brown's survey of over seven thousand people. Brown, *Atlas of the Heart: Mapping Meaningful Connection and the Language of Human Experience* (Random House, 2022), xxi.

Chapter 17 Meltdown Magic

1. Parenting Education Classes (@maryvangeffen), "How to know when you should leave or stay," with Emily P. Freeman (@emilypfreeman), Instagram video, March 15, 2024, https://www.instagram.com/share/BARXYszCrg.

2. Henri J. M. Nouwen, *Reaching Out: The Three Movements of the Spiritual Life* (Doubleday, 1975), 63.

Chapter 18 When Things Get Violent

1. Catherine B. Lo, Jeffery A. Bridge, Jingzhen Yang, and Rachel M. Stanley, "Mental Health Revisits at US Pediatric Emergency Departments," *JAMA Pediatrics* 177, no. 1 (2023): 28–36, https://doi.org/10.1001/jamapediatrics.2022.4592; see also www.abbymedcalf.com to read about the difference between instrumental aggression and impulsive aggression.

2. Andrew Huberman, "Dr. Martha Beck: Access Your Best Self with Mind-Body Practices, Belief Testing and Imagination," *Huberman Lab* (podcast), August 2024, https://open.spotify.com/episode/0wtffMCkSWvPluetaGaY1P?si=rD5Jq-e6RJiS75tC_HrwbA.

3. Ryan Wexelblatt, "Your Emotional Responses to 'Bad' Behavior Are Counterproductive," *ADDitude*, updated November 10, 2021, https://www.additudemag.com/emotional-response-adhd-behavior/.

4. Bruce Perry and Maia Szalavitz, *Born for Love: Why Empathy Is Essential—and Endangered* (Harper, 2010), 29.

5. Valerie June, *Light Beams: A Workbook for Being Your Badass Self* (Andrews McMeel Publishing, 2023), 66. Valerie includes the phrase *immeasurably effervescent*, and it fits your kid perfectly.

6. Keith E. Saylor and Birgit H. Amann, "Impulsive Aggression as a Comorbidity of Attention-Deficit/Hyperactivity Disorder in Children and Adolescents," *Journal of Child and Adolescent Psychopharmacology* 26, no. 1 (February 2016): 19–25, https://doi.org/10.1089/cap.2015.0126; ScienceDirect, "Predatory Aggression," ScienceDirect, accessed April 13, 2025, https://www.sciencedirect.com/topics/neuroscience/predatory-aggression.

7. Actual quote: "The tendency to pay attention to feelings was most associated with the use of touch to convey affection. . . . Individuals open to feelings are more apt to use touch as a means to establish proximity and emotional closeness. . . . Individuals unsure of what emotion they are experiencing are more likely to report a host of negative reactions to touching." Jeffry A. Simpson and W. Steven Rholes, eds., *Attachment Theory and Close Relationships* (Guilford Press, 1998), 411.

8. Made famous by Dr. Becky Kennedy, *Good Inside: A Guide to Becoming the Parent You Want to Be* (HarperOne, 2022), 11.

9. Patty Wipfler, "How to Handle Aggression," YouTube video, accessed April 13, 2025, https://www.youtube.com/watch?v=xMf8TYlVlzg.

10. "Vigorous snuggle" comes from Patty Wipfler, "Playful Parenting: The Vigorous Snuggle," Hand in Hand Parenting, August 7, 2009, https://www.handinhandparenting.org/2009/08/playful-parenting-the-vigorous-snuggle/.

Part IV Find Your FIRM to Keep Away Burnout

1. Neufeld and Maté, *Hold On*, 222–23.

2. Neufeld and Maté, *Hold On*, 222–23.

Chapter 19 Disciplining the Spicy One

1. Cara J. Kiff, Liliana J. Lengua, and Maureen Zalewski, "Nature and Nurturing: Parenting in the Context of Child Temperament," *Clinical Child and Family Psychology Review* 14, no. 3 (2011): 251–73, https://doi.org/10.1007/s10567-011-0093-4.

2. J. E. Bates, A. C. Schermerhorn, and I. T. Petersen, "Temperament and Parenting in Developmental Perspective," in *Handbook of Temperament*, ed. M. Zentner and R. L. Shiner (Guilford Press, 2012), 425–41.

3. Jay Belsky and Michael Pluess, "Beyond Diathesis Stress: Differential Susceptibility to Environmental Influences," *Psychological Bulletin* 135, no. 6 (2009): 885–90, https://doi.org/10.1037/a0017376.

4. Belsky and Pluess, "Beyond Diathesis Stress."

5. Kim John Payne, *The Simplicity Parenting Podcast with Kim John Payne*, "2 by 2 by 1—Giving Directions That Work," episode 162, March 8, 2023, https://www.simplicityparenting.com/podcasts/the-simplicity-parenting-podcast-with-kim-john-payne/episodes/2147889715.

6. Ronald G. Morrish, *Secrets of Discipline: 12 Keys for Raising Responsible Children* (Hushion House, 1998), 80.

7. Jonathan Haidt, *The Anxious Generation: How the Great Rewiring of Childhood Is Causing an Epidemic of Mental Illness* (Penguin Random House, 2024), 53.

Chapter 20 Protect the Sibling

1. Alicia Maples, "Recognizing Glass Children," TEDxSanAntonio, filmed October 16, 2010, YouTube video, 18:01, posted November 5, 2010, https://www.youtube.com/watch?v=MSwqo-g2Tbk.

2. Maples, "Recognizing Glass Children."

3. Cheryl Cardall, "The Glass Child," *Fight Like a Mother* (podcast), March 21, 2024, episode 91, https://podcasts.apple.com/us/podcast/the-glass-child/id1524163171?i=1000650076629.

Chapter 21 When Your Co-Parent Is Triggered by the Spicy One

1. See R. Chris Fraley, "Adult Attachment Theory and Research: A Brief Overview," University of Illinois's Department of Psychology, accessed May 20, 2025, http://labs.psychology.illinois.edu/~rcfraley/attachment.htm.

2. See Samiullah Sarwar, "Influence of Parenting Style on Children's Behaviour," *Journal of Education and Educational Development* 3, no. 2 (December 2016): 222–49, https://files.eric.ed.gov/fulltext/EJ1161470.pdf.

3. See Kari Rusnak, "The Magic Ratio: The Key to Relationship Satisfaction," Gottman, last updated June 24, 2024, https://www.gottman.com/blog/the-magic-ratio-the-key-to-relationship-satisfaction/.

4. Multiple studies found that parenting styles affect children with resistant temperaments more strongly than their easygoing peers. Strong-willed children show significantly better outcomes when parents use reasoned explanations and collaborative problem-solving rather than punishment-based approaches, with the effects being more pronounced than in average-temperament children. See A. D. Stright, K. C. Gallagher, and K. Kelley, "Infant Temperament Moderates Relations Between Maternal Parenting in Early Childhood and Children's Adjustment in First Grade," *Child Development* 79, no. 1 (2008): 186–200, https://doi.org/10.1111/j.1467-8624.2007.01119.x; Belsky and Pluess, "Beyond Diathesis Stress."

5. Lisa M. Hernandez, "Art and Science of Love," Gottman workshop, Costa Mesa, CA, June 9, 2018.

Chapter 22 Healing Apologies

1. E. Z. Tronick and A. Gianino, "Interactive Mismatch and Repair: Challenges to the Coping Infant," *Zero to Three* 6, no. 3 (1986): 1–6, https://psycnet.apa.org/record/1987-15272-001.

2. Grazyna Kochanska et al., "Mutually Responsive Orientation Between Mothers and Their Young Children: A Context for the Early Development of Conscience," *Current Directions in Psychological Science* 12, no. 6 (2003): 193, https://doi.org/10.1111/1467-8721.00198.

3. Siegel and Hartzell, *Parenting from the Inside Out*, 176.

4. A version of my poem was originally published in an Instagram post by Kayla Craig (@liturgiesforparents), September 4, 2023, https://www.instagram.com/p/CwyM4cJpw55/.

Conclusion

1. Meredith Miller, *Woven: Nurturing a Faith Your Kid Doesn't Have to Heal From* (Worthy Books, 2023), 32.

2. Vicky Vox, "Unified Rainbow," Unified Rainbow, accessed July 7, 2024, https://unifiedrainbow.com/.

MARY VAN GEFFEN is an international parenting coach for Moms of Spicy Ones, as well as a Spicy One herself. Mary helps parents practice the spiritual discipline of staying calm, kind, and firm with their strong-willed kids—especially when they don't deserve it. She combines her training as a Simplicity Parenting counselor and Professional Co-Active Coach with hard-earned personal experience raising her own spirited child as well as her mild-mannered child. She has transformed the lives of over eight thousand mothers with her eight-week group program and on-demand digital courses. She shares daily inspirational tips with her 400,000 followers on Instagram. Her greatest achievement is cultivating a connected relationship with her now-adult children. Mary has a master's from Northwestern University and is an ordained elder at her affirming Christian church.

CONNECT WITH MARY:

MaryVanGeffen.com

@MaryVanGeffen

@MaryVanGeffen

@MaryVanGeffen

@Mary-Van-Geffen

@MaryVanGeffen

Mary@MaryVanGeffen.com

A Note from the Publisher

Dear Reader,

Thank you for selecting a Revell book! We're so happy to be part of your life through this work.

Revell's mission is to publish books that offer hope and help for meeting life's challenges, and that bring comfort and inspiration. We know that the right words at the right time can make all the difference; it is our goal with every title to provide just the words you need.

We believe in building lasting relationships with readers, and we'd love to get to know you better. If you have any feedback, questions, or just want to chat about your experience reading this book, please email us directly at publisher@revellbooks.com. Your insights are incredibly important to us, and it would be our pleasure to hear how we can better serve you.

We look forward to hearing from you and having the chance to enhance your experience with Revell Books.

The Publishing Team at Revell Books
A Division of Baker Publishing Group
publisher@revellbooks.com